NEW POLITICAL ECONOMY

Edited by
Stephen Resnick
University of Massachusetts, Amherst

A ROUTLEDGE SERIES

NEW POLITICAL ECONOMY

STEPHEN RESNICK, General Editor

ENCODING CAPITAL
THE POLITICAL ECONOMY OF THE HUMAN GENOME PROJECT

Rodney Loeppky

Routledge
Taylor & Francis Group
NEW YORK AND LONDON

Published in 2005 by
Routledge
711 Third Avenue,
New York, NY 10017
www.routledge-ny.com

Published in Great Britain by
Routledge
2 Park Square
Milton Park, Abingdon
Oxon OX14 4RN
www.routledge.co.uk

Library of Congress Cataloging-in-Publication Data

Loeppky, Rodney, 1969-
 Encoding capital : the political economy of the Human Genome Project /
Rodney Loeppky.
  p. ; cm. -- (New political economy)
 Includes bibliographical references and index.

 1. Human Genome Project--Economic aspects--United States. 2.
Economics--United States. 3. Molecular biology--Research--Economic
aspects--United States.
 [DNLM: 1. Human Genome Project. 2. Genetics,
Medical--economics--United States. 3. Capitalism--United States. 4.
Genetic Research--economics--United States. 5. Public Policy--United
States. QZ 50 L821e 2004] I. Title. II. Series.

 QH445.2.L64 2004
 306.4'5--dc22   2004019544

ISBN13: 978-0-415-64746-5 (pbk)
ISBN13: 978-0-415-97231-4 (hbk)

For my late father,
Rodney David Loeppky, Sr.

Contents

List of Tables and Figures

Acknowledgments

This work, while the product of one, would not have been possible without the support of many. I would like to thank George Comninel—a thought-provoking intellectual, an inspiring teacher and very supportive mentor. At various points during the work's preparation, I have received helpful commentary from Rob Albritton, David McNally, David Castle, Katalin Hudak, Greg Albo, Martin Kenney, Sandra Whitworth, Christopher May, and Shannon Bell. For their support in bringing the work to publication, I am grateful to Stephen Resnick and Kimberly Guinta.

A most heartfelt thanks to my partner, Deepika Grover, without whose intellectual interaction, unending personal support and good-humored friendship, this work would not have been possible. It is a debt I can never fully repay. Finally, a special thanks to the friends who kept me balanced throughout: Julian Ammirante, Michelle Dagnino, Peter Fargey, Andrej Zaslove, Liz Root, Noah Zerbe, Karl Harrer, Alke Firges, Hans-Joerg Schmedes and Chantale Walker.

Chapter One
Introduction

It is unlikely that any scientific undertaking has ever been invested with so much public hope and expectation as the Human Genome Project (HGP).[1] Since its official inauguration in 1990, the project's aim has been to map and decode the full complement of human genetic material. Viewed by some as the 'holy grail' of biology and medicine, the HGP has garnered a formidable degree of political and scientific support, securing a project budget of over $3 billion. To its proponents, the reasoning for such support was obvious, given the substantial benefits that would ostensibly result from the project. James Watson, co-discoverer of the structure of deoxyribonucleic acid (DNA), compared the project with NASA's moon landing, except that,

> the implications of the [HGP] for human life are likely to be far greater. A more important set of instruction books will never be found by human beings. When finally interpreted, the genetic messages encoded within our DNA molecules will provide the ultimate answers to the chemical underpinnings of human existence. They will not only help us to understand how we function as healthy human beings, but will also explain, at the chemical level, the role of genetic factors in a multitude of diseases, such as cancer, Alzheimer's disease, and schizophrenia, that diminish the individual lives of so many millions of people.[2]

This was, indeed, a tall order. Nonetheless, Watson's general tone was repeated across a range of public spaces. The attention of eminent scientists, political figures, the media, leading universities and an overflow of corporations pointed decisively to the socially perceived importance of the HGP. Yet, before 1990, who, besides molecular biologists, knew anything about the inherent value of physical maps and DNA sequencing methods? Near the end of the 1980s, in the wake of the Challenger disaster, the emerging controversy surrounding the costs of the Superconducting Supercollider, and the failed viability of nuclear energy, the HGP seems to have bucked the trend of prevailing pessimism over the benefits of large-scale science-based projects.[3] This gives rise to an important question: why, in particular, was *this* project able to successfully emerge and thrive?

There have largely been two answers to this question. The first, in keeping with the logic resident in Watson's claims, asserts that the HGP was given the go-ahead, because it was both scientifically compelling and would, potentially, bring countless medical and other benefits to society. While such arguments are valuable in many respects, they tend to over-emphasize the altruistic intentions of science and its agents. In such accounts, there is an explicit or implicit portrayal of scientific progress as the result of leading scientists overcoming technical barriers, the misconceptions of public debate or the obstructions of bureaucratic administrators and short-sighted politicians.[4] They tended to construct a teleological history of genome science, in which the political and social 'payoff' is estimated and evaluated mainly through a calculation of potential technical improvements, occasionally weighed against the prospective hazards. However, in the aftermath of a century that witnessed scientific involvement in the hydrogen bomb, as well as the scientific complicities of the Second World War and the Vietnam War, such Mertonian invocations of science and its virtuous intentions seem increasingly hard to sustain, if they ever really existed.[5]

A related, but separate, answer to this question invokes, in one form or another, the technological imperative. In such accounts, one finds varying invocations of technological necessity, the scientific 'idea,' or the 'inevitability' of scientific and technological change used as an explanatory prop. Rather than utilizing a medical or otherwise beneficial 'telos' to explain progress, this approach often volunteers a long explication of the manner in which fundamentally *technological* ideas are advanced through the sinews of political or economic structures, relying, along the way, on the advocacy of specific individuals or organizations. At one end of this category are popularly aimed critical works that tend to portray genome sciences as a dangerous set of developments in which a technological 'can of worms' has been left unattended.[6] Putting aside their polemical tone, a critical analytical problem with (but not restricted to) these perspectives is their penchant for positioning genome science as a 'revolutionary' event. Jeremy Rifkin, for instance, incessantly makes reference to a 'biotech century' in which " . . . convergent forces [come] together to create [a] powerful new social current. At the epicenter is a technology revolution unmatched in all history in its power to remake ourselves, our institutions, and our world."[7] Despite Rifkin's clear awareness of powerful social elements, such as capital or the state, in the unfolding of biotechnology, he systematically depicts this process as one in which detrimental social effects follow—or are determined by—an already-burgeoning scientific and technological development. Although such reverent perspectives towards technology effectively expose some of the latter's more pernicious elements, nowhere is the unexplored 'black box' of technology better left intact.

A subtler version of this thinking is found in the most widely cited source on politics and the HGP, Robert Cook-Deegan's *The Gene Wars*.[8] Cook-Deegan's account considers the project in terms of an institutional process, given a scientific necessity. As such, the author describes his own work as,

> an account of the *origins* of the Human Genome Project. The scientific ideas took hold only after they were publicly aired, provoked a vigorous debate, and were then repackaged to make them politically palatable. The main story line is the creation of a bureaucratic structure to carry those ideas to fruition. The ideas derive from science and technology; the genome project as a sociological phenomenon, however, came from the actions of many people, often working without knowledge of others treading on convergent paths.[9]

This approach, while supplying a valuable detailed reconstruction of the political and scientific events leading up to the HGP's actual promulgation, offers a not-so-compelling analysis of the project's *origins*. Historical analysis aimed at *origins* should, ostensibly, lead to some explanation of *why* a given process has developed in a particular way. This means that the possible social factors that prioritize scientific ideas are precisely what need to be explained. To be sure, such an explanation requires more than a saturated description of the actors and events, which precede and embody a given phenomenon.[10] Cook-Deegan's chronological recounting of the interaction between major policy-makers and scientific elite represents a considerable archival accomplishment, but it does not adequately explain *why* Congressional actors and the scientific community were able to arrive at profound consensus which he describes.[11] Such an explanation would require us to identify the critical social, political and economic forces that historically condition the trajectory of science policy, and how this policy, in turn, has been able to interact with science itself.

While a limited amount of critical literature has also grown up around the theme of biotechnology, none has examined the HGP explicitly, and precious little has provided analytical frameworks with which to understand such scientific practice. The work of Sheldon Krimsky and Martin Kenney are demonstrative of a more analytical approach.[12] Both authors are impressive in their capacities to relate biotechnology thematically to political, economic and institutional practices. Krimsky has, across multiple works, effectively elaborated the distinct political and economic flavor of developments, including the 1970s recombinant DNA (rDNA) debate and the 1980s maturation of the biotechnology industry.[13] Kenney lays out, in a more specific manner, the critical elements that make up an emerging nexus between government, industry and academia. But neither author connects any well-elaborated explanatory framework to their otherwise well-documented empirical research, and each tends, in his own way, to rely on a technologically-driven picture. In particular, Krimsky's later work presents molecular genetics as " . . . a case where a scientific and technological revolution has helped to recast industrial boundaries, fostering entirely new pathways through which economic sectors interact."[14] Although this later research is both meticulous and sensitive to a wide range of important issues, it retains an uncomfortably pure image of scientific research, a somewhat benign view of capital, and an optimistic view of the state (which he feels can regulate any potential problems), weakening its utility as comprehensive social criticism.[15]

Comparatively, Kenney's work positions biotechnology within the upward swing of a long economic wave, led by the rise of certain core technologies. According to Kenney, "[these] technologies or productive forces cannot have such tremendous impact without severely affecting the social relations of a society. In periods of crisis not only are new technologies adopted, but old institutions are transformed or entirely swept away."[16] His argument depends on short references to Joseph Schumpeter and Ernst Mandel, positing 'long waves' as the explanatory mechanism for surges in scientific and technological activity.[17] Kenney's clear attempt to position biotechnology in the wider historical picture is important, but the manner in which science and technology emerges, and exactly how its emergence is connected with social relations, is not especially clear. Ultimately, the status of scientific innovation in Kenney's work is difficult to isolate. On one side, it is represented as a process reflective of the continuing drive of capitalist social relations while, on the other, it is awarded a disconcerting transformative autonomy in the rise and fall of long-term economic waves.[18]

Given the paucity of theoretical development in this area of study, this work undertakes an analytically framed historical exploration of the rise of the HGP in the United States. It does this by utilizing an approach that situates the understanding of contemporary science and technology in the specificities of capitalism as a form of society, with an eye toward locating the project's social and historical significance. Moving away from accounts based on natural 'scientific progress' or 'technological necessity,' which tend to obscure the social origins of change, the work argues that the emergence of the HGP can be properly understood as a function of the social relations of capitalism. In this regard, at political, corporate and scientific-institutional levels, the HGP emerged through processes that reflect the 'logic of motion' of capitalist development. In stark contrast to Watson's views, then, the genome project is interpreted in light of the historical dynamic *peculiar to capitalism:* the pressing systemic need to enhance the possibilities for value accumulation through innovation. The strategy by which U.S. (and other) corporations thrive in the contemporary era has involved, in part, the reassertion of value accumulation through increasingly high-tech, monopoly protected, production processes. In the case of the HGP, the state entered this arena, in order to accommodate the needs of—particularly U.S. based—corporate actors, by providing a research infrastructure valuable to capital in general, but one that would not otherwise have been constructed. This process of 'risk socialization' finds its roots in the increasing historical and systemic pressure on individual corporate actors to perform within a structure that more and more limits their possibilities to do so. Responding to this systemic contradiction, the state politicized a critical part of scientific research on behalf of capital's needs, and research institutions effectively took up the task presented to them by state and corporate actors. Ultimately, the goals of this state-capital imposition were diligently absorbed by lower order institutions in the United States, allowing—indeed, necessitating—the increasingly visible circulation of capitalist social relations at the research level. If genome science is the future staple of capitalist growth that it is purported to be, then it is likely no coincidence that its greatest stimulus (that from the HGP) emerged overwhelmingly in a society with the most extensive reach of capitalist social relations.

To pursue this argument, the work is divided into five parts. Chapter 2 outlines a very brief historical sketch of molecular biology in the United States, as well as a rough explanation of the HGP itself. Intended both as background and as a basis for historical contrast, the chapter contains three purposes. First, it provides the reader with some understanding of the HGP as a scientific project, as well as an initial sense of its potential biomedical effects. Second, it demonstrates that while the science of the HGP can be traced to a trajectory of scientific events, this trajectory has *never been entirely detached* from the social relations of U.S. capitalism. Finally, the chapter offers a basis for historical comparison in relation to questions of contemporary scientific practice, an issue taken up in chapter 6. On this point, throughout the development of molecular biology, scientists exhibited a complicated relationship to external authority, but also demonstrated a semblance of communal autonomy. Particularly during the 1970s debates concerning rDNA research, the scientific community's internal tensions, brought about by the prospect of Congressional oversight, undoubtedly suggested a notion of collective autonomy and 'self-regulation' still largely administered by open and free exchange. Overall, then, the chapter presents both a baseline to think about molecular biology across time, as well as a sketch of the one undertaking that, from its inception, came to symbolize the 'new biology.'

Having elaborated the scientific 'event' with which this work is concerned, chapter 3 sets out the principal aspects of its theoretical framework. It notes the necessity of understanding science and technology in relation to prevailing social forces, and proceeds to examine this connection systematically in terms of political economy. As such, it draws on historical materialist insights with respect to the role of scientific innovation as a particular social tendency, rooted in the 'logic of motion' of capitalism. Insisting on historical process as basic to its theoretical framework, the chapter stresses the increasing importance of information commodities in the contemporary expression of capitalist social relations, as well as the critical role of the state in ensuring their development.

Chapters 4 and 5 are oriented around a historical and empirical elaboration of how the HGP came to be in the United States, specifically in relation to the expectations of capital and the state. Chapter 4 elucidates the connection between the project's emergence and intra-capital relations, emphasizing the historical trajectories of the pharmaceutical and biotechnology industries. It points explicitly to the special motivation and support of capital for the creation and maintenance of the HGP. In direct relation to this, chapter 5 points to the state as the political terrain in which the necessary conditions of capitalist production needs are secured. Linking the HGP directly to such a process, the chapter highlights both the project's instantiation and extraordinary political viability as processes in which the state attended to the structural support of capitalist development in the United States. Importantly, at both the domestic and international levels, state policy procurement is analyzed as a terrain of political struggle, indicating that its favorable positioning *vis-à-vis* the biotechnology and pharmaceutical industries has never been automatic—rather, it is historically constituted in a process imbued with uneven power relations.

Finally, chapter 6, questions how the instantiation of the HGP, with its relationship to both capital and the state, was so effectively orchestrated at the level of the research community. In keeping with the overall suggestion that capitalist social relations have deeply affected the trajectory of molecular biology, the chapter explores the possibility that scientific practice has increasingly taken on the qualities of 'labor.' In this, it points to a clear deviation from the historical trajectory of molecular biology described in the second chapter. After elaborating evidence of this change, the chapter utilizes Michel's Foucault's rendition of 'disciplinary' power relations to understand the shift in the nature of scientific practice. Finally, it examines the HGP as a strong reinforcement of this shift, pointing to both its structural arrangements and disciplinary effects within molecular biology.

The analysis presented in this work may invoke the actions of individuals, but it does so only in the context of prevailing social relations. Kenney, borrowing from Marx, has correctly emphasized the fact that "[s]cientists, university administrators, entrepreneurs, and business executives—all act in a world that is only partially of their own making."[19] In this sense, the point of this work is not to isolate molecular biology *per se* as inherently given to nefarious scientific purposes, such as social control. Undoubtedly, the continuance of genome work will have far-reaching—even negative—social ramifications, but only within a political milieu that permits them. As Erwin Chargaff has pointed out with respect molecular biology, "[w]e think that anything that's not forbidden is automatically allowed. . . . [O]ur era is so appalling that, if Newton were alive today, he'd have taken out a patent on gravity and we'd have to pay to walk around."[20] Thus, rather than villainize the science, the point must be to discern effectively the historical milieu in which scientific research currently lives and breathes. In turn, understanding the motivating social forces that underpin genome research not only helps to elucidate its direct and indirect purposes; it may also offer a basis for more compelling social criticism and, potentially, identify pathways for efficacious forms of public political involvement.

Chapter Two
Contextualizing and Understanding Human Genome Sciences

Throughout the twentieth century, the prominence of large-scale science in American history has been most clearly exemplified by the Manhattan Project and the U.S. Space Program. However, the HGP, as the most recent version of programmatic science, emerged with a degree of fanfare and controversy equal to, perhaps greater than, these famous predecessors. The genome project had the financial and structural backing of the American National Institutes of Health (NIH) and Department of Energy (DOE). However, its presence extended far beyond these state administrative bodies, reaching deeply into the American university system, national laboratory facilities, and corporate departments of research and development. Still, despite its relative enormity as a scientific and public undertaking, the HGP remains an obscure and little-understood endeavor in much of the social sciences and humanities.[1] In recognition of this fact, this chapter offers a brief background depiction of the HGP as a scientific enterprise, as well as a sense of the context from which it emerged. This accomplishes a dual task. First, prior to this work's full-blown political economic analysis, it furnishes the reader with greater insight into the actual object of study—molecular biology and the HGP. Second, it also lays the groundwork for a subsequent argument of this work—that the increasingly overt subsumption of biology under capitalist social relations is manifested in the recognizable shift from autonomous research to the execution of scientific labor (see chapter 6).

Accordingly, the chapter begins by sketching very briefly a historical background relevant to the rise of the HGP. It interprets this background by, first, exploring the early trajectory of molecular biology and, second, investigating the 'high point' of that field's conventional practice, just as the techniques for an era of genetics came into focus. The latter task is undertaken through a discussion of the debate surrounding the emergent use of rDNA research methods, a moment of internal crisis within the scientific community, which reveals an important 'snapshot' of scientific behavior and practice prior to the meteoric rise of biotechnology in the 1980s. Following this, the second section characterizes the scientific form, magnitude and technological potential of the HGP. Ultimately, the non-scientific character of this work renders it incapable of relating a *complete* technical understanding of the genome project. Rather, the intention is to supply the reader with an indication of the HGP's scientific and technical significance while forging a common and accessible basis for further discussion.

MOLECULAR BIOLOGY, BIOTECHNOLOGY AND GENOME RESEARCH

Any historical understanding of the rise of genome science in the U.S. should avoid simple explanations that characterize it as the mere culmination of long-term scientific developments, emerging logically out of the rediscovery of Mendelian genetics.[2] While such representations may convey the excitement and gravity of brilliant scientific moments, they add little to our understanding of the social factors underlying scientific discovery. Instead, the elaboration of preliminary events should serve only as a background, against which explanatory discussion can then follow. Similarly, it is certainly possible to trace certain organizational aspects of contemporary molecular biology at least as far back as the 1930s. This provides limited context for the emergence of genetic research in the 1970s, since, as Lily Kay has pointed out, "the continuities between the 1930s and 1970s [are] as remarkable as the cleavages."[3] Two background themes related to the origins of molecular biology are noteworthy: the role of the Rockefeller Foundation and the changed role of the state in the wake of World War II (WWII). Importantly, because accomplished research has already been carried out on these topics, their mention here requires only the briefest elaboration.[4]

The Rockefeller Foundation understood its own *raison d'être* in terms of an encouragement of research programs, which promoted " . . . procedures in the rationalization of life."[5] During the 1930s, under the direction of Warren Weaver, a classical physicist convinced that quantum physics was going nowhere, the Foundation became outspoken in its vision for the future of biological studies: an application of the logic, method and rigor of the physical sciences and chemistry to the study of biology.[6] Instead of grants to university administrations, the Foundation removed intermediaries, creating direct three-year research grants of $6,700 per year. This 'medium-sized project grant' proved a highly useful mechanism with which to shape the content of Foundation-supported research, favor the most 'efficient' scientists, and weed out less-than-prestigious universities.[7] The achievements of this more directed program included bringing an otherwise disparate collection of molecular-based studies into a coherent overall strategy; demonstrating that science could successfully become the object of management or 'directed autonomy'; and, finally, fostering a new brand of researcher—the scientific entrepreneur. With the Rockefeller program, one can discern a shift from autonomous scientific research, to research focused on socially appreciated objects of study, the latter of which helped to secure resources for subsequent research. Ultimately, the Foundation was able to channel the progression of molecular biology, such that its scientific achievements could be viewed as a resource subject to the country's national interest.

Also noteworthy was the manner in which increased state involvement in scientific research grew out of activities during WWII and its aftermath. The most obvious example of this is the Manhattan Project, but this period also witnessed the rise of active federal participation in the area of biomedical research. Practical questions relating to malaria, aviation medicine, penicillin production, blood substitutes and transfusion took a predominant role in new government programs.[8] In addition to these practical research exigencies, the astounding fact that around one-third of all enlisting men were proclaimed physically or mentally unfit for service catalyzed the government's commitment to a more energetic role in health-related research.[9] A critical element in this process was the extension of pre-war managerial science programs, combined with a scaled-up version of industrial (but largely government-regulated) involvement. The essential structure of 'directed autonomy,' based on coordinated project grants, remained intact, even as the war effort subsided and the National Institutes of Health (NIH) emerged as the new patron of research in molecular biology. The rapid rise in resources and power of the NIH (its budget skyrocketed from $700,000 in 1939 to over $1 billion in 1968) brought with it a buildup " . . . of highly specialised experts, grouped together in universities and medical schools, and the categorical institutes of NIH, with a broad, long-term relation to hospital-based, technologically intensive clinical medicine."[10]

Within this buildup, biology within the U.S. was transformed into an arena of considerable competition, a process involving scientists and their institutions alike. Scientists adapted quickly to an intensified system of competitive project grants, as well as doctoral and post-doctoral support. As a direct result of work done by Weaver, within both Rockefeller and the NIH, this allocation system greatly encouraged the shaping of research 'baronies,' leading accomplished scientists to draft the best graduate students and post-docs as insurance towards productivity and topical research.[11] Universities, for their own part, sought out researchers who had the capacity and where-withal to construct and maintain such research empires. Open grants for molecular biology allowed these institutions to seek out aspiring or success-ful scientists who " . . . were required to manage [their projects] as an asset in the race with colleagues for results which would secure further disbursal of funds."[12] It is important to note that a competitive atmosphere, in which peer review internal to the field determines funding distribution, lends itself quite effectively to the loose enforcement of a particular (molecular) ap-proach to biological research. In this sense, history points already to a com-plex picture of research practice within U.S. biology: it developed as a competitive, self-policing (dominated by peer review) practice, to which in-dependent researchers contribute, and yet transpired under the umbrella of application-oriented institutions (particularly the NIH).

The rDNA Break

Molecular biology is striking in terms of its consistent ontology of 'biologi-cal program,' surviving the shift in scientific focus from protein base to DNA base, as well as that in patronage from private to public sources.[13] In certain ways, the current trajectory of molecular biology remains largely within the parameters set by Weaver, culminating in an understanding of the genetic program as an 'enabling concept.'[14] Nonetheless, there is no denying the enormity surrounding Stanley Cohen's 1973 announcement at the Gordon Conference concerning the insertion of genetic material from a South African clawed toad into a common laboratory bacterium E. coli, inaugu-rating a new era of genetics and recombinant DNA research. Indeed, the present work is concerned with the political economic trajectory that pro-pels the scientific and technological aftermath of this event, a process that finds its maximum expression in the genome project. However, it is also im-portant to understand the scientific justification that dovetailed with the ul-timate direction of genetics research, production and regulation in the United States. In this sense, it is insightful to highlight the reaction of the mo-lecular biology community to the new rDNA reality, particularly in terms of its interface with public institutions. This interface is a complicated one, in-volving elements of self-regulation, self-protection and technological opti-mism on the part of the scientific (and regulatory) community. In this instructive moment of change, it is still possible to view both old and new visions of scientific practice, providing both a reference with which to con-sider the institutional behavior of science in the current period (chapter 6) and a relevant depiction of the technical context that would ultimately give rise to the HGP.

Controversy came to the fore almost immediately with the publication of a letter by Paul Berg and ten other distinguished scientists, outlining the need for a temporary moratorium on certain experiments and requesting the creation of a NIH evaluation committee on the hazards of rDNA research. Three classes of experiments were identified: i) experiments using antibiotic resistance factors or toxins manipulated and reproduced by way of extra-chromosomal, circular pieces of bacterial DNA known as plasmids; ii) experiments inserting genetic segments from cancer-causing viruses into bacterial plasmids; and iii) experiments involving the random combination of animal DNA with plasmids. The letter suggested a temporary moratorium on the first two types of experiments while the third was to be 'handled with care.'[15] This call for oversight warranted considerable attention on the part of the scientific community, attention that culminated in the 1975 Asilomar conference on biohazards.

The Asilomar process was an attempt to identify those aspects of research, which should be subject to public scrutiny. It should be borne in mind that, in large part, this initiative was undertaken by the scientific community in order to diffuse potential criticism of its activities. Certainly scientists were concerned about the problem of potential biohazards emanating from their laboratories, but they were more concerned about having regulatory guidelines imposed on them from actors external to the scientific community. Sheldon Krimsky points out that,

> [as] a policy-making model for the rDNA debate, Asilomar was severely limited in the following ways: selection of participants; clarity of the decision-making process; boundaries of discourse; public participation, and control of dissent. In the matter of selection of participants, the meeting was subsequently criticized for drawing its scientific expertise from far too few fields. Most participants were from disciplines that would draw benefits from the new research program. There was little representation from the health sciences and no participants representing environmental interests.[16]

While its guest list did not include actors concerned with ethical or social matters, Asilomar did include representatives of major corporate industrial laboratories, including *General Electric,* the Merck Institute, the *G.D. Searle & Co.* and the Roche Institute for Molecular Biology.[17] Nonetheless, it is important to note the complicated dynamic in which external actors threatened to influence or regulate the direction of research while scientists resisted with a form of self-regulation in order to *stem the tide of outside intervention.*

The conference closed with a consensus statement restricted almost exclusively to technical issues, calling for four containment categories related to gene-splicing experiments and endorsing the notion that the NIH should promulgate the federal guidelines for research. This latter task fell to the NIH rDNA Advisory Committee (RAC), which after 16 months of consultation issued its guidelines in 1976. In broad strokes, they followed the spirit of the Asilomar:

1. In the light of current information, certain experiments may be judged to present sufficiently serious potential hazards so that they should not be attempted at this time.
2. The group of experiments that pose either lesser or no potential hazards can be performed provided
   i.   the information to be obtained or the practical benefits anticipated cannot be obtained by conventional methods.
   ii. appropriate safeguards for containment are incorporated into the design.
3. The more potentially hazardous the experiment, the more stringent should be the safeguards against escape of the agents.
4. There should be an annual review of the guidelines.[18]

The strategy, of course, was to promulgate guidelines that were entirely a product of the molecular biology community. Despite this, their suitability was almost immediately challenged. Partly because the guidelines had made the possibility of genetic research a greater public issue, and partly because their regulatory force applied to only those projects supported by federal funding, the expansion of rDNA research had come to constitute a source of public and governmental concern. Public anxiety made itself apparent in Cambridge, MA, where the City Council requested Harvard University to supply a justification for its construction of new P-3 biohazard containment facilities. After acrimonious debate, the Council, which eventually softened its position, blocked Harvard and MIT from engaging in this level of experimentation until a review board could make recommendations. This process was repeated around the country in regions where genetic research was prominent. Moreover, between 1976 and 1978, over a dozen legislative bills were introduced into Congress regarding the national regulation of genetic research.[19] The combination of potential local control and national regulation, the most significant of which was that promoted by

Senator Edward Kennedy, reinforced the fears of the molecular biology community. While the prospect of federal legislation was clearly preferred to local control, both were largely perceived as a potential threat to the freedom of scientific investigation.

As a result, the scientific community organized itself in order, first, to resist the possibility of over-regulation and, second, to demonstrate the 'exaggerated' nature of the public reaction to genetic research. Major university research centers, in conjunction with industry, resorted to lobbyists on Capitol Hill to ensure that legislative momentum would not take a turn for the worse. Harvard, Stanford, Princeton and the University of Washington all engaged in professional lobbying during this time.[20] A line of eminent scientists and industrial figures (especially the Pharmaceutical Manufactures Association (PMA)) ensured that Congress was aware that "[c]umbersome and punitive legislation [was] not needed. The financial cost of overly cautious containment and enforcement, the delay in achieving benefits, and the penalties incurred by restricting freedom of inquiry [were] real risks to be considered in setting up regulations."[21] The aim here was to ensure that if there was to be federal legislation, it should be kept within the confines of the NIH, and it should override any potential local regulation.

At the same time, scientific evidence was garnered to preempt excited arguments condemning the safety of future research. An important meeting at Falmouth, Massachusetts considered the possibility of pathogenicity in the standard laboratory *E coli* KI2, the bacterium of choice for most rDNA experiments. This meeting is important, in particular, for the manner in which its results were communicated to the wider scientific community and public. It would also foreshadow later scientific findings, which were deployed 'optimistically' in a manner conducive to both industrial production and an image of research safety. The meeting set out to determine whether pathogenic effects were possible in three ways; in the bacterium itself; as a medium to other potential pathogens; and as an instigator of autoimmune syndromes. Despite the fact that it could conclude scientifically only on the first question—that *E coli* K12 could not become pathogenic, as other *E coli* strains had—the Chair's conclusions were far more suggestive.

> The participants arrived at unanimous agreement that *E coli* K12 cannot be converted into epidemic pathogen by laboratory manipulations with DNA inserts. On the basis of extensive studies already completed, it appears that *E coli* K12 does not implant in the intestinal tract of man. *There is no evidence* that non-transmissible plasmids *can* be spread from *E coli* K12 by insertion of known plasmids to other host bacteria within the gut. Finally, extensive studies in the laboratory to induce virulence in

E coli K12 by insertion of known plasmids and chromosomal segments coding for virulence factors, using standard genetic techniques, have proven unsuccessful in producing fully pathogenic strain. As a result of these discussions, it was believed that the proposed hazards concerning *E coli* K12 as an epidemic pathogen have been overstated . . . *E coli* K12 is inherently enfeebled and not capable of pathogenic transformation of DNA inserts.[22]

This statement, although very strong in its suggestion that *E coli* K12 poses little to no risk, masked the meeting's far more limited conclusion, that the question of pathogenic effects required further scientific evaluation. Note the extraordinary leap in Gorbach's logic: it has not been demonstrated conclusively that plasmids within *E coli* can be transferred, *ergo,* they cannot be. Ultimately, this interpreted consensus proved crucial because of its consistent use in the regulation debate as a way to emphasize the overreaction concerning potential pathogenic risks.[23]

Another set of experiments at the NIH, conducted by Malcolm Martin and Wallace Rowe, involved the simulation of a worst-case scenario in which polyoma (cancer-causing) viruses spliced into *E coli* K12 were transported into laboratory mice and hamsters. The aim of these experiments was to determine the degree to which rDNA molecules could be transferred into mammalian cells, pointing to the possible risks of pathogenicity of vector-induced molecules. There is little doubt that these experiments—which, like the Falmouth meetings, were widely cited as demonstrative of the innocuous properties of rDNA research involving *E coli* K12—resulted in scientifically controversial findings. On the one hand, there were concerns that *E coli* K12 was not a natural settler in the intestinal tract of mice; indeed, it was known to be expelled quickly by this organism. Thus, the claim that this was a simulation of a worst-case scenario for rDNA transfer was a false start. As one commentator has noted, it was " . . . rather like crash-testing a sponge-rubber dummy for auto injuries, and the Bethesda scientists knew it."[24]

At the same time, the experimental results were the subject of contestation in both mice- and hamster-based polyoma inducements. In the former, the existence of positive results in one of the four case studies were classified by the NIH as theoretically plausible, or 'expected.' The point that investigators highlighted was that the rate of infection from rDNA molecules was significantly lower than that from an unmanipulated, natural virus. The controversy, then, largely dismissed by the scientific establishment, emerged over the degree of significance to accord to these positive results. Were they to be understood as a risk lower than that which occurs in nature or, alternatively, should it have been emphasized simply that *E coli* K12 contained the capacity to transfer infectious molecules into a higher organism? The NIH, along with the prominent journal *Science*, weighed in decidedly in favor of the former conclusion. Krimsky, however, has contrasted this decision with the text of the original experimental protocol:

> In particular, since we are very concerned that a negative result will be misinterpreted as indicating that there is little biohazard in DNA recombinant work, we feel that a number of variables must be evaluated, and that the experiments should be designed to maximize the chances of a positive result. Also, if negative results are obtained with a given system, we feel that the *experiments should be continued with modified systems until we are reasonably convinced that a positive result is just not going to occur.*[25]

The seeming insistence on the part of the NIH to see the first polyoma experiments as conclusive of insignificant risk was compounded in the second set of hamster-based experiments. In this set of studies, suckling hamsters were used because of their high susceptibility to even incomplete polyoma viral DNA. While infections resulted from inoculation with free polyoma DNA (9 out of 17 cases), as well as those inoculated with bacteriophage containing single and double copies of polyoma DNA (1 and 3, respectively, out of 16 cases), no infections occurred from inoculations of polyoma-equipped *E coli* K12. The experimenters' conclusions emphasized the importance of the negative outcomes, implying that *E coli* K12 constitutes an effective barrier to any incorporation of pathogenic DNA into eukaryotic cells.[26] Again, the critique of this conclusion, predominantly from Barbara Rosenberg and Lee Simon, was based on how to interpret the significance of results. Rosenberg and Simon's paper—which contested the limited sample size, the downplayed significance of tumorigenicity of viral DNA, and the narrow, enfeebling manner in which *E coli* K12 was induced—was rejected by *Science* and largely ignored by the NIH.[27]

Finally, an important experiment involved some of the early scientific actors in the genetic regulation debate: Stanley Cohen and Annie Chang. One of the more tenacious scientific counter-arguments leveled at proponents of rDNA research concerned the risks of crossing the species-barrier. A species within nature is defined by those barriers that block the possibility for reproductive interactivity or, for geneticists, the mixing of genetic material. Crossing the species barrier became a rallying point around which several active groups and some prominent scientists charged that the risks of rDNA research were far greater than the benefits. One such critic was Robert Sinsheimer who, ironically, would much later become a leading figure in the pursuit of a publicly funded human genome project. In the days of rDNA regulation debates, however, Sinsheimer's message was considerably less sanguine:

> [to] introduce a sudden discontinuity in the human gene pool might well create a major mismatch between our social order and our individual capacities. Even a minor perturbation such as a marked change in the sex ratio from its present near equality could shake our social structure.[28]

Ewin Chargaff went one step further, in stating that,

> [you] can stop splitting an atom; you can stop visiting the moon; you can stop using aerosols; you may even decide not to kill entire populations by the use of a few bombs. But you cannot recall a new form of life . . . An irreversible attack on the biosphere is something so unheard of, so unthinkable to previous generations, that I could only wish that mine had not been guilty of it.[29]

The crucial question to be answered here relates to the extent of damage that is possible due to a transgression of the species barrier. Since this subject had become a magnet for public criticism, the experiment performed by Cohen and Chang was, not surprisingly, aimed at downplaying the significance of such a transgression.

The researchers started with the most fundamental of all perceived species barriers: the almost universal exclusion of genetic interchange between prokaryotes (bacteria and algae) and eukaryotes (cells with identifiable nucleii). They placed plasmids (circular pieces of DNA) in *E coli* in proximity to cut fragments of mouse DNA, restriction endonucleases (enzymes found in bacteria which cut up foreign DNA at specific sites) and DNA ligase (enzymes which connect DNA). The absorption of some DNA fragments by the bacteria was, in the researchers' opinion, ample evidence that the species barrier is likely crossed in nature. They stated that because there are widespread restriction and ligase enzymes in nature, as well as abundant eukaryotic DNA from dead cells, it was reasonable to infer that DNA transfer may also play a role in the natural evolution of chromosomes.[30] This conclusion came under major scientific suspicion, as it is highly questionable whether such controlled experimental conditions allow for any reasonable comparison with even simple organisms. Yet, this untidy aspect of the story became even messier. In 1977, when major legislation was being discussed in Washington, unpublished drafts of the Cohen-Chang experiments were passed around to influential Congressional committee members. This circulation of prepublication material, in blatant disregard of scientific etiquette and peer review, played an important role in shaping the minds of policymakers in the US Congress.

Ultimately, this stream of scientific evidence, despite its clearly controversial nature, played a crucial role in both weakening the possibility of ramped-up Congressional oversight of rDNA research and encouraging revisions of NIH guidelines, allowing a wider array of genetic research. Indeed, by 1978, Congressional regulation seems to have been largely resisted by the scientific community, and even prominent bills put forward by Senators Kennedy and Rogers had lost their steam. After charges of 'Lysenkoism' were directed at Congress, even the possibility of regulation with respect to an emerging commercial sector dissipated.[31] Not surprisingly, the NIH issued new guidelines in 1978, 1980 and 1981, wherein the overwhelming majority of experiments would no longer be classified as high-risk experiments. None of this is to claim that the consultation and experimentation engaged in by scientists to demonstrate the low-risk nature of rDNA research was executed in bad faith. Even before the meetings at Asilomar, molecular biologists were taking unprecedented steps to consider some of the long-term consequences of their research. However, it is difficult to overlook the fact that all social and ethical considerations were explicitly excluded from discussion, and that scientific ramifications were debated almost entirely in terms of laboratory safety. Moreover, as Krimsky has rightly noted, it should not go unnoticed that the principle public sponsors of rDNA research, the NIH, were also handily made into its regulators.[32] Corporate researchers, not subject to NIH guidelines, supported this development, enabling the appearance of regulation where there was, at best, only voluntary compliance. Ultimately, debate and subsequent regulation was successfully restricted to a minimalized form, acceptable to the closed ranks of the scientific community.

Given these research-friendly policy results, the development of rDNA research progressed rapidly in a favorable regulatory and socio-economic context. As the regulatory debate waned, the prominence of 'biotechnology' as a scientific and economic practice gained momentum. There are differing viewpoints on the age of biotechnology, but it is certainly clear that its conception—the application of biological processes for the synthesis of useful products—has existed for some time. The long tradition of beer brewing, requiring the biological process of fermentation, provides a simple demonstration of this point. Many have, however, spoken of a 'new' biotechnology, which has emerged only in the post-rDNA period. This biotechnology is no longer concerned with processes in which microorganisms work on behalf of industry, such as fermentation. Instead, it pertains to a set of techniques devised to manipulate the molecular operation of organisms such that they become economically useful within productive processes. While an analysis of this commercialization will play a major part in a subsequent chapter of this work, it is also necessary here to note the parallel significance of a burgeoning commercial presence in relation to the weakening U.S. regulatory framework.[33]

In the midst of the 1970s rDNA debate, a series of companies came into being with an expressed interest in developing such techniques for commercial ends. By 1978, Genentech's early production of insulin and somatostatin (human growth hormone) by way of genetic manipulation demonstrated the potential commercial viability of basic research. Not surprisingly, from this period onward, one also notes a dramatic push from actors external to the scientific community to help change the circumstances in which research proceeds. The contract between Eli Lilly and Genentech led the former to push for a relaxation of NIH guidelines. It requested and was granted an immediate exemption from the prohibition of experiments exceeding the volume of 10 liters. During the following five-year period, when industrial amplification was well under way, Susan Wright has referred specifically to a regulatory transition.[34] According to Wright,

> countervailing pressures for caution were enormously weakened both by the demise of regulatory legislation and by the successes of a corporate campaign for general deregulation, which the Carter administration to an extent and the Reagan administration entirely endorsed. When it became clear, toward the end of 1978, that Congress was unlikely to act to control genetic engineering, public advocacy groups had almost no leverage in the policy arena.[35]

Pressure from the PMA and individual corporations combined with the scientific community to ensure the weakening regulation of rDNA research. Testimony of these actors in front of House and Senate subcommittees converged around the idea that controls were an excessive barrier both to scientific progress and a newly maturing arena of industrial development. Beyond the limits on industrial scale-up, representatives were made aware of the increasing body of investments at stake, the need for proprietary protection, and the objection to data disclosure within the NIH-RAC.[36]

Of course, the most dramatic effects came about through an increasing investment and contractual arrangement of the biotech industry. Eli Lilly's licensing agreements for market distribution of insulin and growth hormone would help form a model for future connections between academic researchers, start-up corporations and multinational firms throughout the

1980s. Already between 1971 and 1981, 79 biotechnology enterprises were launched, some of the more prominent of which were Cetus Corporation (1971), Genentech (1976), Genex (1977), Collaborative Research (1978), Hybritech (1978), Biogen (1978), Molecular Genetics (1979), Monoclonal Antibodies (1979), Calgene (1980), and Genetic Systems (1981).[37] And by 1983, virtually every large pharmaceutical and chemical corporation had made multi-million dollar investments or started their own in-house research programs. This, combined with a groundswell of venture capital and public stock offerings, predisposed policymakers to take account of the commercial prospects of genetic research. Thus, by the early 1980s, one finds no serious discussions concerning the regulation of rDNA research— indeed, by 1982 the NIH guidelines were *de facto* inoperative.

All said, it is striking to consider the affinity between intention and effect from the very earliest days of molecular biology. The scientific and social goals on which supporting agencies set their sights ultimately became the basis upon which the field modeled itself. The directed autonomy under which the science proceeded lent itself well, in certain senses, to the potential for sharpened competition (through commercialization) and a managerial agenda. Indeed, reminiscent of certain aspects of Weaver's Rockefeller program, genome sciences are now more directly aimed at a mechanistic control of the human body, national development and US corporate growth. Importantly, however, the continuity in this historical picture with the present day should not be overdrawn. It is fair to say that by the late 1970s, even for the molecular biology community, this debate had likely become deeply fused with the future of biotechnology, as well as corporate and state agendas. But what remains notable prior to this is the capacity of scientists to register their public criticism, expose themselves to internal debate, and insist on the autonomous character of their practice as a community. In the rDNA debate, for instance, although scientific community members certainly 'circled the wagons' in a manner that was not especially admirable, their intentions in doing so had more to do with preserving communal autonomy than anything else. Fear of Congressional, or any other, external oversight helped to precipitate a process of self-examination which, however problematic, exhibited the continuing hold of past scientific norms: public and open criticism of prevailing scientific ideas, free exchange of information, and a continuing drive to sway (rather than fully isolate) colleagues. Thus, while their actions may have eventually dovetailed with corporate intentions, scientists' actions during the transition to 'new biology' reveal a widespread desire to preserve their conventional sense of internal self-regulation and relative autonomy from direct external pressures. Ultimately, as subsequent chapters will point out from both theoretical and empirical perspectives, this sense of autonomy could not hold within the social relations giving rise to the HGP. However, prior to elucidating these social relations and their significance *vis-à-vis* molecular biology, it is necessary to provide some overview of the empirical reference point of this work: the HGP and its scientific significance.

THE HUMAN GENOME PROJECT: WHAT IS IT?

The idea of an HGP came to fruition in the latter half of the 1980s. Any analysis of this project requires, from the outset, a general conception of its scientific and technical nature. As the pharmaceutical and biotechnology industries increasingly searched out viable product conceptions stemming from genetic information, there developed a greater need for comprehensive information on the human genome. This, in broad strokes (and discussed below in greater detail), was the problem addressed by the HGP. Instigated by the NIH and DOE in the late 1980s, the HGP was a directed undertaking by several American universities, national laboratories and private corporations to create a readable 'map' of the human genome. This entailed a process of locating the position of genes and genetic material on human chromosomes, as well as reading (or sequencing) the nucleotide 'code' of DNA from which genetic material is constituted. The overall aim of the project, then, has been to produce a public database, revealing the sequence order of approximately 3 billion nucleotide bases and the location of what was then estimated at 50,000 to 100,000 genes within the 46 human chromosomes. The significance of this 'mapping' process lies in the numerous possibilities it renders for cellular control and protein synthesis.

The central dogma of molecular biology is that DNA is transcribed into messenger ribonucleic acid (mRNA) and then translated into polypeptide chains of amino acids that are, in turn, processed into proteins, the building blocks of life. To understand the significance of this dogma in relation to any genome map, it is important to grasp two relevant processes: *transcription* and *translation*. The structure of DNA is composed of four different nucleic acids which bind to each other to form the well known double-helix: adenine, guanine, thymine and cytosine (or, for short, A, G, T, C). Based on structural compatibility, A only binds with T and G only with C. During *transcription* (the transcribing of DNA into RNA) DNA separates and an enzyme known as RNA polymerase attaches itself to the template or 'antisense' strand of the DNA. From this, it matches ribonucleic bases according to the binding principle above, although it uses uracil (U) instead of thymine (T). This is a highly simplified description of actual events, but the point is that the sequence of DNA relates directly to the sequence of mRNA. With the introduction of a rhibosome into this picture, the cell is able to engage in *translation*. Every three bases of the RNA—and, thus, DNA by association—forms a codon, which corresponds to one of twenty possible amino acids, the building blocks of proteins. This genetic code is nonoverlapping: once the reading frame is established from a particular codon, it precedes every three nucleotides from that point on, adding amino acids until a termination codon is reached.[38]

There are roughly three billion nucleotide bases in the human genome, most of which exhibit an unknown function. It was estimated early on that only 3–5 percent of this material actually constitutes the functional complement of human genes. Understanding the location and exact sequence of these genes could provide an unprecedented capability to intervene in the abovementioned molecular process, so integral to the operation of cellular life. However, producing a map is no simple endeavor. In fact, the creation of a genome map was composed of three different elements: genetic linkage mapping, physical mapping and sequencing. With respect to linkage maps, the discovery of restriction endonucleases—a defensive bacterial enzyme that cuts foreign DNA at specific (code-dependent) points (digestion)—played a critical role. Near the end of the 1970s, it became apparent to scientists that the result of digesting different individuals' DNA with particular restriction enzymes always yielded a series of pieces with varying lengths. These restriction fragment length polymorphisms (RFLPs or 'riflips') were utilized, especially by David Botstein and Collaborative Research (a private biotech company), as a means to create a genetic linkage map.[39] Linkage refers to the fact that when two given genetic traits are located on the same chromosome, they should, theoretically, always be inherited together. Occasionally, however, in the meiosis stage of reproduction (in which the reproductive cells split into gametes), chromosome pairs (chromosomes always come in pairs) perform a 'crossover' in which they exchange genetic material, a process known as recombination (because genetic material with one chromosome is recombined with that of its pair chromosome). Because this process is unpredictable and rare, it is logical to deduce that the closer two traits are to each other, the more likely their linked status is to survive the recombination process (that is, they are too close together to be separated). Indeed, the frequency of this occurrence allows one to infer something about the relative distance of the two traits: the closer together the markers, the less likely they are to recombine. By studying genetically related populations on a generational basis, one can deduce the relational distance between traits by determining the frequency of their deviance from linkage, or their recombination. The importance of RFLPs in this process is that they offer natural markers that are passed through generations. While it is unbelievably rare for any two people to have indistinguishable sets of RFLPs, particular fragments are quite traceable throughout families. If one can demonstrate that such fragment lengths travel with a particular trait—that is, they are subject to linkage—then determining the number of recombinations or unpredicted outcomes (those with the trait but without the fragment length, or vice versa) gives a fair estimate of their genetic distance from each other. Importantly, this is not a physical distance, but a relational one, measured in centimorgans (cM) or map units (mu). By continually calculating the relational distances between a range of markers, scientists can acquire a linkage map—its resolution given in cM—which " . . . could anchor a map, and be used to search for genes expeditiously, *even if one knew nothing more than the pattern of inheritance in a family.*"[40]

If linkage maps enable one to have a picture of where genes and particular genetic markers lie in relation to each other, there is still some difficulty in determining precisely where to find the gene within the chromosome. The distances estimated in linkage maps differ from the actual physical distances between genes. Thus, the point of the physical map is to locate a marker's actual position on a particular chromosome. A central mechanism in this form of mapping involves what is known as bacterial DNA 'cloning.' DNA is separated into short pieces and incorporated into cloning vehicles: plasmids, phages, yeast artificial chromosomes (YACs) or bacteria artificial chromosomes (BACs).[41] Each of these can hold varying amount of DNA, but in all cases the cloning vehicles are inserted into bacteria and multiplied. The idea is to create library collections of such clones, whereby sections of DNA are represented in multiplicity. By identifying within each fragment particular sequence tag sites (STSs), short stretches of DNA which have already been randomly decoded (i.e. their nucleotide bases have been identified), the aim is to find points of overlap between the cloned fragments. This process of reconstruction connects DNA fragments into continuous segments (or 'contigs') that, optimally, will grow in size and eventually connect with each other. Complimentary to this, a labeled probe containing a known series of nucleotide bases can be used to create fluorescent probes which hybridize to their correct position on the chromosome (fluorescent *in situ* hybridization or FISH). In sum, physical mapping is intended to provide locational 'anchor' points, in relation to which DNA segments can be physically ordered. Whatever more detailed work gets done with these ordered segments, their general position will already be known.

Typically, physical mapping has been used to lay the groundwork for large-scale sequencing—the process whereby the detailed order of nucleotide bases within DNA is determined. Sequencing a cloned segment reveals the order of its nucleotides and its location in the genome. This completed the finite goals of the HGP: to locate and sequence the full complement of nucleotide bases in human DNA. Sequencing technology, while progressing rapidly in the last decade through automation, has generally relied on the same principle. In the original method, a section of DNA is multiplied (by cloning or by PCR[42]) and separated or 'denatured' in a solution. This solution is then subdivided into four equal parts and mixed in a solution with DNA polymerase (an enzyme which reconstructs DNA in singular direction during replication), a primer to activate the polymerase, and free floating nucleotide bases (as new 'building blocks'). Each solution also receives one of four dideoxynucleotide triphosphates (ddNTPs), corresponding to one of the nucleotide bases: A, T, G or C. While these ddNTPs are used freely by the polymerases to construct DNA (just like nucleotides), their structure, which lacks a hydroxyl group in a crucial part of the phosphate molecule, blocks the polymerase's capacity to add any subsequent nucleotide bases. With countless polymerase-based constructions proceeding simultaneously, each solution will show all of the stop points for one of the four nucleotide bases. The resulting DNA fragments from each solution are then subjected to gel electrophoresis, a polar-charged gel, which causes the differing, fragments to migrate according to their mass (which corresponds to their different lengths). When all four gels are laid side-to-side, one can read off from shortest to longest which lane—A, T, G or C—holds the fragment with the ddNTP. In this way, the exact order of nucleotides in this stretch of DNA is revealed. In the now automated methods, a fluorescent-labeled ddNTP is used, and the fragments are separated and forced at different speeds through a capillary tube (capillary gel electrophoresis). In this process, all DNA fragments can be loaded into the tube (each differing from the next by only one base), again separated by voltage and caused to migrate in order of the length, and then, on exit, have their fluorescent ddNTP excited by a laser and read by a detector. This has greatly accelerated the speed of sequencing since the outset of the genome project, enabling a single machine to read as many as 500,000 nucleotide bases per day.[43]

Since its inception, sequencing may not have changed a great deal conceptually, but the strategies toward its use have varied. The approach utilized by the HGP relied on the compilation of successful clone libraries from which subclones were subjected to sequencing methods. Assuming the clone has already been mapped, this 'top down' strategy has the advantage of already knowing the broad location of the sequence (based on the known lo-cation of the original clone) and a less complicated reconstruction (based on the *limited* number of fragments contained the original clone). It also en-sures a relatively high degree of accuracy, because overlapping clones can be more effectively checked against each other for accuracy.[44] However, it is also a more time-consuming process, requiring a step-by-step compilation of clone libraries. A more controversial approach, orchestrated by J. Craig Venter of Celera Corporation in competition with the HGP (more on this below!), was high-throughput 'shotgun' sequencing. This more direct method has been labeled a 'bottom up' approach to sequencing because it skips over the stage of mapping. Instead, the whole genome is broken into random fragments, which are then run into very high-powered sequencers. Once the fragment sequences are all obtained, a powerful program utilizes algorithms to determine overlaps for the reconstruction process.[45] The con-troversial aspect of this approach, despite its apparent success with the se-quencing of *Drosophila* (fruit fly), was the potential inaccuracy of DNA fragment reconstruction.[46] Human DNA is composed of a high degree of repetitive material, much of which can exceed the length of DNA molecules to be sequenced. Consequently, "sequences containing very similar repeats will be automatically assembled into the same contigs, and careful reanaly-sis will be necessary to detect and correct such misassemblies."[47]

In sum, the HGP emerged in the late 1980s and 1990s as a project combining linkage maps, physical maps and sequencing, although it should be noted that linkage analysis has existed for most of this century. Their combination afforded a powerful and vast information resource with which innumerable subsequent scientific and technological developments are pos-sible. As is well known, complete or partial maps of genome material are not inherently instructive in relation to biological function, but they do provide a powerful tool for genetic comparison and experimental manipulation. With every complete sequence, the possibilities increase to understand gene activity, determine new protein structures and function, and synthesize med-ical and non-medical products related to the human body. Although this complement of research activities was not properly within the mandate of the genome project, it is difficult to separate from its underlying reasoning. The HGP signals, scientifically, the long culmination of a research trajectory within molecular biology based on cellular control and, practically, the foundation for an entirely new range of products and methods aimed at medical and commercial utilization.

While this is not the place for an extended discussion of activities de-rived from basic HGP science, some initial understanding of their character and significance is necessary. By way of illustration, three such applications include genetic diagnostics, human protein synthesis, and gene therapy. The specter of genetic diagnostics has been the source of much criticism.[48] The markers gathered in both genetic and physical maps can, logically, be used to diagnose the presence of ostensible genetic dispositions in individuals. The search for reliable markers related to numerous medical conditions is well under way, resulting in diagnostics for conditions such as breast cancer, Huntington's disease and sickle-cell anemia. Controversy continues to emerge in relation to the medical significance, utility, and social ramifications of such information.[49] Even assuming the identification of an already mapped and sequenced gene, the predictive significance of such tests can differ widely. On the one hand, late-onset cancers, given their strong environmental component, are extremely difficult to attribute to genotype. PKU disease, on the other hand, is now subject to a reliable and life-saving predictive test. Nonetheless, many late-onset cancers are the focus of diagnostics development. Moreover, problematic statistics are often used to interpret the presence of a given genotype, pointing to the subsequent 'odds' of developing a given condition in one's lifetime. Such figures—which are probabilities averaged out over average lifespan across wide populations—can obscure the fact that until old age, the likelihood of symptomatic expression is several orders of magnitude weaker. Even if the determination of genotype could lead to accurate predictions, including the time of onset, their utility would remain questionable on moral grounds. For example, in the case of late-onset conditions for which there is no medical preventive or cure, what purpose does this knowledge serve? Would it cause anxiety or resignation? Is a life that *may* include a serious condition late in life not worth living in the first place?[50] Finally, there are important questions concerning how this information will be disseminated and used. Here, the central problem is whether the availability of such information can lead to socio-economic discrimination.[51] These questions will, for obvious reasons, remain unanswered here, but it is crucial to note the association of immediate genome mapping technologies with the development of techniques that have profound implications for public and corporate medical communities.

Human protein synthesis constitutes another logical outcome of gene mapping. If the sequence code of a given gene is determined, the amino acid sequence of the protein to which it is associated can also be deciphered. Consequently, the HGP is of vital importance to the study of proteins, or 'proteomics,' because its data is revealing about the structure, function and regulation of human proteins. Human proteins take part in virtually every biochemical action within the cell and organism and are, thus, constitutive of countless substances in the human body of medical interest. Some obvious examples would include insulin, interferon, human growth hormone and monoclonal antibodies (large proteins produced by white blood cells which perform search and destroy tasks). There is a deep connection here between the HGP and the ongoing development of a productive healthcare industry:

> Many diseases are caused by the absence or impaired function of proteins, and synthesising and purifying these from cloned genes is an important medical application of genetic manipulation. The majority of biopharmaceuticals on the market are recombinant therapeutic protein drugs. Until the use of recombinant DNA technology, the only source of these proteins was animal or body fluids; however, these techniques now allow many more possibilities. Genetic engineering also offers the possibility of improving natural human molecules by replacing or changing the order of some of the amino acids in the protein—making 'designer' molecules.[52]

Again, the social utility of these products varies and can be the subject of some contention—an example is Eli Lilly and Genentech's mass production of human growth hormone to address growth deficiencies and, potentially, aging.[53] Nonetheless, already by 1997, there were over 50 such products available and around 450 under development, 120 of which had already reached Phase III clinical trials in the United States.

A final example of the HGP's relevance lies in the area of gene therapy. The incubation of gene therapy as a research endeavor came about at roughly the same time as the HGP, but the latter must be viewed, at least in part, as constitutive of the former. Without mapping the location and characterizing the gene(s) in question, it is fruitless to speak of any widespread use of this medical technique. The concept of gene therapy entails the delivery of genetic information to a critical number of cells within an organism, such that they can have a desired medical effect. This larger categorization is subdivided into germ-line and somatic therapy. The former involves alteration of reproductive cells such that individuals would pass on genetic alterations to their offspring. This would, primarily, involve procedures on early-stage embryos.[54] Somatic therapy involves treatment aimed at human cells that are not passed on through reproduction. At present, only somatic therapy has been attempted clinically, beginning with William French Anderson's treatment of children with adenosine deaminase (ADA) deficiency.[55] In this procedure, the aim was to extract, treat and reinsert stem cells—cells located deep within bone marrow which divide and produce most red and white blood cells—but there have also been many trials involving an *in vivo* delivery process.[56] The genetic material is usually delivered by way of a viral vector which has had its deleterious genetic material deleted, ostensibly disabling its pathogenic effects. This, theoretically, allows for a transfer of the desired DNA into specific cells where it can multiply and be expressed. There is still much uncertainty in relation to this form of medical research, but the degree of interest it has garnered should not go unnoticed—the NIH already has increased its yearly budget in this area to over $200 million, and there are over 500 approved human trials.[57]

In the end, the HGP was an audacious and productive scientific endeavor, managing to accelerate and accomplish most of its goals ahead of time.[58] While the above description by no means represents an exhaustive account of the project, or the activities to which it is associated, it should provide insight for the reader into its general scientific and technological contours. In its scientific form, the project has raised an enormous degree of social fanfare and derision, scientific hope and criticism. As a result, in any attempt to evaluate the project's merits, goals or effects, this elaboration of its scientific features and potential effects constitutes a necessary, but only preliminary, part of a wider historical understanding.

CONCLUSION

The burden of this chapter has been to provide context for a critical analysis of the HGP. It has briefly cast the history of molecular biology in the light of external structures that were influential in its development, by highlighting the prevalence of 'directed autonomy,' oriented around an early alliance with particular social goals. More specifically, in relation to genome science, it has provided a critical background concerning the later rDNA debate, as well as the ensuing regulatory regime that accommodated the rise of the biotechnology industry. In addition to this historical picture, the chapter has elucidated, for introductory purposes, the HGP's scientific contours, along with some indication of their (especially medical) significance. Clearly, the initial rDNA developments of the 1970s can be scientifically related to the HGP, but, interestingly, there is no *necessary* historical path from one to the other. Thus, while there are certainly elements of continuity between the history of molecular biology and the HGP, we should not contrive to 'uncover' the latter within the former. As later chapters will make clear, while the earlier practice of molecular biology conformed more closely to the conventional norms of scientific practice, the emergence of the HGP signaled a considerably altered scientific context on both individual and institutional levels. Thus, it is critical not to mistake this transition as a 'natural' evolution in scientific practice. Ultimately, any compelling explanation of the HGP's origins requires a clear elaboration of its social basis. This, in turn, depends on a theoretically informed discussion of the social, political, and economic factors which have brought genome science to the fore, and made necessary the construction of a genome map—a task to which this work now turns.

Chapter Three
Understanding Science and Technology: A Political Economy Framework

The period in which genome research came to the forefront in biology witnessed no shortage of analyses addressing scientific and technological change in the face of larger social processes.[1] However, much of this material inadequately explains the predominant factors that condition the emergence of particular scientific practices. With respect to the HGP, there remains a marked absence of works that offer compelling conceptual and historical accounts of the project's emergence. The prevailing tendency to reconstruct a record of scientifically significant events in narrative form, either chronologically or thematically, fails to provide any explanatory framework within which the HGP can be situated historically. While interesting in its own right, empirical research of this kind is only useful insofar as it enhances or detracts from the tenability of relevant explanatory mechanisms.

Bearing this in mind, this chapter introduces a theoretical framework informed by political economy, with an eye towards understanding scientific and technological advance in its concrete political and historical context. It offers the conceptual apparatus with which the science and technology of the HGP will be interpreted in later sections, situating their development within the progression of capitalism in both the United States and the wider advanced industrial world. As such, it sets the groundwork for the central contention of this work: that the primary forces that incited and conditioned the American genome project are to be found in capitalist social relations. The chapter opens with a general discussion of the important relation between dominant social forces and the progression of contemporary science and technology. It then proceeds to situate this progression in relation to capitalism's specific 'logic of motion.' Drawing upon systematic accounts of the competitive market pressures that induce innovation within production, and informed in particular by Karl Marx's account in *Capital,* the chapter underlines the critical role played by scientific and technological innovation within the contemporary expression of capitalist development. Explaining this role on a theoretical level, the chapter turns to a discussion of knowledge as a commodity form, pointing to the actual utility of science and technology within capitalist production. Finally, and importantly, the chapter closes with an elaboration of the state and its critical role in both the reproduction of these social relations and the proactive facilitation of scientific and technological development.

THE SOCIAL NATURE OF SCIENCE AND TECHNOLOGY

In *The Sociology of Science,* R.K. Merton insisted on the untainted nature of science as a social practice.[2] Understanding scientific practice as emerging from a Protestant ethic, Merton argued that there exists a deep friction between science and governing social institutions. In this sense, Merton insisted on the preservation of a normative conception of science—one that would protect the objectivity of its own practice from ever-encroaching social pressures. However, in the aftermath of events such as WWII and the Vietnam War, the objective and disengaged nature of scientific practice has become increasingly difficult to sustain as either theoretically or practically relevant. Indeed, science and technology are now frequently referred to as invested with socially derived interests, revealing their practitioners as open to externally derived subjectivity and hierarchy.[3] A form of analysis emerging out of sociology deals with the social construction of technology. It purports to, "look very closely at the artefacts and varieties of technical knowledge in question and at the social actors whose activities affect their development."[4] However, its frame of reference tends to be very narrow, with a clear avoidance of any larger social context. As Langdon Winner has pointed out, the social and political context tends to emerge as a balanced outcome of the overall set of, 'pushes and pulls' within an essentially pluralist and fundamentally conservative framework.[5] In contrast to such ethnographic approaches to the behaviour of scientists, the emphasis of this study is on the set of wider social forces that condition the direction and character of scientific and technological change.[6] Here, 'social forces' refer to the predominant set of social relations that underlie production in capitalist societies. The point is neither to establish an 'anti–scientific' perspective nor to accept, naïvely, the inherently progressive character of scientific practice. Instead, the aim is to understand science and technology in the totality of their setting—a goal not unlike some sociologists in science and technology studies. Sheila Jasanoff, for instance, refers to the importance of a

> full-blown political analysis of science and technology [which] seeks to illuminate the 'co-production' of scientific and social order—that is, the production of mutually supporting forms of knowledge and forms of life—with all the detail and specificity that such a project entails.[7]

Similarly, Hans Klein and Daniel Lee Kleinman argue that

> [to] understand the capacity of groups to shape a technology, we need to know where the groups are situated within some structural matrix. We need to know further what the relative power of the contending groups is and what sources and varieties of this power are. We should understand potentially relevant social groups in relationship to one another and their structural characteristics and should be clear about the resources they have to draw on in their efforts to shape a technology.[8]

An approach embedded in Marxist political economy is useful to this end, because it provides, " . . . a social/historical interpretation that encompasses both science and technology, explaining their development in relation to large economic, political and ideological transformations."[9] And while it is true that Marx never systematically investigated science and technology as a set of practices, they nonetheless play an important role in his critical analysis of capitalism. In fact, in his exploration of capitalism as a historically specific set of social relations, Marx suggests that science and technology fulfil an integral and historically unprecedented function within the capitalist 'logic of motion.'

In relating science and technology to issues of political economy, it is important to differentiate the approach presented here from certain problematic accounts, particularly those that suggest technological determinism. For instance, Joseph Schumpeter, regularly taken as an alternative to Marxist analysis, has had a rather dramatic influence on writers on both the left and right with respect to questions of technology and development.[10] Schumpeter sees clusters of 'creative destruction' as instrumental to waves of capitalist development.[11] However, he arbitrarily divides 'invention' from 'innovation,' leaving questions related to the conditions surrounding the emergence of particular sciences and technologies completely out of his analysis. Moreover, even within his discussion of innovation (which, ostensibly, happens at a later point), he advances the claim that such activity emerges out of individual entrepreneurship. Indeed, he scolds Marx for failing to recognize that innovation emerges out of 'leadership' and not class struggle—entrepreneurs are, for Schumpeter, not a social class and need to be separated conceptually from capitalists.[12] Here we have no recognisable motive for the introduction of either 'inventions' or 'innovations' (assuming our temporary acceptance of their separation within capitalism). Following this theoretical scheme would certainly relate scientific and technological development to capitalist social formations, but it would treat the former as a mercurial origin of change, explaining, rather deterministically, only the cyclical development of advanced industrial societies.

A more current notion of scientific and technological change can be found in the now well-known work of Manuel Castells, who states quite adamantly the manner in which science and technology should *not* be understood. He dismisses explanations that attribute this to "a response by the capitalist system to overcome its internal contradictions," or "a way to ensure military superiority."[13] Instead, the emergence of new technological developments "must be traced to the autonomous dynamics of technological discovery and diffusion, including synergistic effects between various key technologies."[14] These synergistic effects include creative and dynamic interactions between actors in a 'network' configuration. Despite Castells' attempts at complexity, his network conception suggests that a description of all possible strong and weak connections between technology and society already provides an adequate explanation of the former's existence. Unfortunately, while such approaches quite correctly stress the importance and multiplicity of the social elements of innovation, they supply neither a method to identify the most crucial associations nor a way to ascertain *why* they occur. As such, their explanatory capacity goes no further than the allusion to complexity between an endless array of social and scientific factors.

In distinction from these approaches, a guiding principle of historical materialist analysis should be to prioritize historical process over technological determinism. Ellen Wood quite rightly expresses an intellectual opposition to those perspectives that, explicitly or implicitly, understand historical change as a function of scientific and technological change. In particular, she problematizes the assertion that " . . . evolution occurs because *the level of development of the technology outgrows the particular form of the social organization, which comes to constrain and fetter it.*"[15] This is not to deny that technological change is associated to historical process—indeed, the claim is just the opposite. Rather, the point is to question whether particular trends in science and technology constitute, in any way, " . . . the dynamic force that motivated historical change—either (causally) before or ('functionally') after the fact."[16] Since much of this criticism is directed at analyses of the 'left,' any framework relying on Marx's work must by necessity address Wood's challenge: to provide an explanation which does not assume the generalized march of an inherently innovative (even immanently capitalist) historical development and, instead, understands innovations within the location of their specific social forms. Importantly, Marx himself sought to understand the specific functions of science and technology within the specific social form of capitalism. Here, it is worth quoting Wood at length:

> Beginning early in his career, Marx never deviated from the view that the capitalist drive is specific and unprecedented and that whatever progressive tendencies may be generally observable in history, the specific logic of capitalism and its specific compulsion to improve the productivity of labour by technical means are not reducible to these general tendencies. They require a specific explanation. . . . Marx conducts his critique of political economy, the core of his mature work, by differentiating himself from those who take for granted and universalize the logic and dynamic of capitalism without acknowledging the historical specificity of its 'laws' or seeking to uncover what produces them. Marx, unlike the classical political economists, and indeed a host of other ideologues of 'commercial society,' did not assume that 'progress' embodied in modern society was simply the outcome of drive inherent in human nature or natural law, but insisted on the specificity of the capitalist demand for productivity and the need to find an explanation for it.[17]

The power of Marxist analysis lies precisely in the fact that its central task is to locate the *differentia specifica* of social relations within the present historical era of capitalism. If there is a case to be made for the historical specificity of capitalist social relations, then it is reasonable to surmise that there exists a historical specificity of the scientific and technological development that occurs under the auspices of those relations. Thus, as in the study of capitalism as a social form, the task must be clear from the outset: explain the progressive scientific and technological innovation of the current era beyond merely referring to the thing itself.

Wood's interpretation of Marx provides a valuable entry point into an understanding of the relation between capitalist social relations and science and technology. Prior to engaging this theoretical task, however, it is crucial to state unequivocally that the statements offered here do not dismiss, out of hand, any autonomy for scientific practice. One cannot assume that the entire history of science, a good deal of it occurring outside of the historical boundaries of capitalism, should be explained by a materialist understanding of capitalist social relations. Neither is it tenable to assert that all modern scientific achievements are, in a simple sense, the result of capitalism. Rather, for Marx, it is in the company of developed capitalist industry that science and technology take on a special significance. While there is most definitely innovation prior to this—namely, the rearrangement of the production process into detail labor—the critical moment " . . . is completed in modern industry, which makes science a productive force distinct from labour and presses it into the service of capital."[18] The shift from pre-capitalist social forms to industrial capitalism is also that from technologies circumscribed by the abilities of human beings and their physical endowment to an active engagement with mechanical laws that regularly surpass these boundaries. As Marx states it, "[the] principle, carried out in the factory system, of analysing the process of production into its constituent phases, and mechanics, of chemistry, and of the whole range of the natural sciences, becomes the determining principle everywhere."[19] It remains, therefore, possible to speak historically about general technological progress. However, this progress pales in comparison to the specific development of scientific and technological forces resident in capitalism. This historical shift demands our attention, insofar as it sheds light on the contemporary, and seemingly inexorable, push for large-scale scientific and technological progress. As such, it is in the social and historical circumstances of capitalism, first properly elucidated by Marx, that genome research needs to be properly situated.

SCIENCE, TECHNOLOGY AND THE 'LOGIC OF MOTION' OF CAPITALISM

Having set out the reasoning behind a social and historical analysis of scientific and technological processes in the context of capitalism, actualising such an analysis means following the contours of Marx's own argument concerning social relations, as well as certain Marxist interpretations which have followed in his wake. While it is seemingly distant from the issues of science and technology, it is important to begin where Marx does in his critique of political economy: with the nature of commodities. In the opening sections of *Capital,* Marx identifies two aspects of a commodity, its use-value and its exchange value. The former refers to the utility of the commodity, which is realized only through its consumption.[20] Marx intentionally excludes use value from the investigation of the workings of political economy, because it is not, strictly speaking, an expression of social relations in capitalism.[21] Instead, he emphasizes the exchange value through which commodities relate to one another, but this is not based on a quantitative estimation of their utility or use value. Instead, he turns to a third factor that is common to all commodities, from which their exchange values can be derived.

> Along with the useful qualities of the products themselves, we put out of sight both the useful character of the various kinds of labour embodied in them, and the concrete forms of that labour; there is nothing left but what is common to them all; all are reduced to one and the same sort of labour, human labour in the abstract.[22]

Value (which Marx uses to signify exchange value), then, amounts to the expression of abstract labor, emptied of its particular concrete elements (for example, varying skills), and represented through labor-time invested into production. Importantly, *exchange* cannot be identified only with the historical era of capitalism. The separation of exchange from use value begins with barter, and this development, like trade in general, is common to a wide array of historical social forms.[23] Even in the case of commodity exchange supported by the institution of money, there is no necessary connection to capitalism, as Marx understood it. Instead, a unique and fundamental element of capitalism is that it features *production that is directed explicitly for the purpose of exchange.*

What, then, are the distinctive elements that constitute this historically unprecedented rearrangement in the social relations of production? Marx does not equivocate on this point.

> The historical conditions of its existence are by no means given with the mere circulation of money and commodities. It can spring to life, only when the owner of the means of production and subsistence meets in the market with the free labourer selling his labour-power. And this one historical condition comprises a world's history. Capital therefore, announces from its first appearance a new epoch in the process of social production.[24]

In this sense, 'value' is not a metaphysical entity that is somehow innately connected to labor. Rather, value is the quantitative expression of how production relations are organized and, as a result, how social distribution proceeds. Marx arrives at this position by connecting his own insights concerning labor and exchange value with an issue central to the capitalist system: profit. He asks: if labor is the source of value, and if laborers are reimbursed for the labor they expend (equivalent exchange), how is profit at all possible? Any commodity sold at a price that deviates from its value would be an anomaly within equivalent exchange, and further rounds of production would bear this out, as other 'capitals' (in this usage, the term corresponds roughly to corporations) raise their prices concomitantly.[25] Marx's point here is that profit simply cannot be explained metaphysically in the realm of exchange, although it is in exchange where profit is realized. Given this reality, understanding the source of profit in capitalism requires a more sophisticated approach to the realm of production.

For Marx, analyzing production means dividing it more precisely into its constituent parts, beginning with the separation of constant (c) capital (fixed capital, raw materials, etc.) and variable (v) capital (that capital expended on labor). In terms of value creation, Marx puts aside constant capital, because it can only transfer value, not produce it.[26] With his sights set on variable labor, Marx's exceptional insight into capitalist social relations avails itself, as he identifies the notion and significance of 'labor power.'[27] Marx makes clear that it is not labor which the capitalist purchases, but labor power—the *capacity* of the laborer to perform useful labor that s/he can sell on the market for a stipulated time period. Labor power, in other words, is the sole commodity that laborers have at their disposal.[28] The laborer sells her/his capacity to perform work based on the prevailing value of labor power as a commodity. However, "[in] contradistinction . . . to the case of other commodities, there enters in the determination of the value of labor-power a historical and moral element."[29] The value of labor power amounts to the socially determined minimum costs required to sustain or reproduce the laborer's existence—a value differing considerably in varying social contexts. Whatever the value of labor power, the capitalist pays it out (or promises it at a later date) on the premise that it will be returned through work performed—a process called 'necessary labor' by Marx. The crux of the matter is that the performance of necessary labor only ever equals a portion of the full benefits which labor secures for the capitalist. The remaining 'surplus labor' (s) creates value accrued not by the worker, but by the capitalist. In other words, variable capital does not amount to equivalent exchange between capitalist and laborer. As such, the differential between paid (necessary) labor and unpaid (surplus) labor corresponds to the surplus (or expanded) value accumulated by the owner of the means of production.

In such a system, the capital-labor relation remains, at its foundation, deeply antagonistic, while the mutual relations between capitals are constituted by ceaseless competition—any capitalist failing to ensure optimal surplus value production can rest assured that others will do so. Indeed, as will be made clear below, an increase in surplus value for any one capital quite regularly comes at the direct expense of other capitals. Thus, it is imperative for each to maximize the creation of surplus value in production, such that it is able to maintain at least the average rate of profit. To raise the surplus value, each capital has at its disposal different possibilities. On the one hand, there are those methods referred to by Marx that result in absolute surplus value (ASV): expanding the scale of production or expanding the amount of unpaid labor performed.[30] Quite obviously, the expansion of unpaid labor in this manner has certain physical, human limits. Subsequently, when absolute surplus value can no longer be extracted, capitals must turn to what Marx terms relative surplus value (RSV). RSV also implies an expansion of unpaid labor, but the important difference lies in the methods used by capital. RSV involves an alteration in the means of production, such that the rate of surplus value (s/v) can be enhanced—that is, an alteration that decreases the time necessary to reproduce variable capital (to compensate capital for the amount paid out to necessary labor) and increases the portion of labor devoted to unpaid surplus production. Usually, this signifies either an alteration of the production process or a technical innovation. This is a point which remains relevant quite independent from Marx's thought. Corporate strategists, by necessity, both account for and pursue the productive effects of technological innovation, because to do otherwise would be to ignore a powerful element of the marketplace. And this is also the first manner in which Marx implicates science and technology in capitalist social relations.[31] Science and technology serve each capital in its inherently antagonistic relation with labor and its competitive relation with other capitals. It is not merely that the capitalist 'opts' to use science and technology as a tool. Rather, s/he must do so. A failure to respond to these relations would effectively nullify one's capacity as a capitalist—ultimately expressed in concrete terms by relative weakness in the production of surplus value.

Beginning, then, with its implication in labor-saving innovation, science and technology play a complicated role in the development of capitalism. To unravel this complicated role, it is first necessary to consider the question of profit realization. In day-to-day practice, individual capitals' concerns are not directed at the quantity of value production but, rather, at the relationship of their commodities to prevailing price. In Marx's understanding of the market, prices must even out with value only in the context of the total system of production.[32] The more immediate reality, however, is that price deviates regularly from value, although the former remains beholden to the latter through " . . . a tendency toward equalisation, seeking the ideal average, i.e., an average that does not really exist, i.e., a tendency to take this ideal as a standard."[33] According to Marx:

> Whatever the manner in which the prices of various commodities are
> first mutually fixed or regulated, their movements are always governed

by the law of value. If the labour-time required for their production happens to shrink, prices fall; if it increases prices rise, provided other conditions remain the same.[34]

Importantly, price in a given sector is linked to value, but this connection exists within a field of unregulated individual capitals pursuing optimized rates of profit. While in all spheres of production there is a tendency for the average rate of profit to be reflected by a market price, both constitute little more than a moving target. It is, in fact, rare that the individual values realized by capitals actually coincide with either the average rate of profit or price. Because competition compels changes in the costs of production, as changes in productivity and innovation are regularly introduced, different commodities are sold at the same social value (reflected in the average rate of profit and price) but realize an actual rate of profit (and individual value) above or below the social value. Each differentiation between individual value and market price has, in turn, its own effects on the average rate of profit and price. As such, competition among capitals ensures that the average rate of profit, reflected in price, is always dynamic and tendential, constantly shaping and being reshaped by production practices among capitals. This is true within branches of production and is amplified to an even greater extent across branches. This means that market competition within capitalism can never be viewed as governed by the principle of equilibrium, because the anarchical structure of production ensures a complex array of challenges to the outward manifestation of supply and demand: average rate of profit and price.[35] In this sense, Marx's value-oriented analysis comes to terms with conventional economic analysis based solely on price. Marx emphasized value as a category separate from price, because it was necessary to demonstrate that profit is affected, above all, by changes in labor organization that bring about changes in social distribution. Ultimately, both Marx and conventional economic theory attempt to show profit in relation to prevailing price, but Marx utilizes an analytical category that actually explains profit in material terms.

For individual capitals, this opens up a field of possibility. If price equates with prevailing social value, and its deviation from value depends on total social production, an extra incentive presents itself to individual capitals regarding the augmentation of production, particularly by way of innovation. The introduction of techniques to cheapen production costs amounts to the realization of extra profit (beyond the average). It may also offer the possibility to undercut the prices of competitors, potentially leading to an appropriation of greater market share. As a result,

[the] special productivity of labour in any particular sphere, or in any individual enterprise of this sphere, is of interest only to those capitalists
who are directly engaged in it, since it enables that particular sphere, vis-
à-vis the total capital, or that individual capitalist, vis-à-vis his sphere,
to make an extra profit.[36]

The ongoing process of scientific and technological application within the
parameters of capitalist production is, on the one hand, a means of survival
and, on the other, a route to extraordinary gains. The process is, of course,
perpetuated by the necessity of other capitals to adapt and generalize
whichever productivity measure has been introduced. It is further amplified
by the tendency of capital to follow profit across production spheres—
amounting to the movement of capital from low profit to high profit areas.[37]
At a very fundamental level, then, capital must turn to science and technology in view of both its antagonistic relation with wage labor and the inter-
capitalist competitive relation.

In a recent work, Chidem Kurdas confirms this role for science and
technology within the accumulation process, but strictly curtails its parameters.[38] She argues that there actually exist two ways in which science and
technology are connected to accumulation. There is, first, the 'routinized'
way, in which capital-intensive and labor-saving innovation is driven by the
ever-present necessity of growth among capitals. The second, more 'radical'
manner, however, implicates science and technology in the emergence of new
accumulation trajectories. According to Kurdas, it is only the routinized version of scientific and technological development that is addressed by Marx's
theoretical work.[39] As such,

> Marxian growth theory is focused on accumulation that takes place
> within a given technological and organizational framework, and that
> embodies the one type of innovation consistent with this framework. . . .
> [Thus], technological and organizational changes that do not fit the
> specified form cause the functions to shift, and the shifts of the growth
> path are outside the explanatory power of the theory.[40]

This is a very serious charge indeed. Not only does Kurdas see Marxian theory as incapable of explaining a major facet of scientific and technological
development, but she also associates a form of technological determinism to
Marxist arguments. Supposedly, the Marxist assumption is that 'path-shift-
ing' science and technology originate from external (and unexplained)
sources. Ultimately, the shortcoming of Marx and Marxists is that they fail
to identify the 'special stimulus' that must be present to motivate radical scientific and technological change. However, this is a reading of Marx that

fails to account for the overall logic of his work, and it certainly cannot be said to represent subsequent Marxian positions on science and technology. While Kurdas is correct to identify the importance of new areas of accumulation as a critical element of scientific and technological development, understanding this element through a Marxist framework requires a closer reading of Marx's laws of motion—particularly with respect to the pressure of market forces.

In fact, the increasingly active engagement of science and technology, as a method by which to compete, introduces a difficult systemic problem. As this process unfolds, there is an inexorable propensity for capitals to aggravate one of the central contradictory elements of capitalist production—the effort to lessen reliance on the special commodity upon which the expansion of value ultimately depends: labor power. The introduction of labor-saving technology leads to climbing productivity, but in the process, this heightens competition among rival capitals.[41] This is true of the production and circulation system as a whole, but it manifests itself especially at the level of the individual capital in terms of increasingly aggressive competition. Importantly, not all capitals feel this process equally. Indeed, further rounds of scientific and technological innovation constitute, for the individual capital, a potential escape route—along the lines of either intensified labor-saving technology or an innovative detour into new lines of production. In this sense, science and technology constitute for the capitalist both a problem and its solution, although s/he is only cognizant of the latter. Over the long-term, the move to introduce yet more technology tends to compound the contradictions inherent in capitalism, manifested concretely in overproduction and difficulty in the realization of profit. This underlying systemic pressure hardly resonates with individual capitals, because the more immediate reality of inter-capital relations consistently points to 'progressive' scientific and technological change as a method of surmounting market pressures.

Thus, within capitalism, there is not only an impulse built into the class dynamics to subordinate science and technology, but this impulse is also reinforced by an intensifying systemic pressure, urging competing capitals to approach science and technology as a 'solution.' This reaction to market pressure proves to be a critical counter-tendency. While Kurdas seems to understand the role of science and technology within the intensification of market pressure, she does not account for the fact that Marx outlined a systemic logic, continually moderated by multiple *countertendencies*—periodic processes that rejuvenate the system's tenacity. There are a number of counter-effects listed by Marx, and this list can easily be augmented in the contemporary context. He refers to increases in the intensity of exploitation (for example, prolongation of the working day, or the use of family labor); the depression of wages; a cheapening of the constituent parts of constant capital; the depreciation of already existing capital; the utility of a relative over-population (an increase in unemployed laborers); and the outlet of foreign trade. Joachim Hirsch has argued that Marx understood these tendencies mainly in the context of class struggle, in which capital either encourages or orchestrates the 'reorganisation of the conditions of production.' For Hirsch, there are three historically critical features to this reorganization: changes in capital itself (monopolies, property forms, credit, etc), the quantitative and qualitative expansion of the world market, and acceleration of scientific and technological progress.[42]

On the subject of alterations to capital itself, it should come as no surprise that the most astounding growth rates this century in advanced industrial countries came on the heels of one of the greatest capital-destroying endeavours ever undertaken: WWII.[43] Destruction of capital, more regularly through obsolescence and redundancy than through war, creates breathing space for capital to re-expand the production process described above. In a related sense, it also should not come as a surprise that recent rounds of 'deindustrialization' have occurred concomitantly with the rise of 'merger mania' and the introduction of new production technologies, such as 'just in time production.' These movements, particularly in the U.S. economy, have removed or consolidated large portions of pre-existing fixed wealth in order to make room for technologically more advanced constant capital. This is part and parcel of what Marx described as the centralization of capital—a process that necessitates the development of large-scale credit, the creation of joint stock companies and a socialization of production, in which the mobilization of capital no longer depends on the individual property owner.[44] As such, new opportunities are opened up for investment, as enormous amounts of surplus value are mobilized under one coherent scheme. Thus, the process of capital reorganization helps form conditions in which investment outlets become paramount to the functioning of the system.

At the same time, there is a "contradiction between the progressive development of the productive forces and the narrow basis of the relations of production."[45] With a constant need to overcome the boundaries of the market as it exists, expanding production requires an increasing number of market outlets, such that production value can be realized according to, at minimum, the average rate of profit. This absolute growth, however, must be constantly augmented by the procurement of relative surplus value. This, according to Marx, requires the production of new consumption; requires that the consuming circle within circulation expands as did the productive circle previously. Firstly: quantitative expansion of existing consumption; secondly: creation of new needs by propagating existing ones in a wide circle; *thirdly:* production of *new* needs and discovery and creation of new use values. . . . The value of the old industry is preserved by the creation of the fund for a new one in which the relation of capital and labour posits itself in a *new* form. Hence exploration of all of nature in order to discover new, useful qualities in things; universal exchange of the products of all alien climates and lands; new (artificial) preparation of natural objects, by which they are given new use values.[46]

This passage points to the manner in which Kurdas' argument has gone decisively awry. Even assuming that Marx does not explicitly relate science and technology to the formation of new needs (as he, in fact, does on the very same page), it is still directly within logic of capitalist accumulation that any 'special stimulus' for radical innovation should be understood. The counter-effects of capitals' behaviour *vis-à-vis* market competitors ensure that there is a prevailing social motivation for quantitative and qualitative assessments of production and market realization. Any failure on the part of capital to react in an innovative and dynamic manner to the tendential pressures related to production for the market would, most likely, rapidly precipitate its own decline. Ultimately, however, a major factor contributing to the systemic longevity of capitalism is precisely capital's historic tenacity in seeking out the means to overcome emergent barriers to its own social reproduction.

This leads to the third feature related to the reorganization of the conditions of production: the increasing subsumption of science and technology under the process of capital accumulation. In keeping with the motivation to both minimize costs and create new needs, "the development of science and technology represents an increasingly important counteracting influence to the tendency towards crisis and collapse in the developed capitalist countries."[47] As indicated above, a major part of this influence is directed at those areas that have not yet been the object of market relations. In this sense, it seems that Paul Sweezy was premature to claim that it " . . . is difficult even to imagine a series of new industries which would today have a relative importance comparable to that of the textile, mining, metallurgical and transportation industries in the eighteenth and nineteenth centuries."[48] Indeed, there is a case to be made that the recent round of capitalist development, drawn primarily from the realm of science and technology, is just such a 'series of new industries.'

Thus, understanding science and technology within the logic of accumulation means more than its mere association to innovation in the production process. Rather, such an understanding must relate science and technology to fundamental capital-labor social relations which give rise to the contradictory forces encapsulated by Marx. Moreover, it is critical to understand the Marxist emphasis on countertendencies, which slow and, at times, even reverse the tendential logic of capitalist production relations. Science and technology not only play an integral role in an ever-intensifying competitive logic, but also actively contribute to countertendencies that deflect or attempt to overcome the harshest effects of this logic. In other words, the same social and historical utilization of science and technology, which constitute a counter-tendential outlet for capitals, also "magnifies at the same time the inherent contradictions of this [capitalist] mode of production and progressively creates its absolute barrier."[49] It should hardly be surprising, then, that science and technology have increasingly been brought to the forefront of investment and production schemes. In fact, the pressures are so extreme that the distinction between science as 'pure research' and technology as 'knowledge application' has become increasingly blurred. This pressure results in an ever increasing pace and scale of scientific and technological development, such that the active reproduction of material conditions necessary for productive growth are often even beyond the means of socialized capital. One consequence of this is an expanded role for the state in the process of capitalist accumulation, in an attempt to position the 'national' economy for optimal scientific and technological competitiveness. Before exploring this role, however, it is necessary to address more specifically how scientific and technological knowledge actually fit into the social relations of capitalist production.

KNOWLEDGE AND ACCUMULATION

Given the manner in which science and technology interact with the contradictory set of social relations inherent to capitalist production and reproduction, it remains necessary to outline their more exact utilization within that process. If it is the case that value is an expression of the total distribution of social effort *versus* social wealth appropriation—ultimately understandable within capitalism in terms of the capital-labor relation—then what role can science and technology possibly play in value accumulation? What gets produced and who are the producers? One possible answer is suggested by the concepts of 'new economy' or 'information economy,' which imply that there is something unique and unprecedented in the current production process. Richard Florida and Martin Kenney argue that, presently, there is a shift to 'innovation-mediated' capitalist production.[50] They assert that this shift is characterized by a greater integration of 'knowledge,' which is directed almost solely at the search for value. As the authors state,

> [t]he new model of capitalism involves the blurring of the lines between production and innovation. The distinctions between the factory floor and the R&D laboratory are neither hard nor fast. Overlap between the two occurs frequently, and is increasingly promoted. Innovation becomes a continuous process. Experimentation and the recording of the results of manufacturing become a part of the production process itself. Workers, in conjunction with production and design engineers, are engaged in performing experiments and analysing results. Thus the roles and activities which were once thought of as involving only physical labour are transformed into information-rich arenas where knowledge and intelligence are applied.[51]

This picture is at once both fair and slightly misleading. It is certainly correct to maintain that the domain of production is encroaching more and more on activities of research and knowledge application (a claim compatible with the argument presented in this work). But while it is one thing to describe shifts within capitalist production, it is worth cautioning against claims of 'qualitative new levels' in the system's evolution.[52] As Ellen Wood quite correctly states,

> while we track the endless process of change in this uniquely dynamic system, we have to be very clear about what defines capitalism as a specific social form throughout all its transformations. We have to be very clear not only about what changes but about what stays the same: the unique systemic logic of capitalism, the specific 'laws of motion' or 'logic of process' common to capitalism in all its forms—the very logic that generates those constant changes.[53]

In this sense, even though Florida and Kenney's perspective is attentive to the fundamental importance of capitalist production, it obscures the historical continuities of the present period. This leads the authors to imply that it is only in the recent historical period that science and technology have come to be derived through research and development 'teams' and that capitals are only now subjected to 'perpetual innovation.'[54] While the former may be *increasingly* true, the latter has always been central to capitalist social relations. Taking this historical context seriously, it is of utmost importance to determine the operational role of knowledge within the capitalist production process, rather than assume the appropriateness of a 'new model.'

The labor process has always contained a particular element of pre-existing knowledge and, as such, material transformation brought about by human action always requires intellectual labor. In the same vein, mental transformations have very often required some material element.[55] Thus, to say that knowledge is a 'new' basis for economic development is already to subtly misrepresent the concrete, historical reality of the production process. Moreover, avoiding this tendency in the study of capitalist production in no way implies that mental and material transformations are, in an analytical sense, not worth holding separate. Guglielmo Carchedi sees value in this explanatory separation because, " . . . the *objects* of transformation differ: they are material objects in the case of material transformations and knowledge in the case of mental transformations."[56] For Carchedi, in order to understand the object of transformation in relation to commodity production, it is necessary to conceive of the use value of knowledge. This can be understood in a manner not unlike material commodities—knowledge has a use value insofar as it helps us relate to the material world. Since the production process is oriented around the transformation of use values, the use value of knowledge is also subject to transformation. As a result, the production of knowledge involves its transformation into new ways of relating to the material world.[57]

Ultimately, material and mental determinants of new use values can only combine in the labor process. While the productive labor process always exhibits both material and mental elements, any particular labor process can be expressed as either mental or material, based on the character of the use value to which it leads.[58] Thus, in its more pure form, mental labor can lead to knowledge that 1) is consumed in commodity form and/or 2) contributes to a 'deposit,' which leads to subsequent forms of transformation. By way of example, an immediately consumable knowledge might be DNA screening tests for a particular genetic disposition. The commodity consumed is knowledge, but its value is realized through its implication in various transformations of our relationship to human 'conditions' and medical practice. The same piece of knowledge—based, as it is, on the search for RFLP markers (see the previous chapter)—will also be added to the depository of knowledge constituted by gene mapping and contribute to later transformations of use value. At the same time, however, mental labor can also play an integral role in various manifestations of material production of commodities, which are also subject to consumption and/or future rounds of transformation. Here, an example might be knowledge involving sequencing methods and automation, which can lead to concrete, automated high-speed sequencing machinery, subject to immediate exchange as a material commodity. And this same material commodity is integral to the various forms of future transformation, such as DNA sequencing, the search for single-nucleotide polymorphisms or future work on 'proteomics.'

Ultimately, a stronger reach into spheres of scientific and technological innovation means that capital must direct ever more control over its progression. This is not to say that the scientific community—or the genome research community—is without autonomy. There is little doubt that the collective labor of science has a kind of immediate capacity to affect or transform prevailing realities. However, this capacity occurs within an ethos that can no longer properly be described as 'free.' This implies that,

> definite limits are set to the production of scientific results on the basis of capitalist commodity production. These limits show themselves concretely in the fact that individual capitals are increasingly unable to produce and to realize (from the point of view of production technique) the mass of scientific and technological knowledge necessary to stabilize the system as a whole, and indeed are less able to do so the greater the required mass becomes and the less it is possible to fall back on knowledge gained outside capitalist commodity production as a 'free productive force.'[59]

This somewhat complicated picture of scientific and technological development contains two important elements. First, the content of scientific and technological research has been drawn directly into the orbit of the productive capital. Second, the productive demands placed on science and technology have burgeoned to such an extent that, for the most part, the use of pre-existing scientific knowledge is no longer a 'luxury' within capitalist production. The agenda of scientific and technological change has, at once, both grown and become more specialized. Capitalist production exhibits a range of needs that must be satisfied in increasingly specialized and directed ways. As competitive systemic pressure mounts, individual capitals have no choice but to encourage and direct knowledge production that accords with their own area of valorization. 'Freely-conceived' knowledge is rarely of use to the single-minded producer. On the other end of knowledge production, scientists certainly do not own those means of production necessary for their research. Particularly within genomic research, laboratory costs are growing even beyond the budgets of many universities and institutions. This means that those involved in scientific and technological research are compelled to effect mental and material transformations that are increasingly defined by the needs of capital.

As capitalist development draws scientific research closer and closer into its sphere, there is not only a need to control the general direction of study, but also to control the manner in which its results are demonstrated.

Consequently, knowledge is now increasingly subject to the relations of private property. This means that knowledge that has been subject to mental transformation is now either an element of production or a commodity of exchange, the value of which is realized as price in the market. Within the contemporary expression of capitalism, the ever-intensifying expression of this process gives rise to, and continually exacerbates, a relentless pursuit of new and marketable information derived through science and technology. This proves difficult, however, given the easy dissemination of information relative to material commodities. As such, " . . . the consumption of knowledge is easily collectivized but is difficult to privatize. Capital has responded by trying to use the political arena to guarantee its private appropriation of socially produced knowledge."[60] The use of the patent, sanctioned by the state, allows capitals to invoke a form of artificial monopoly over the dissemination of particular forms of knowledge. Having secured this political right, scientific and technological advancement have become the predominant means to carve out new areas through which monopoly profits can be secured. Although referring more specifically to 'machinery,' Marx understood the significance of this process quite clearly:

> Machinery produces relative surplus-value; not only by directly depreciating the value of labour-power, and by indirectly cheapening the same through cheapening the commodities that enter into its reproduction, but also, when it is first introduced sporadically into an industry, by converting the labour employed by the owner of that machinery, into labour of a higher degree and greater efficacy, by raising the social value of the article produced above its individual value, and thus enabling the capitalist to replace the value of the day's product. *During this transition period, when the use of machinery is a sort of monopoly, the profits are therefore exceptional.* . . . The magnitude of the profit whets his appetite for more profit. . . . As the use of [same] machinery becomes more general in a particular industry, the social value of the product sinks down to its individual value, and the law that surplus-value does not arise from the labour-power that has been replaced by the machinery, but from the labour-power actually employed in working with the machinery, asserts itself.[61]

Consequently, the results of scientific (mental) labor lead to transformed knowledge as a commodity, which can be aimed at new use values—accelerating and reinforcing a system of competitive, uneven growth. At the same time, securing monopoly over a knowledge commodity, by way of rapid advancement and patent protection, makes possible profit accumulation among individual capitals, despite the continuing pressures of declining profitability and the intensely competitive environment of industrial sectors fighting this tendency.

KNOWLEDGE, ACCUMULATION AND THE STATE

The particular case of the HGP appears to confirm the need to identify a 'special stimulus'—external to either capital-labor or inter-capital relationships—that underlies the emergence of radical science and technology. After all, strictly speaking, the HGP was not the direct product of individual capitals, but was instead orchestrated 'externally' by the state. This raises important questions regarding how the state is related to both capitalist social relations and science and technology. On the former, the debate concerning Marxist state theory has been extensive, to say the least, and it cannot be settled here.[62] It is, for the purposes of this work, adequate to suggest that capital has, throughout its development, made subtle use of extra-economic measures to ensure its ostensibly 'pure' economic ends. This means that class domination does not, and cannot, propel itself by way of some natural chain of economic logic, against which political struggles mean little. Indeed, it is just the opposite. The social relations of capitalism, by their very nature, require a regularized set of behaviors, as well as the assurance of conducive interaction between classes. The focal point of that interaction with respect to capitalist development continues to be the state, an entity that enforces an environment amenable to the capitalist 'logic of motion.' As an entry point to this subject, it is instructive to realize that,

> the strategic lesson to be learned from the transfer of 'political' issues to the 'economy' is not that class struggles ought to be primarily concentrated in the economic sphere or 'at the point of production.' . . . The division of labour between class and state means not so much that power is diffuse, but, on the contrary, that the state which represents the coercive 'moment' of capitalist class domination, embodied in the most highly specialised, exclusive, and centralized monopoly of social force, is ultimately the decisive point of concentration for all power in society.[63]

In this context, the state can hardly be seen as a secondary, much less a passive, agent in the contemporary push for scientific research aimed at commodity production. But if the state represents a critical non-economic factor in the advancement of scientifically facilitated growth, how should we characterize it, and what is its role?

It is vital to point out that a role for the state *vis-à-vis* the progression of capitalism does not necessitate that the former be seen as epiphenomenal to the latter. The fact that the state, as a historical apparatus, predates the emergence of capitalism means that "we cannot take . . . for granted that there do not cling to it features which can be accounted for by the conditions of its formation."[64] It is of particular interest that advanced industrial states have had varying relationships with the development of capitalism, owing in part to the staying power of certain pre-capitalist elements.[65] As such, the aim is to understand the particular form of the state in relation to a set of historical, material conditions prevalent under capitalist social relations. These conditions do not *create* the state, but they affect its development, such that it takes on trappings (form and functions) that are historically unique. Consequently, while capitalist social relations do not tell us everything about the state, the "historical concretization of state functions is essentially to be determined from the context of crises so defined and from the political movement to which the crisis gives rise."[66] The broad strokes of this 'historical' concretization are considered here, while a more specific and detailed exploration of the American state in relation to the HGP follows later (particularly chapter 5).

Historically, and especially following the exceptional expansionary period following the second world war, capitalist states have undertaken a series of steps which "always establishes, as if by a trick of reason, exactly that which can be regarded as functional at the time for the concrete conditions of capital accumulation."[67] These can be viewed as the external reproduction of conditions necessary for production, but they are also *necessary* to the reproduction of the state as a political entity. Because the appropriation of surplus value by capital depends on the principle of equal exchange, free wage labor and competitive accumulation, the social reproduction of these processes must be guaranteed. Consequently, the form taken by the capitalist state is unique, in that free wage labor and equal exchange require the removal (at least in appearance) of the direct means of domination from the owners of the means of production. As such, the social relations of capitalism, for the first time, require that "control over the means of force . . . be localized in a social instance raised above the economic reproduction process: the creation of formal bourgeois freedom and equality and the establishment of a state monopoly of force."[68] Given this *nominal* separation of the political from the economic, the state is at once both external and integral to the immediate social relations of capitalist development. In order to ensure the reproduction of social relations, as well as its own form (raised above production and extra-economic coercion), the state must not only maintain a surface 'neutrality' in relation to both the capital-labor relation and market outcomes, but simultaneously underwrite the general and external conditions of the capitalist production process.

Consequently, the advanced industrial state is associated with a political-legal form ostensibly based on equality and independence from economic interests. At the same time, it requires a technical capacity to foster conditions favorable to the material well being of production and, by association, the state. The political-legal realm remains the most outward expression of class antagonism, manifested in specific democratic forms (such as legislatures, councils and judiciaries), but largely obscured by a prevailing ideological conception of the 'general will.' Important to any analysis of the state in relation to class, the democratic institutions of the advanced industrial state are the frontline terrain of social struggle, in which the general predilections of the state as an apparatus are chosen. However, while this arena may be a site of struggle, it remains so within a historically structured process, dependent currently on the material reproduction of capitalism. There has been a consistent trajectory of state intervention, in order to ensure the ongoing preconditions for development. This is why outcomes in the capitalist political process, while never in any way absolutely determined, are hardly invulnerable to predictability.[69] The forms of these interventions have varied "as the economic and social basis is modified by the process of the accumulation of capital, the technological revolutionization of the labor process and the course of capital crises."[70] Hirsch identifies three 'moments' in this process, the latter two of which are *most* pertinent to this study: 1) the imposition of capitalist class structure; 2) the centralization and concentration of capital in concert with the extension and consolidation of the world market; and 3) the development of 'infrastructure' policy.[71]

Pertaining to the centralization and concentration of capital, the state has taken an interventionist role, in order both to allay the difficulties of reproduction, as well as ensure the legitimacy of the capitalist political form. The exceptional circumstance of the capitalist state stems, in part, from its capacity to raise revenue and undertake measures that stabilize the system, all the while remaining independent of the accumulation process. These measures include both 'incomes policy' and 'state consumption.' The former aims "to prevent the wage earners from realizing their cyclical opportunities on the market, in order gradually to lower the rate of increase of real wages, if not to bring about real cuts in wages."[72] The latter involves a set of practices aimed at redistribution as a means to social reproduction (social policies, family wages, unemployment insurance), as well as the drawing of surplus value into the unproductive sphere. Investments that redirect surplus value in this way are either 'wasted' or do not produce subsequent rounds of self-expanding capital accumulation (a good example is government procurement through the military-industrial complex). This slows growth in constant capital investment relative to productive labor, and it means that states typically provide a major release valve that counteracts pressures related to profitability. Moreover, the state also contributes to 'demand' insofar as it enacts policies that affect the circulation of capital, modifying productive cycles and the immediate direction of profitability. However, while these measures demonstrate the complex managerial capacities of the state, their effects are ultimately temporary, because they only delay the underlying structural contradictions inherent in capitalism's long-term development.[73]

In the pursuit of sustained effects on capitalist production, the state is more likely to turn to infrastructure policy, as it implies the possibility of structural alterations. For instance, in order for capital to exit from overproduced lines with chronic profitability problems, the state must provide certain tangible, advantageous preconditions. This implies the pursuit of growth policy, necessitating the facilitation of infrastructure, the establishment of which assumes the state-organized supply of finance. The reasons are many-fold, including the possibility that,

> their establishment or their management is insufficiently (or not at all) profitable (e.g. because of extremely long capital turnover times) or too risky; exclusiveness of use for the individual capital ('principle of exclusion') cannot be guaranteed—either because the . . . specific use-value structure cannot enter into commodity circulation (qualification of labour power, research results), or because the organization of the value return would hinder the whole process of reproduction excessively (e.g. road tolls). In all cases, [however], it is necessary that the relevant precondition of production is 'general' in so far as its *absence* represents a considerable hindrance to the process of production and reproduction, with the result that its establishment is forced on the state apparatus, if need be by crisis.[74]

These factors speak directly to instances of large-scale scientific and technological projects. It is significant that such 'infrastructure,' in the face of a rapidly growing world market, has taken on a central necessity in the rejuvenation, or survivability, of even the most concentrated and centralized individual capitals. Since the obsolescence and costs of scientific and technological knowledge continue to accelerate within capitalist social relations, the perceived risk factor in producing 'general' (unapplied) science and technology has risen considerably. For this reason, "the systematic generation of science and technology . . . becomes an important area of the functions of the state administration in guaranteeing 'the general external conditions of the reproduction process.'"[75] Relatively separated from the circumstances of accumulation and competition, the state assumes the task of 'socialized risk.' Public policy is utilized to direct a transfer of social surplus value into particular high-risk sectors, such that individual capitals are given extra incentives to develop scientific research and technology in ways they would otherwise rarely undertake. This transfer of value can take place *via* a direct transfer, orchestrated through the outright public funding of projects that significantly further the cause of a developing industry. Alternatively, it can occur indirectly through tax allowances for those capitals undertaking innovative research and development. Whatever specific avenue the state takes, the mobilization of counter-tendencies to capitalism's systemic logic is the ultimate effect, extending the market to create 'new needs' and, by association, new areas of accumulation. The significance of such an explanatory framework with regard to the HGP is unmistakable: as a large-scale project, it should properly be understood as socially mobilized infrastructure, aimed at strategically countering waning profitability tendencies in advanced industrial economies. [76]

None of this occurs in a mechanical (econometric) manner but is, instead, the immediate subject of political struggle. The state's involvement in the development of science and technology hardly stops with maintenance of the 'general good.' Rather, it represents a field within which particular groups can gain ascendancy while fighting for the most advantageous policy. Indeed, the state can, against the will of many capitals, force the procurement of scientific and technological advance. As such, "[state] technology policy can . . . not be interpreted as the smooth reaction to the requirements of reproduction; it is rather moulded in a particular way by the conflict between the partial interests of monopolies and the general reproduction demands of capital as a whole."[77] The theoretical portrayal of the state in relation to technology must, like all state functions, be mediated through the course and results of political (class) struggle.[78] In this sense, not only is the examination of state policy at once an examination of fundamental social relations, but the specific case of 'big science' offers an illustrative example of its contradictory tendencies, wherein the state's ostensibly neutral mobilization is systemically impressed with the partial interests of selected industries. In the 'best case' scenario, particular industrial sectors will be encouraged (or will have the luxury) to invest *en masse* in a sphere of entirely under-exploited technological competence.

The historical context of this ongoing political struggle has by no means been contained within state borders. For some time, it has been noted that the conditions that are conducive to the reproduction of capitalist social relations are the subject of internationalization.[79] With the increasing pressures of the accumulation process, states have taken it to be in their interest to assure such developments at a national and international level. Particularly in the post-1973 era, state institutions have increasingly understood an important part of their task in relation to the shaping of strategic advantage. And since the 1990s, this has become virtual policy dogma. As Leo Panitch points out, the rules of global restructuring

> take place in, through, and under the aegis of states; [they are] encoded by them and in important respects even authored by them; and [they involve] a shift in power relations within states that often means the centralisation and concentration of state powers as the necessary condition of and accompaniment to global market discipline.[80]

In everything from an increasingly technical and specialized education structure to the advocacy of international competitiveness, the state has reoriented its priorities in favor of the latest motion of capitalist development. States, and the policymakers who nominally direct their actions, appear compelled on an international level to act in accordance with the competitive logic of capitalist development.

This translates, above all, into the "public promotion of flexible production and technical innovation in those particular sectors which can 'win' in a global export-led competitive race."[81] Thus, the endorsement of science and technology policy must also be seen within the context of an increasingly international competition—an individual state's failure to set the conditions amenable to productive arenas of scientific and technological research assures only one thing: its eventual slippage into the position of technological 'laggard.' In keeping with this logic, advanced capitalist states also act to effect a political-legal form suitable to international competition, complete with familiar notions of freedom (sovereignty), equality (trade, non-discrimination) and justice (dispute settlement mechanisms). On this front, the development of binding international agreements extends the possibilities for strategic advantage. Viewing this concretely, one need only look to such instances as the General Agreement on Tariffs and Trade (GATT), the structural adjustment policies of international lending institutions, and the relatively recent creation of the World Trade Organization (WTO).

While such organizational schemes seem somewhat distanced from scientific and technological development, the former have direct bearing on the latter. The conscious construction of this international regime intensifies the market imperative, opening up individual capitals to a wider realm of competition, and transforming the exigency of scientific and technological progress into one of national survival.[82]

Ultimately, although on a superficial level the state can be viewed as a stimulus external to capital accumulation, its 'autonomy' needs to be heavily qualified. Neither independently orchestrating nor mechanically reacting to the tendential pressures of innovation-heavy accumulation, the state can be understood as a historically structured realm of political struggle which, by reason of its current material circumstances, has shifted its focus to emphasize international strategic advantage, capital mobility and rapid technological advance. There is, in other words, no logical reason to view the state as disassociated from capitalist development, and its pronounced involvement in science and technology does not shelter the latter from the effects and influences of capitalist social relations.

CONCLUSION

This chapter has advanced a framework for understanding the emergence of (especially, but not limited to, large-scale) scientific and technological innovation in the contemporary age. It has, at a general level, argued that any attempt to discern the driving force behind current science and technology needs to be understood in relation to social forces. Political economy, informed by Marx, forms the most effective basis of this framework, because it affords the opportunity to relate scientific and technological progress to dominant social, economic and political processes. Situating this progress within such a framework also renders an explanation that emphasizes the contradictory tendencies and effects of capitalism's tenacious advance. Contemporary science and technology are properly understood to emerge within the historical parameters of this advance, heightening its contradictions while also serving as the preferred means to overcome them. In such circumstances, the state mobilizes important counter-tendencies by socializing risk, promoting scientific and technological advance, and regulating the property relations that govern the production, circulation and realization of potential knowledge-based commodities.

It is worth noting that this chapter has, momentarily, put aside the question of *how* this scientific agenda emerges at the institutional level—a critical element in the political struggle around the private ownership and utilization of knowledge. In addition to an empirical account of this process, chapter 6 will further this work's theoretical framework by discussing the ways in which the scientific community operates within and, subsequently, reproduces prevailing power relations. Prior to this, however, chapters 4 and 5 apply the conceptual framework developed above. As such, they are devoted to a historical account of both capital and the state in relation to the U.S. HGP.

Chapter Four
U.S. Capital, Innovation and the HGP

In spring of 1998, Dr. Craig Venter issued a challenge to the federally funded HGP: in concert with Perkin-Elmer Corporation, he would sequence the entire human genome within three years. The presence of this newcomer within the mapping/sequencing scientific world quickly came to be depicted in terms of a 'public' *versus* 'private' competition to map and, ultimately, control the human genome.[1] This curious depiction implied that the HGP was somehow detached or neutral with respect to corporate biology and capitalist production. However, only in the most superficial sense can the accelerated pace of genome mapping in the ensuing period be depicted as a public/private 'showdown.' It is, in fact, misleading to disassociate the federally funded project from the context of either corporate competition or the needs of particular sectors to carve out new areas of value production. It is, of course, important to recognize that the constituent parts of scientific programs always contain conflicting motivations and practices—scientific ideals may be subject to capitalist structures, but they need not always be capitalist *in nature*. Recognizing this, however, does not free the HGP from the structured process of history—a process which has, particularly in the post-war period, positioned science and technology in ever-closer service to prevailing capitalist social relations.

Consequently, rather than point to the conflicting natures of government-orchestrated and privately funded projects, it is surely more useful to track the historical processes which conditioned the rise of genome research, the HGP's promulgation, and the ongoing manifestation of competition related to genome research. In this sense, the HGP needs to be empirically contextualized, at least as far back as the commercial processes of the mid–1970s. The task of this chapter is to discern the degree to which the project grew out of the dynamics of capitalist social dynamics, as well as to highlight some of its most significant aspects of commercialization and technology transfer. Bearing out the foregoing theoretical framework, it points to the industrial trajectories most closely related to genome sciences, particularly those involving the pharmaceutical and biotechnology sectors. With an eye toward the systemic imperatives imposed on these sectors, the HGP is properly seen as an extensively developed set of production tools, enabling the intensification of competitive accumulation among a particular range of capitals.

The chapter begins by emphasizing the industrial changes in the pharmaceutical sector during the 1970s and 1980s. During this period, this sector came under a series of pressures that enforced a more innovative outlook on production techniques, a process that must be closely associated with the emergence of the biotechnology sector from the late 1970s onward. Overlapping with the peak in pressure on the pharmaceutical industry, the advent of industrial biotechnology translated into the generation of new value appropriation, both creating an arena of 'start-up' firms and reinvigorating the appropriation capacities of existing firms. In bringing this context to the forefront, the chapter proceeds to highlight corporate motivations and support for the HGP, underlining its integral role in fostering the development of a highly competitive industrial sphere. In the final section, the ramifications of the HGP and the explosive activity of biotechnology and pharmaceutical sectors is considered as a reciprocal dynamic in which the increasingly competitive drive between capitals expresses itself overtly through stepped-up research and development (R&D) programs.

U.S. PHARMACEUTICALS AND COMPETITIVE NORMALIZATION

In order to gauge the environment from which genome research emerges, it is necessary to examine the development of the pharmaceutical industry. This is due to the fact that, in terms of industrial involvement by major corporations in genome research, pharmaceutical corporations have been consistently dominant. Since the late 1970s, the pharmaceutical industry has paid increasing attention to biotechnology-related R&D. This is clearly borne out by the fact that biotechnology companies too have maintained "a strong focus on human health care products, largely because capital availability has been greater [from] pharmaceuticals than for food or agricultural, due to the prospect of greater market reward."[2] In fact, in terms of patentable material, during and after the rise of a biotechnology industry, biotechnology-related patents were held mostly by pharmaceutical companies. These corporations controlled 56.3 percent of biotechnology-based patents, with the chemicals sector a distant second (15.2 percent).[3] But the high visibility of the pharmaceutical industry with regard to biotechnology does not, beyond correlation, *explain* its integral role in the emergence and proliferation of genome research. For that, it is necessary to consider the development of this industry in the post-war context, in order to provide a historical motivation for its surging interest in biotechnology from the late 1970s onward.

The birth of the 'modern' pharmaceutical industry is typically located between 1940 and 1960, a period frequently referred to as the 'golden era.' This era began largely under the dominance of German chemical firms. Because of their pre-war superiority in industrial chemicals, German firms such as Hoechst and Bayer were able to take considerable advantage in the discovery and production of antibacterials. In the pre-war era, German firms commanded 40 percent of the world market, along with 52 percent of the patents.[4] Their successes helped set off a wave of innovation and discovery in the drug industry after WWII, although it would be American and not German firms that dominated the market. During this period the development of drugs such as *streptomycin, tetracycline,* and *cortisone* brought a new rush of research and development in pharmaceuticals that overwhelmingly found their way to the market in the mid–1950s.[5] From 1953–1963, the introduction of new chemical entities (NCEs) increased approximately four-fold. Importantly, this wave of industrial research and development activity was crucial in changing the expectations for pharmaceutical profit margins. Rather than 'falling into' therapeutically useful compounds, these companies began to orchestrate concerted programs to develop, with an eye to the market, numerous NCEs with medicinal value.

Much has been said about the profit margins of the pharmaceutical industry—namely, that they are very high. Figures differ considerably depending on the source, but the industry consistently exhibits profits that exceed other areas of manufacturing. This was not always so. During the 'golden era' of discovery, before multiple NCEs had worked their way into firms' profit margins, the pharmaceutical industry was still operating within a typically competitive marketplace. Indeed, in the immediate post-war economic surge, pharmaceuticals enjoyed roughly equivalent profit margins with the rest of industry. Most of its products were long past patent expiry, and generic drugs were a considerable force in the marketplace. According to Heinz Redwood, it is only after the mid–1950s, when a flood of R&D-derived products came into the marketplace, that profit margins between pharmaceuticals and other manufacturing begin to diverge.[6] From the mid–1950s through the mid–1980s, the return on equity in the drug industry was between 40 and 89 percent higher than in all areas of manufacturing.[7] This stark change in profit levels dispels the notion that there is some "Law of Nature which decrees that the pharmaceutical industry always yields a higher return than all manufacturing."[8] It is only with the mass introduction of patent protection on countless products, concomitant with the aggressive squeezing out of generic production, that the pharmaceutical industry began its post-war trend of above average profits.

It is important to keep in mind that other areas of manufacturing, without the extensive protection of monopoly patents, experienced a falling profitability in the post-war period. Robert Brenner has recently analysed the post-war manufacturing sphere of the three leading advanced industrial economies—the U.S., Germany and Japan—and demonstrates a falling profitability and heightened market pressure on capitals beginning in the 1965–1973 period.[9] Increased productivity, particularly in Japan and Germany, led to international over-production, " . . . forcing down manufacturing profitability in the advanced capitalist economies taken in aggregate, with US producers bearing the brunt of the fall."[10] From 1973–1990, profitability continued to languish, never even peaking at the 1973 levels, and far from the years preceding it. The main explanation for this is to be found in insufficient 'exit' by manufacturers from over-crowded production lines, manufacturers' willingness to swallow the reduced profit rate (sometimes attempting to make lines even more efficient, further exacerbating the over-capacity situation), and the use of debt and public spending to stave off collapse.[11] As such, in line with the logic of capitalist production, the U.S. economy exhibited a rising rate of productivity throughout the post-war era, which, in turn, made more stringent the conditions under which profitability could occur. Fred Moseley estimates that both surplus value and production investment of capital increased by 58 percent and 14 percent, respectively, in the period between 1947 and 1987, leading to increased market pressure, as the rate of profit declined from 22 percent in 1947, to 10 percent in 1980, to 15 percent in 1994.[12]

Thus, while there was slow decline in profitability exhibited across US manufacturing, the pharmaceutical industry quite clearly remained advantageously sheltered from this pressure. Its capacity from the mid–1950s through the 1970s to establish patent-based sales, allowing for exclusivity within each therapeutic class, made it relatively unique among manufacturing sectors. This was, nevertheless, a process requiring renewal, as the competitive market would eventually erode or take away the market dominance enjoyed through pharmaceutical patents. As such, members of this growing market invested in and utilized R&D capabilities, with an aim toward finishing first in the introduction of therapeutic products, allowing them to exploit further their temporary monopoly powers.[13] It is hardly a surprise, then, as Figure 4.1 makes clear, that the pharmaceutical industry maintained a high expenditure on R&D as a percentage of sales. From 1970 to 2000, R&D, as a percentage of sales, roughly doubled from just over 10 percent to over 20 percent.

It is also notable in Figure 4.1 that, although pharmaceuticals maintained a healthy profit margin through the 1960s and 1970s, there is a dramatic upswing in research and development from around 1980 onward. Why, if there is no substantial drop in profit margins, should R&D investments increase so dramatically? By 1970, the 'over the counter' (OTC) market had been reduced to less than 25 percent, with 'ethicals' (or prescription drugs) accounting for the rest. The focus of industry had clearly moved in the direction of patentable prescription drugs, sought out through aggressive R&D. The only major challenge to this market security occurred within therapeutic classes where there existed openings for the production of 'me-too' drugs—R&D-derived improvements on already existing drugs. Realistically, however, 'me-too' drugs also required long-term R&D investments, effectively limiting inter-capital competition to those firms with considerable resources. In other words, even with 'me-too' drugs, high market entry barriers were maintained for would-be drug producers. The apparent sheltering effect of R&D commodities, however, could not last indefinitely, because leading firms' high profits had been based on a combination of patent control and a lack of price control in the United States healthcare market. By the end of the 1970s, the number of patent expiries was growing, and many core product lines would be opened up to market competition in the 1980s.[14]

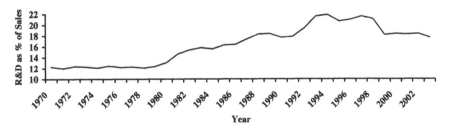

Figure 4.1. R&D as a percent of U.S. sales, ethical pharmaceuticals, research-based pharmaceutical companies, 1970–2002. Source: Pharmaceutical Research and Manufacturers of America, *PhRMA Annual Survey,* 2004.

Patent expiry presented one among several interrelated pressures challenging pharmaceutical profit levels by the end of the 1970s. It is worth elucidating these pressures, as their structural effects continue to be felt into the current period. While the avalanche of research-derived products from the mid–1950s onward had effectively destroyed the generic drug industry, its increasing 'revival' in the late 1970s and 1980s was alarming to industry officials. Research progress from the 1950s and 1960s had been effectively exhausted, and the possibility for 'follow-on' products was rapidly depleting (that is, there was a saturated market for product improvement and 'me-too' drug production). By 1980, the increasing presence of generics, which are generally said to enter the market with a price 25 percent lower than 'pioneer' drugs, had already cornered a 23.3 percent share of the prescriptions market.[15] In other words, the production of 'ethicals'—now the core of production within the pharmaceutical industry—was being threatened with the possibility of exposure to regular capitalist market pressures, entrants of cheaper production lines, and an inevitable downward pressure on industry prices.

For the industry, this situation was simultaneously exacerbated and ameliorated in 1984, with the passing of the Drug Price Competition and Patent Term Restoration Act (the Waxman-Hatch Act). The aim of this act was to address Congressional and public concerns over rising drug prices in the U.S. market while not grossly offending the considerably powerful pharmaceutical lobby. On the one hand, it makes the entry of generic drugs onto the market easier, by not requiring repetition of the Food and Drug Administration's (FDA) approval process for generic drugs shown to have equivalent active ingredients of already approved drugs.[16] These 'Abbreviated New Drug Applications' (ANDAs) substantially reduce the amount of time and investment required to bring generic drugs onto the market. At the same time, the act grants up to five years of patent restoration to research-derived products for time lost during the FDA approval process. Since the instantiation of this legislation, research-based firms have represented generics as engaging in aggressive 'cannibalization' of their product revenues. Added to this has been a widely circulating perception that pioneer drug producers, following patent expiry, lose over half of their market share within one or two years.[17] However, a report from the U.S. Office of Technology Assessment (OTA), in a study of 35 therapeutic compounds that lost patents between 1984 and 1987, estimates that post-patent losses are not nearly as intense as is commonly claimed. According to the OTA, "three years after patent expiration, the mean annual dollar sales of the original compound were 83 percent of mean sales revenue in the year of patent expiration."[18] Nonetheless, while the impact of generics on research firms' bottom line is difficult to finally ascertain, it is clear that the former's 'revival' has come to symbolize a growing threat to the latter.

The threatening presence of generic substitution in the pharmaceutical market is augmented by other institutional and market pressures which emerged more forcefully toward the end of the 1970s. Quite clearly, the FDA has played an integral role in the development of the industry. This government agency, formed by the 1938 Food, Drug and Cosmetic Act, plays an active role in much of the drug development process.[19] This has been especially true since the 1962 Kefauver-Harris Amendments, brought about by the tragic consequences of widespread use of thalidomide in 46 countries.[20] The amendments intensified safety and efficacy regulations considerably, requiring the Investigational New Drug (IND) application for all pharmaceutical NCEs. Submitted by firms prior to clinical testing, INDs require full reports on safety and efficacy in relation to model organisms, as well as protocol for three phases of 'double-blind' clinical trials. Following these trials, the firm must prove efficacy in its New Drug Application (NDA). This approval process is one of the most rigorous in the world and, from the perspective of capitals, represents a large hurdle for the introduction of NCEs. By the late 1970s and into the 1980s, the increasing fear of major firms was that the regulatory process was effectively devouring the time of patent protection. Until 1995, patent protection was for 17 years in the United States, and the pharmaceutical industry expressed its displeasure concerning the amount of time taken up by the FDA approval process. Any barrier—state-derived or otherwise—that gobbles up production time is viewed by capital as a considerable drag on value accumulation. This placed serious pressure on capitals to reconsider the organization of their production processes, given the prevailing perception that there was less and less market time free of generic competition.

An additional, perhaps more serious, pressure bearing down on drug-makers was the changing structure of the American healthcare market. As the 1970s drew to a close, an increasing emphasis was placed on the need to reduce public healthcare expenditures. With, by far, the greatest degree of privately provided healthcare in the industrial world, the United States has, typically, been least inclined to administer any kind of pharmaceutical price control.[21] Thus, prior to the late 1970s, pharmaceutical firms operating in the U.S. market had a unique position. Not only was there no regulatory—or even market—barrier to pricing, but purchasing decisions were made by a group who were not the products' effective consumers—physicians. Given these peculiar arrangements, pharmaceutical marketing operated almost wholly on product differentiation and perceived efficacy. This situation began to change over the course of the last twenty years with the rise of cost-containment strategies in public healthcare programs, hospitals and 'managed care' organizations. By 1990, Congress passed a law requiring drugmakers to give rebates on prescriptions paid for by Medicaid, a rebate that is pegged to inflationary practices.[22] Systemic pressure on research-based profitability is said to result from policies that encourage price discounts and generic drug substitution. According to Stuart Schweitzer,

> [the] most powerful development in the private health care market has been the dramatic shift toward managed care, in which an enrolled population receives health care for a prepaid fee, and the organization uses administrative techniques to control utilisation rates, cost, and quality of care. Both public and private health care sectors have used similar programs to contain costs of pharmaceuticals for their members. These include negotiated manufacturer discounts and rebates, the use of formularies to limit the types of drugs that a physician can prescribe and a pharmacist can dispense, the use of generic and therapeutic substitutions in place of more costly brand-name drugs, drug utilisation review committees, and physician information and education programs.[23]

The degree to which pharmaceutical corporations experience this range of pressures, of course, waxes and wanes with political fortunes. The important point here is that, in line with a building political sentiment for health-care reform in the late 1980s and early 1990s, the industry faced considerable pressure to either lower prices or demonstrate the social utility of its highly-priced products.[24]

None of this should convey the impression that major pharmaceutical firms simply became passive victims of regulatory red tape, cost cutting or generic 'cannibalization' since the late 1970s. Indeed, research-based firms have countered aggressively with strategies that maintain the longevity of their market share. Such strategies include converting patent-protected products to OTC status prior to patent expiry. This is intended to corner brand loyalty (copyrights on brands have a much greater longevity than patents) before competitors enter the market. They have stepped up marketing and information campaigns aimed at medical staff and care providers, utilizing marketing budgets that easily rival or surpass the amounts spent on industrial R&D. At the sectoral level, capitals have engaged in massive horizontal and vertical integration schemes. Since the mid–1980s, horizontal mergers have continued at a feverish pace, creating pharmaceutical giants with tremendous research, development, production, distribution and marketing capabilities.[25] Such integration increases market share and allows for greater capital leverage in everything from R&D to marketing. Vertical integration has involved the takeover of health maintenance organizations (HMOs) and pharmacy benefit managers. Examples here include the purchase of Medco Containment Services by Merck for $6 billion in 1993, the $2.3 billion purchase of Diversified Pharmaceuticals by SmithKline in 1994, the acquisition of PCS Health Systems by Eli Lilly in 1994 for $4 billion, and the broad alliance between Pfizer and Value Health of Connecticut.[26] With the U.S. market moving increasingly towards managed care in 1990s, pharmaceutical corporations were also increasing their leverage to ensure system-wide acceptance of products. All of this is in keeping with the expected reaction of capitals. As our theoretical approach suggested, the first line of defense against encroaching market competition is the process of centralization and cost-cutting measures.

Above all, however, the reaction of research-based corporations has been a dramatic increase in R&D investments (along with marketing). Thus, the upturn in R&D activity after 1980, as highlighted in Figure 4.1, is attributable to an eroding patent base, increasingly market-oriented healthcare delivery, and an accompanying realization of market competition from generics. Research-based firms were becoming increasingly vulnerable to the regular pressures placed on profitability by a capitalist production system. All too aware of this normalizing process, pharmaceutical firms undertook a vigorous effort to re-establish product differentiation and renewal. As O.B. Parrish, then president of the pharmaceutical group at *G.D. Searle & Co.*, stated, "the only way to play the ethical drug game is to have something different. . . . Companies that don't have that will fade out."[27] Redwood, writing in the early period of this R&D upswing, and still unaware of the significance of biotechnology, pointed out that the U.S. market had become a tougher place for pharmaceutical firms, and a 'return to the norm' of fully competitive pricing was an encroaching possibility. According to Redwood, the only way for the industry to counteract such a possibility was a creative turn to new R&D, one that would allow dominant firms to maintain their research-based oligopoly within different therapeutic classes.[28] While this may seem somewhat removed from the advent of the HGP, it is precisely this amplified need among capitals for creativity that forms a crucial precursor to the rise of genome-based sciences. The pressures experienced by the pharmaceutical giants during the late 1970s help foster a necessity for new techniques in health-related research, based on a groundswell of interest in molecular biology.

PHARMACEUTICALS, BIOTECH AND THE 'NEW BIOLOGY'

As pharmaceutical firms came to grips with the difficulties of competitive normalization, they engaged increasingly in basic research as a means to productive innovation. It was already the case that linkages to universities and other research institutions made up an important part of firms' research activities.[29] However, their decisive shift into rDNA research by the end of the 1970s took on a special significance for future research in molecular biology. Because most major pharmaceutical corporations were facing long-term droughts in terms of new-product lines, an obvious market niche opened up to supply innovative new technologies. In relation to this, Sheldon Krimsky has stated that 'biotechnology' emerged in the 1970s as a technological revolution that recast certain industries, as well as the way in which different industrial firms and sectors interact.[30] As we will see below, this is true in only a limited sense. It is obvious that the Cohen-Boyer experiments were chronologically prior to investment in genetic engineering by major corporations. But if we are to avoid the pitfall of technological determinism, matters of chronology should not automatically be equated with causality. Rather, it is historically more significant that pharmaceutical and chemical corporations were casting around for new parameters of innovation and ways of interaction in the face of economic slowdown, both real and perceived. The rise of biotechnology as an industrial phenomenon must be seen in this social context—an opportunity for value creation at the level of individual capitals and, systemically, a growth strategy rendered possible almost solely in the context of American capitalism.[31] In this sense, its emergence offers a striking example of an instantiated counter-tendency to impinging price competition in the broader health industry.

Biotechnology as a full-blown industry is really a phenomenon of the 1980s, although it is certainly true that an industrial dynamic existed from the outset of rDNA research. Even the Cohen-Boyer 'moment,' in which rDNA work got underway, was immediately subject to patent application, undertaken by both Stanford University and the University of California system.[32] Luigi Orsenigo has highlighted that a major development in the 1970s was the notion of the 'spin-off' corporation, born out of the university laboratory. In spite of the swirling debate surrounding rDNA research during the mid–1970s (see chapter 2), scientists increasingly became involved in so-called 'start-up' corporations, seeking to apply their research in various ways to the commercial sector. This notion of scientist as 'entrepreneur' is a critical issue, to be dealt with more thoroughly in a later chapter. For the moment, however, it is important to highlight that the growth in significance of biotechnology occurred through the early development of capitals. Early entrants included corporations such as Cetus (1971), Genentech (1976) and Biogen (1978). But a claim that biotechnology grew merely as a result of individual scientists' entrepreneurial activities is problematic. As is well known, in the mid–1970s, representatives of venture-capital funds went looking for new areas of investment. Indeed, as far as proactive behavior goes, "the whole process of commercialization of biotechnology was initiated by . . . venture capitalists, who identified commercial opportunities, scientists and premises, and orchestrated relationships with other necessary organizations."[33] But even the catalytic symbol of venture capitalists needs to be understood in a more sophisticated manner than Schumpeter's notion of entrepreneurs as 'leaders' and not 'owners.' As has been pointed out by a number of authors, the venture capital that found its way to such 'start-ups' in the 1970s was a direct result of the value accumulated from the microelectronics industrial growth that preceded biotech.[34] Moreover, venture capital did not merely migrate toward biotechnology because of its sponsors' desire for risk. Indeed, the risk factor may have been much lower than is usually assumed in biotech's early days. As Koyin Chang points out,

> [m]ost NBFs [new biotechnology firms] have relied on other established firms for investments. The role of established enterprises as investors in NBFs is suggested by the fact that between 1976 and 1985, they provided 56 percent of the total funds invested in NBFs. [The] dependence of NBFs on corporate partners is further illustrated by considering the role of contract R&D for two of the oldest and largest NBFs: *Genentech* and *Cetus*. Revenues from development contracts funded 70 percent of Genentech's total R&D between 1976 and 1980. Contract R&D undertaken by Cetus accounted for 65 percent of its total R&D expenditures in 1981. . . . Although not the intention of the NBF founders, the biotechnology industry, in its early years, took on the characteristics of a specialised R&D supply sector. Indeed, it could be argued that the biotechnology industry emerged as a market for R&D, with NBFs on the supply side and established chemical and pharmaceutical enterprises on the demand side.[35]

It is an obvious point that venture capitalists expected a return on their investment, but this expectation cannot be equated with mere 'hope.' Rather, it was a product of both systemic necessity and relative investment certainty. Those in control of post-microelectronics investment income could not simply 'sit on' their money. Price inflation in the context of the 1970s and early 1980s ensured that capital would, over time, substantially decrease in value.

Venture capital always gravitates to those areas in which there is a credible expectation that new value can be extracted, and venture capitalists had the clear expectation that, even during the deep recession of the late 1970s and early 1980s, biotechnology could 'bust through.'[36] Thus, with the well-known situation of the pharmaceutical giants in the 1970s, the placement of start-up capital at the door of rDNA research was only partially a risk-oriented event.

In spite of large corporations' early involvement, it has almost become a truism to say that the pharmaceutical industry was a 'latecomer' to the biotech process. While this entrepreneurial narrative may hold for the pharmaceutical industry as a whole (that is, some 5000 firms worldwide), it makes little sense with respect to industry leaders. This is critical, because the pharmaceutical industry can be characterized as a two-tier industry, in which the top 25–30 firms account for well over half of world sales and almost all of its R&D expenditures.[37] Orsenigo has made clear that in the U.S., "firms like Upjohn, Eli Lilly, Smith, Kline and French, Merck and Abbot Laboratories . . . had already significant interests and capabilities in biotechnology and close contacts with the academic system."[38] Moreover, in addition to the presence of large capitals in the early days of biotechnology, Figure 4.2 makes clear that biotech's rise as an industry correlates powerfully with the new R&D commitments of pharmaceutical corporations.

If we take 1978–79 as the rough point in which the pharmaceutical industry initiated considerable increases in pharmaceutical R&D (Figure 4.1), the rapid growth of biotechnology must certainly be one of its direct effects. Of course, this does not explain the rise of every biotechnology company, but the overall pattern seems difficult to explain any other way. One potential counter-explanation involves the allure of public stock offerings. However, public offerings remained relatively rare, and the required business credibility for such an event was, in large part, based on the new companies' involvement with established capitals. The groundbreaking offering of Genentech in 1980, for instance, exceeded every investor's expectations. But this offering came only in the wake of Genentech's already successful contractual connections to companies such as Eli Lilly.

Ultimately, then, biotechnology and the burgeoning field of genetic research was motivated by far more than the mere allure of entrepreneurial science. Science is certainly important, but it is the legal, political and economic realm that structures the limits of the possible. It is crucial to avoid analyses that position biotechnology as an inevitable development, stemming from rational progress in molecular biology. Even if we were to set aside the politico-economic flavor of molecular biology's historical

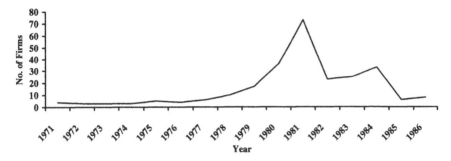

Figure 4.2. Founding of U.S. Biotechnology Firms, 1971–1986. Source: U.S. Office of Technology Assessment, 1988.

development (see chapter 2), the circumstances of capital accumulation for large capitals in the 1970s should dispel such naïve understandings of progress. Structurally, biotechnology's growth is directly tied to the needs of powerful corporations operating in the parameters of the U.S. economy. These production needs—played out in terms of a technological re-tooling—were pursued above all in the United States, because they played to the strength of leading corporations and helped ensure their continuing dominance.[39]

It remains to be explained, however, what such R&D expenditures, as well as the fostering of an emergent industry, could actually accomplish for the pharmaceutical industry's 'bottom line.' The development of biotechnology-based research offered, on a production level, considerable opportunities to rationalize further the value accumulation process. Conventionally, the industry approached the R&D phase of this process in a 'trial and error' manner. This was operationalized through the randomized screening of thousands of compounds, in order to determine their biological activity and potential therapeutic value. Estimates vary wildly, but it seems clear that only one in several thousands of compounds realized anything in the way of therapeutic potential. Importantly, however, this was not a situation that was forced upon the pharmaceutical industry. Rather, its decisions concerning R&D have always been rationalized in terms of the economic return that they would yield. According to Alfonso Gambardella, it is important,

> to recognize that this was a deliberate economic decision of firms. . . . [In] order to invest in fundamental knowledge, firms need to have some expectation that they can comprehend problems in generalized forms. But when problems are very complex, the costs of comprehending them in general forms can be enormous. Trial and error is then economically more advantageous, even though it yields only localized knowledge.[40]

This decision-making process led companies to engage in 'blind' experimentation, with little or no attention directed at an intricate understanding of molecular processes being observed. The classic example of this is *aspirin.* Introduced by Bayer in 1899, it proved to have several therapeutic effects over the course of time. However, because of a lack of knowledge about its chemical or biological functions, companies were not able to create new aspirin-based medicines until the mid–1980s.[41]

This situation began to change, not surprisingly, as both the need for new product lines became acute and the limits of screening-derived compounds became apparent. Indeed, because drug 'productivity' had been dropping heavily for some time, the mid–1970s witnessed a general pessimism in the pharmaceutical industry concerning the long-term viability of 'trial and error' methods. Randomly screening up to 75,000 compounds for an ever-decreasing number of therapeutic products did not translate into bright prospects for the industry.[42] The fact that molecular biology had witnessed several developments since the early 1960s allowed for opportunities that did not exist in the 'golden era.' It is important to state, however, that there was no necessary connection between existing scientific knowledge and drug-discovery approaches. Much had been done on protein analysis and the importance of receptor sites well before industry decided to take them up in a process of 'discovery by design.'[43] Ultimately, however, the deliberate decision of pharmaceutical capitals to take up such approaches meant investigating far more closely the molecules with which they had been dealing. Before the biotechnology 'hoopla,' drug companies had already been taking a more targeted research approach to compounds. Gambardella uses three examples: Tagamet (SmithKline), an anti-ulcer drug which required extensive study of receptors of acid-secreting cells in the stomach; Capoten (Squibb), the atom-by-atom constructed compound that blocks the production of angiotensin II, a protein that raises blood pressure; and lovastatin (Merck), the active ingredient in Mevacor, which blocks the production of an enzyme HMG-CoA that, in turn, starts the production of cholesterol.[44] *Merck,* as one of the leading pharmaceutical giants on the world market, exemplifies the emergence of 'discovery by design.' In the mid–1970s, Merck's head of research argued that "the key to developing new drugs is understanding how diseases affect the chemistry of the body. Instead of the old grind-it-up-and-test-it approach, he ordered researchers to target the biochemical reactions that a disease triggers and then devise a chemical bullet to stop them."[45] The company's successful move into genetic sciences was neither a 'fluke' nor mere reaction—it was a deliberate production decision that had been in play for some time.

This new move involved research of cellular mechanisms and target-oriented discovery methods, and it made the utilization of genetic research a must for competing capitals. It has allowed corporations to focus on very specialized aspects of the body, such as proteins that are produced in problematic proportions, or not produced at all. Since entry of research-firms' new product lines into the marketplace is largely based on differentiation, rather than competitive pricing, a specialized R&D basis could greatly benefit individual firms' capacity to accumulate. As one senior executive in the industry expressed it,

> [m]olecular biology is the foundation of modern drug discovery, specifically rational drug discovery, because it permits biology to be mechanistic rather than merely descriptive. The process is one of tearing apart the body's cells to identify specific molecules against which we can define drug action. That is, biotechnology permits science to tell not only what is happening in the human body, but why. With that insight comes the rational understanding that permits us to design drugs to carry out specific tasks. . . . These therapeutic interventions should do well in a cost-constrained marketplace where only innovative products will be the dominant factor in market penetration.[46]

In the early stages of genetic research, precisely this logic was applied to genetic sequence and protein production. If DNA sequence data could be isolated, amplified, and deciphered, its use value would most certainly be transformed, such that it could be subject to immediate commodification and made integral to subsequent productive techniques. Indeed, its role in the creation of diagnostics and the genetic synthesis of useful proteins represents precisely such a development. More illustrative examples of this utility are provided below, but it is sufficient to say that an improved target orientation, leading to enhanced drug differentiation (and, potentially, efficacy), was the primary motivating factor for industrial forays into genetic research and molecular biology.

Another reason for the adaptation of molecular biology by the pharmaceutical industry receives little attention in the bulk of literature. Not only can cellular and genetic knowledge be aimed at the industrial conceptualization process, it can also be utilized defensively in the early development stages of production. Thus,

> [m]olecular biology and genetic engineering have . . . given a great impetus to the possibility of predicting and controlling side-effects. Scientists have found that many receptors in different human organs have similar structures. Thus, drugs that are designed to bind to a

certain receptor may also bind to similar receptors in other parts of the
body, thereby causing side-effects. If scientists could devise the specific
regions of the receptor molecules that differentiate otherwise similar receptors, they would be able to design drugs that fit uniquely the target
receptor sites.[47]

In this sense, the 'prediction of failures' resulting from R&D is as important
as product development.[48] With an ever-growing knowledge of biochemical
pathways and cellular control, researchers can discard those drugs or drug-
derivations that are likely to lead to side effects or inefficacious treatment.
From the perspective of capitals engaged in competitive specialization and
extended, expensive clinical trials, the removal of potential 'dead-ends' is
central to the maintenance of high profitability.

Related to this, the question of 'risk' is ever-present within discussions
concerning the benefits or disadvantages of molecular biology. Indeed, the
notion of risk is often associated to the pharmaceutical-biotechnology nexus
as a justification for existing profit levels. In relation to immediate R&D
costs, numerous authors claim that risk has increased with the advent of molecular biology research methods.[49] The allusion to increasing total R&D
costs (including successes and failures) is generally used to highlight the need
to provide strong incentives (patent protection, sustained profit) for industry's entry into such research. The OTA went so far as to say explicitly what
other authors implied: risk itself must be understood, quite literally (and
metaphysically), as a cost. According to the OTA, if "investment in the pharmaceutical industry is riskier than in [other] firms, then the cost of capital
will be higher."[50] While such assertions offer little in terms of a compelling
explanation of this claim, their centrality as a prevailing perception of the
drug industry should not be discounted.[51] But how the risk element of the
drug development process is affected by molecular biology remains somewhat controversial. The fact is that such risk—a function of fear involving
the costs of potential failures—is more likely to be minimized by increased
knowledge of molecular processes. At any rate, the possibility of avoiding
pitfalls through a more focused drug discovery and production process is
certainly difficult to interpret as *increased* risk.[52]

Beyond the production process, the greatest benefit of rationalization,
seen through the eyes of capitals, is the possibility of *new* areas of value accumulation. Carving out new areas of scientific application offers the possibility of 'first mover' advantages that can bestow market exclusivity benefits
on a given capital. The capacity to reach the marketplace first with a product will bring about a period of sales monopoly, in which profits are extraordinary. These 'first mover' advantages are, of course, greatly strengthened by

the full power of patent protection. On the one hand, patents ensure that the innovation itself will be largely protected from imitative competition. And since there is a lag between patent application and approval, drugs may be well through a large part of the clinical trials before the patent is issued. This too provides companies with a substantial clinical lead to secure a large part of the marketplace, often with the help of enormous marketing and sales staff (commonly referred to as 'detailers'). Pharmaceutical companies count on this lead-time to instigate, to the greatest possible degree, brand loyalty. Later, when the patent comes due for expiry, brand loyalty can prove an additional weapon in maintaining powerful market leverage. On the other hand, patents offer a negative incentive insofar as they act as "a means of protecting the output of basic and applied research . . . an important factor in raising the incentives of firms to invest in upstream research."[53] Because patents on biotechnology-related research are generally quite complex, more so than conventional chemical compounds, their effects are genuinely more difficult to reproduce in a non-obvious manner. Additionally, as basic research increasingly becomes subject to patenting (such as on genes or even partial genes), the ability to control the productive potential of such research means that capitals can 'block' potential competition. Taken together, these factors mean that in areas of new value accumulation, derived from biotechnology- or genome-based research, the opportunities for competitive 'me too' drug production are becoming increasingly limited.

This is why, by the second half of the 1980s, there was already a rush of biotechnology-related patents. Indeed, by the mid–1980s, the Industrial Biotechnology Association (IBA) and the Association of Biotechnology Companies (ABC) felt compelled to plea to both Congress and the Patent and Trademark Office (PTO) to accelerate the patent application and approvals process. There were, by 1986, already 4051 biotechnology-related applications pending, and that figure jumped by 21 percent in 1987 to 6907 applications.[54] As an important aside, this explosion has often been explained as a direct result of the now well-known 1980 Supreme Court decision in *Diamond* vs. *Chakrabarty*, in which General Electric scientist Ananda Chakrabarty was awarded a patent on a life form, an oil-eating bacteria. However, too much historical weight has been placed on this judicial ruling, making the subsequent deluge of patents appear as the mere manifestation of a legal decision. Not only was the Chakrabarty case suffused with precedents, namely the Plant Patent Act of 1930 and the Plant Variety Protection Act of 1970, but by the time it reached the Supreme Court, it was clearly a symbol of larger social and economic processes. By 1980, there was already substantial investment both in start-up biotechnology firms and by pharmaceutical and chemical companies. In fact, the original decision of the PTO to take the case as high as the Supreme Court was based entirely on the PTO's desire for clarity—not to stop patenting on life forms. Gerald Bjorge, the Associate Solicitor in the PTO, has made clear that the central reasoning in the decision to go to court was the "belief that living products could be patented [and] would call forth considerable investment in biotechnological enterprises."[55] By the time of the 1980 hearing, ten *amicus* briefs had been filed on the side of *Chakrabarty* by major corporate and institutional actors, including the University of California, *Genentech*, and the Pharmaceutical Manufacturers Association. Indeed, Genentech made very clear in its original 1978 brief that patents were "an important if not indispensable factor in attracting private capital support for life-giving research in the pharmaceutical field."[56] The company asserted, with respect to arguments against patenting, that it was not the responsibility of the Supreme Court, "to attempt, like King Canute, to command the tide of technological development."[57] While this case may have come at a critical juncture in patenting history, its symbolic value has taken on an air of causality that its actual historical role cannot bear. It seems that far more than the *Chakrabarty* case, the dramatic push for patenting was a function of the already swelling range of investments in biotechnologies, the Bayh-Dole Act of 1980 (which encouraged patenting of federally-funded research) and even other patent claims, such as the Cohen-Boyer patent, finally granted in 1980.

In this dramatic rush to carve out yet another area of the 'commons' for privately-appropriated value production,[58] capitals have attempted to secure areas of value appropriation and augment their own 'learning' capacities. In the decade before the HGP, large capitals greatly expanded their efforts to tap into the value-producing potential of biotechnology. Quite clearly, the rise in venture capital and the use of public offerings on the stock market was exceptionally helpful in raising cash for start-up scenarios. However, none of this would have been likely, if not for the rapidly growing interrelationships between already existing pharmaceutical corporations and growing biotechnology firms. These arrangements varied in nature, but they included research and development limited partnerships (RDLPs), licensing agreements, joint ventures, equity purchase and even outright acquisition. As Orsenigo suggests, "contract research and equity investments in a number of specialised companies provided the opportunity to diversify efforts and gradually to acquire capabilities and experience in a wide range of new areas. The financial outlays were relatively small and could yield high rates of return."[59] As a necessary complement to this, major firms could only utilize this acquired knowledge by simultaneously developing their own 'in-house' complement of R&D. In the first three years after 1980, while biotechnology companies increased their employee base by 80 percent, major firms increased their own biotechnology-based personnel by 4 times this amount.[60] Thus, by the 1980s, the development of numerous industrial alliances, substantial investment in in-house research, and the now-burgeoning connection to academic molecular biology laboratories (see chapter 6) had combined to create a large and growing complex of potential new value appropriation in the U.S. economy.

Despite the fact that, by the end of the 1980s, much of the R&D activity within the biotech sector had yet to show any substantial value return, investment growth continued at impressive levels. By 1988, over 400 biotechnology firms had emerged with supporting funds from over 70 major corporations. Indeed, the emergence and continuing viability of most biotechnology endeavors was, during this period, largely premised on their commercial value and marketability *vis-à-vis* major corporations. In many cases, the goal of these start-ups was not necessarily to develop into fully profitable companies, but instead to fill some particular research need in the emerging biotech market. As such,

> [c]ompanies were founded with the intention of developing one idea or targeting a niche market and, perhaps, being acquired. . . . According to a recent . . . survey, 39 percent of all companies . . . expect to be acquired by a large firm within the next 5 years, and 32 percent expect to merge with and equal-size firm in the same period.[61]

While there existed an overall paucity of demonstrable profitability, the potential for such profitability had been symbolized by the successes of a few select companies—Genentech, Amgen and Chiron. Their synthesis and production of various diagnostics and therapeutic compounds, such as tissue plasminogen activator (t-PA), human growth hormone, insulin, and erythropoietin (EPO), provided evidence of the potential for biotechnology-derived commodities. Indeed, even certain large firms such as Dow, Monsanto, and DuPont, unwilling to overlook such successes, had undertaken processes to drastically restructure their future innovation and production structures.[62]

Consequently, as the HGP emerged conceptually in the second half of the 1980s, biotechnology was being considered as nothing less than a 'locomotive' that could pull the economy out of its doldrums. It is telling that the sector survived the economic slowdown of the early 1980s and the investment retraction of the mid–1980s.[63] Even in American governmental and regulatory circles, there was considerable desire to promote the well being of the U.S. biotechnology nexus, as well as maintain its international lead. In the mid–1980s, Martin Kenney made the claim that biotechnology had achieved its successes with minimal interference of the state.[64] This is a contestable claim, and it is decreasingly tenable in relation to the second-half of the 1980s. Here, the case of Genentech's development of t-PA proves instructive. This product, derived through rDNA-based protein production, received preferential treatment over its rival product, streptokinase (SK), produced by foreign firms Kabi Vitrum and Hoechst. T-PA was selected, after heavy pressure from Genentech advocates, to be used in massive NIH-directed (and funded) clinical trials. Moreover, t-PA's rejection and SK's approval by the FDA in 1987 *should have* given substantial 'first mover' advantage to the latter compound. In fact, at the time, American media mourned the fact that "pending final approval by the FDA, Hoechst and KabiVitrum plan to get [SK] to market within two months. Genentech, in the view of most analysts, is unlikely to get t-PA approved for another year."[65] Perhaps not so surprisingly, however, things did not turn out as such.

> [The] $64,000 question that has never been answered was why the approval of streptokinase was held up for six months, until t-PA's was imminent. It certainly looked as though the fact that this was the first drug from America's biotechnology industry played a key role, and the lives that could have been saved by streptokinase in the interim apparently didn't enter into the FDA's calculus. . . . Reaction from the proponents of streptokinase was even more pointed. 'The real scandal' maintains Karl Mettinger [of KabiVitrum], 'is that under pressure from the White House, the FDA delayed our approval for six months. Otherwise, we could have been in the marketplace before Genentech had a chance."[66]

Not only is t-PA's efficacy open to considerable contestation with respect to its effects *vis-à-vis* longevity, but also its price tag is certainly an issue. While SK can be administered for $200 per dose, t-PA costs upwards of $3000. It is hardly a wonder that Genentech advocates were deeply concerned that t-PA would not reach the marketplace in an advantageous timeframe.

Even more critical during the 1980s, however, was the support for biotechnology development provided through the orchestration of large-scale molecular biology. If Gambardella's claim concerning complexity and economic R&D decisions by U.S. capitals is correct, then anything that supports an increase in available understanding of complex biological systems would prove helpful to health-related corporate production methods.

> Clearly, greater economic incentives to invest in understanding the properties of drugs are reinforced by the externalities produced by the

growth of *public knowledge*. Firms can focus on problems that have already been clarified, in large part, by public discoveries, and hence that have greater potential for economic returns.[67]

In the case of biotechnology and genome-related R&D, any scientific advance on the 'public' front offers an invaluable resource. According to the FDA, between 1981 and 1991, only 12 of the 348 drugs introduced by the 25 largest firms represented a demonstrable therapeutic advance. And 70 percent of those were a product of government-based research.[68] Not only is it considered high risk to venture out into new therapeutic entities, but there is no doubt that corporate capital relies, even insists, on the governmental development of advantageous tools for new product development. Thus, as major capital investment and biotechnology's development continued, the rationale for a federally-funded 'map,' dealing with the *complexity* of the human (and other) genome(s) found its appropriate historical place.

THE HGP AND THE TOOLS FOR INDUSTRY

Quite clearly, by the late 1980s, the growing and complementary needs of the pharmaceutical and biotechnology industries were bound to be felt within political circles. As is well known, the HGP emerged formally out of state-led attempts to address those needs. Indeed, from its initial conception, the project was almost entirely a government-orchestrated project. While the next chapter is devoted to an extended discussion concerning the character of this state involvement, it is important here to consider the creation of such a project specifically in light of capital's interests. Importantly, pharmaceutical and biotechnology capitals, among others, demonstrated their receptivity to genome mapping efforts previous to any federally devised project. By the time the U.S. government began to take seriously the prospect of a HGP, the competitive environment of biotechnology was already giving rise to mapping as an innovative process. As the OTA published its report on the possibility of a HGP in 1988, capitals had either undertaken or were planning mapping as part of their business strategy. Corporations, such as Collaborative Research and Integrated Genetics, were substantially involved in creating genetic linkage maps of the human genome. At the same time, two companies under formation—Genome Corp. and SeQ, Ltd.—expressed the explicit agenda of mapping and sequencing the human genome.[69] While the existence of these strategies among capitals does not change the fact that the immediate catalyst and support for the HGP's emergence was a state-led initiative, the project's necessity was prefigured in corporate attempts to carve out niche-areas of value accumulation.

More important than specific companies' plans around mapping or sequencing, however, was the industrial interest in the general implementation of such research. In the face of reordered production processes among existing capitals and the overwhelming growth of biotech 'start-ups,' the possibility of a 'map' (or several maps) which could introduce order into the mind-numbing complexity of the human genome became a tangible industrial imperative. In 1987, the International Biotechnology Association (IBA) released a survey of its members on the utility of, and potential support for, federally sponsored initiatives in mapping and sequencing the human genome. No one company, or group of companies, had the capacity to muster the kind of effort necessary to undertake such a complete mapping project. As such, the IBA recommended that,

> genome mapping and sequencing work should be carried out primarily in university laboratories and national laboratories. Only a minority of those who support a genome initiative believe that a government/ industry/university consortium or a new center created for this purpose would be appropriate.[70]

Strangely, despite the fact that the IBA, in concert with industry members, remained convinced that the private sector should not provide the financial backing for such a project, it had no difficulty recommending that 20 percent of those involved in oversight be drawn directly from industry.[71] Its respondents "clearly support[ed] a role for industry in planning and using the results of mapping and sequencing projects, while indicating that the Federal Government should pay the bill."[72] Ultimately, industrial members had their expectations exceeded, with 25 percent representation on the NIH Program Advisory Committee on the Human Genome.[73]

Members of industry had no direct need to control such a project, but they certainly wished to influence its overall direction and ensure that they remained well informed of its progression. As the previous chapter points out, the state facilitates the amenability of emerging science to industry, and in the United States, the latter's concerns are generally focused on questions of technology transfer. In this sense, IBA's member firms' comfort with research confined to universities and national laboratories speaks to the high degree of industry-friendly technology transfer practiced in the United States. During 1988 Congressional House meetings dealing with the OTA report on genome mapping, Mark Pearson, then Director of Molecular Biology at DuPont Corporation, expressed the degree of concern on this issue among major U.S. capitals. When asked about barriers to exchange, Pearson responded that increasingly that barrier which I think has been in part a figment of the imagination of the scientific communities on both sides of the fence, is rapidly dissolving. The Technology Transfer Act has done much to simulate the ready exchange of materials and development, indeed, of collaborative scientific projects. . . . I think we have a chance in this country to in fact run another experiment through this program, and that is the development of a much more cooperative scientific endeavor nationally, where there is stimulated cooperation between industry and academic scientists.[74]

With such confidence in the capacity of the U.S. scientific community to translate research into industrial utility, it is hardly surprising that the HGP, as a federally based project, had no visible detractors within industry. Indeed, during earlier Senate Hearings concerning the DOE's first proposal for a Human Genome Initiative (HGI),[75] Jack McConnell, corporate director of advanced technology for Johnson & Johnson, went so far as to express the view that there should be a concerted, government-funded sequencing project, undertaken without the barrier of peer-review and the burden of regulatory review, and that this should be tailored to U.S. industrial needs.[76]

Not only did industry express its devotion to technology transfer, but it also made clear that the information stemming from the project would prove substantively beneficial. The more detailed the map, the more productively it would serve as a research and design tool, helping to sort through the vast complexity of genetic makeup and gene expression. Among industrial advocates, the possibility of an HGP undoubtedly raised expectations to a level similar to that during the late–1970s shift to 'drug by design' production methods. McConnell, who not only supported the idea of a mapping project, but also assisted in drafting the first Congressional bill regarding the DOE's proposal for an HGI, put things in a rather stark manner.

> If we want the U.S. to maintain its position as a dominant force in the pharmaceutical industry in the world, I cannot imagine our letting this opportunity pass us by. Someone has said that the group that first gains access to the information from mapping and sequencing the human genome will be in position to dominate the pharmaceutical and biotech industry for decades to come.[77]

And the 1988 OTA report maintained, somewhat more specifically, that

> genome projects could produce both direct and indirect economic benefits. Some projects are expected to yield directly marketable products

(e.g., DNA sequenators, analytical instruments, DNA probes for diagnostic tests). Others would accelerate development of products (e.g., maps, repositories, and databases).[78]

Again, Pearson's testimonial support also reinforces the two-sided advantageous character of a genome project. His words fly in the face of the widely circulating impression that industrial interest emerged as a *reaction* to the technological exigencies of the HGP.

> The near-term benefit of this project for industrial research and development in America is the immediate stimulation of technology development for rapid, accurate, and inexpensive diagnostic tests for human genetic diseases and for many infectious diseases will have a profound effect on U.S. agriculture and on the detection of microbial contamination in the food industry. It will help ensure that American citizens have available the best health care and the highest quality food in the world. . . . Longer-term, in a decade or more, I expect profound benefits to come from the application of DNA sequence information to the design of therapeutic drugs and to gene therapy for the treatment of a variety of presently untreatable human diseases.[79]

The emphasis on both short-term gains and long-term returns (as the project would proceed) reflected the prevailing view that what was being undertaken was more than mere scientific endeavor. It was evident to industry and non-industry members that what was at stake was the 'rejuvenation' of one industry and the blossoming of another. As Pearson himself noted, the large majority of examples concerning the benefits of gene mapping refer, directly or indirectly, to a commodifiable product.[80]

Even while the government project went about exploring the possibilities for decreased costs in sequencing technology, short- and long-term benefits would accrue for companies involved in genome research. Speaking to Congress on behalf of the IBA, Genentech CEO Kirk Raab stated several reasons why industry supports the project, including,

- The increased speed for industrial problem-solving.
- The productive breadth of a genetic 'dictionary.'
- The utility of the results *as they emerged,* rather than having to wait for the project's completion.
- The scale, which made the federal government's lead necessary.
- The profitable effects on industry, including pharmaceuticals.
- The potential increase of a tax base, which would, eventually, allow the project to pay for itself.[81]

In participating circles, there was a proactive engagement with economic reasoning behind the project's emergence. The HGP offered the prospect of an overwhelming amount of useful information, enhancing greatly the potential for sophisticated and highly rationalized approaches to product design in the biotechnology and health industries. The upcoming information made available by the HGP would mean that "[w]hoever cracks the design code [for genes and gene products] is going to have a significant competitive advantage not only in understanding the disease but also the ability to produce drugs whether they be classical drugs or recombinant products."[82] Ultimately, *Business Week* quite rightly depicted the prevailing industrial perspective, when it asserted that the HGP was leading to a competitive 'pot of gold.'[83]

The scientific community expressed a view that, in large part, remained compatible with the industrial understanding of the project's ultimate utility. Scientific advocates testified before both Senate and House hearings in favor of a concerted scientific effort, reinforcing the two-fold economic value of the HGP. In a set of obviously coordinated testimonies, high profile scientists such as James Watson, Maynard Olson, Charles Cantor and Leroy Hood made clear that mapping would have immediate returns, particularly in the area of diagnostics. At the same time, they also cautioned that it was sensible to put off a full-scale sequencing effort until such a time that the prevailing technology would be more economically efficient.[84] This accomplished not only the 'selling' of this project to public officials, but it also conveyed a genuine belief that an entirely new array of technologies and industrial development was on offer.

From this, however, it would be inaccurate to conclude that there existed only unity with respect to the project. On the contrary, the tendency of scientific circles to close ranks when dealing in the political arena obscured the reality of a certain degree of struggle over how federal funds should be appropriately utilized. Characterized by a distinct economic undertone, debate focused on the value of such a project in the face of an already successful trajectory in molecular biology. Indeed, during initial meetings concerning the scientific viability of the HGP, and through the early years of its promulgation, criticism was directed at whole genome mapping and sequencing, questioning its scientific usefulness. These 'early skirmishes' appear to bubble to the surface at a meeting in 1986 at Cold Spring Harbour on Long Island, entitled 'The Molecular Biology of *Homo Sapiens*.' The initial mapping proposal from the Department of Energy (DOE) was already making rounds in the scientific community, and the meeting's keynote speaker, Walter Bodmer, utilized the opportunity to pitch the idea among his scientific colleagues. Significantly, he made reference to the project's utility, stating that "it is no good getting a man a third or a quarter the way to Mars. . . . However, a quarter or a third . . . of the total human genome sequence . . . could already provide a most valuable yield of applications."[85] This thinking, supported by the likes of Watson and Paul Berg, came under fire from other scientists, led by David Botstein, who stated that,

> if it means changing the structure of science in such a way as to inden-
> ture all of us, especially the young people, to this enormous thing like
> the Space Shuttle, instead of what you feel like doing . . . we should be
> very careful . . . [and] not go ahead under the flag of Asilomar, okay, be-
> cause we are amateur politicians and we're about to be dealing with the
> professionals. . . . [Molecular biologists] maybe accept the goal, but not
> [to] give away our ability to decide what is important because we have
> decided on the Space Shuttle.[86]

In particular, the perception of 'mindless' sequencing stirred dissatisfaction among many scientists. Robert Weinberg of the Whitehead Institute went so far as to state that he could not believe that "consenting adults have been caught in public talking about it . . . it makes no sense," and that scientists would be "wading through a sea of drivel to merge dry-shod on a few tiny islands of information."[87] Letters drafted by Martin Rechsteiner and Michael Syvanen, and used as templates by at least 50 disgruntled scientists, made early assertions that large-scale mapping and sequencing efforts were a waste of funds.[88] From this perspective, it was questioned why scientists should support a mapping project of the whole genome, an estimated 97 percent of which exhibited no known function. Why not just continue on the same task-oriented basis, investigating genes known to be associated with particular traits or conditions?

It is worth stressing that this controversy, with its emphasis on identi-
fying the most productive use of federal research funds, never placed in any question the centrality of capital to contemporary molecular biology. Thus, the one consequence of the debate—putting whole scale sequencing efforts on hold (while waiting for sequencing technology to evolve)—was accepted easily by the project's main advocates, because it fit very well into an overall picture of basic genome research in relation to biotechnology and the pharmaceutical industry.[89] Indeed, Hood, a leading figure in sequencing technology, who would later be central in the Perkin-Elmer/Applied Biosystems effort to greatly accelerate privately funded genome sequencing, stated that "[it] would be a serious mistake to jump into a full-scale sequencing effort with the cottage industry techniques we have at the moment. . . .

If we make the proper investment in developing technology then in 5 years time we will be able to do the job more effectively, both technically and financially."[90] In large part, putting the emphasis on linkage and physical maps as the initial goals of the project meant that visible benefits could be derived in accordance with the degree of effort expended.

On one level, these discussions may be interpreted as purely scientific in character, not especially concerned with the economic facets of project proposals. After all, Robert Cook-Deegan's representation of the HGP argues that it, "was borne of technology, grew into a science bureaucracy in the U.S. and throughout the world and is now being transformed into a hybrid academic and commercial enterprise." [91] Similarly, in 1999, Charles Cantor, a prominent scientific participant in U.S. genome efforts, claimed that commercial interests were never a factor in the initial mapping endeavors.[92] His claim was based on the fact that he had attempted with colleagues, at the outset of the HGP, to begin a private venture based on genomics (the utilization of mapping and sequencing data). Unable to raise capital from investors, his conclusion many years later was that the market value of this information could only have been evident much later. This rather troublesome claim ignores not only those genomics companies that were already in existence, but also turns a blind eye to the benefits expected within the burgeoning biotechnology industry and otherwise well established firms. It is true that, on the surface, technical meetings directed a good deal of the project's early movement. And, of course, the more technical the debate, the more likely were leading scientists to engage in heated interaction. But to decouple these scientific exchanges from either the economic reality of the new biotechnology sector or large-scale corporate restructuring tends to cast both scientific and non-scientific participants in an excessively innocent and naïve light.

Without attempting to allocate individual responsibility (this would contradict the structural-historical component of this study), most participants were never disassociated from the material prospects and consequences of genome research. Indeed, in keeping with the historical trajectory of molecular biology described above, it is hardly surprising that,

[the] torrent of investments in genetic engineering from the late 1970s onwards encouraged practitioners to form a variety of new affiliations with the private sector. Scientists formerly cloistered in academe, became equity owners, corporate executives, members of scientific advisory boards, and industry consultants. By the early 1980s, it was said to be difficult to find a genetic engineer without a corporate connection.[93]

Thus, controversies over the utility of genome research, its scale, and the direction of its proposed program should not be represented as a mere technical curiosity. Instead, proposed funding was (and continues to be) viewed in a scientific and industrial climate that placed a very high premium on investment returns. As with any set of investments, the focus of its participants was centered squarely on the potential for short-term gains, as well as long-term benefits.[94] There could certainly be no mistaking the testimony presented by lead scientists in appropriations hearings in 1990. Participants in these critical meetings appeared highly cognizant of the fact that industrial growth, particularly in biotechnology and pharmaceuticals, was the central aim of the project. Watson stated directly that encouraging technology programs, such as those under the umbrella of the HGP, had the clear effect of developing new industrial capacity and economic prowess. According to Watson,

> [the] biotechnology industry will benefit from the trained manpower, data, and techniques developed by the Human Genome Project and will generate many useful applications of the new knowledge that is produced. . . . Rapid transfer of technology developed under the Human Genome Project to industries that can develop medically and economically useful applications is a major goal of the Genome Project. The U.S. biotechnology industry considers the Genome Project critical for maintaining and increasing U.S. competitiveness.[95]

Cantor, in the same hearing re-emphasizes the point by stating that

> [the] biotechnology industry in this country is young but growing quickly. In 1989 the biotechnology industry had a combined revenue of over $1.2 billion, a 33% increase over the previous year. . . . Many of these companies, including Cetus, Genentech, and Perkin-Elmer are already collaborating with the human genome initiative. Future technological advances developed by the human genome initiative will greatly aid in allowing the biotechnology industry to continue to grow and provide both new jobs and medical products.[96]

Finally, Hood brings the point home by referring, as Watson regularly had, to the impending threat of the Japanese.

> As we all know, America is currently the world leader in biotechnology. This leadership is unequivocally being threatened by the Japanese. The human genome project, both through technology and the creation of a powerful infrastructure, is helping to insure this future world leadership. . . . Hence, when we are technologically competitive, we can generate a positive trade balance. The human genome project to develop a variety

of new biological tools and technologies is going to spawn new industrial opportunities that will on the one hand create new industries and
on the other hand will give the old industries new opportunities. . . .
[The] . . . genome project will prime the American economic pump. It is
a critical time to develop these new technologies. If we decline to do so,
rest assured our competitors will fill the vacuum.[97]

Such forceful testimony makes clear that even the project's scientific advocates were able to clearly identify and elaborate on its economic motivations. Hood's recognition of 'critical timing' points to far more than a
convenient explanation, used to secure appropriations from Senatorial representatives. It exhibits an understanding of the overall systemic role that the
project could fulfill in the U.S. socio-economic setting. Ultimately, this injec-
tion of economic motivation, so closely attuned to scientific interests, is one
of the most poignant characteristics of the process by which the genome proposal emerged. Not only did advocates argue in terms of economic benefits,
but they positioned the project in relation to America's survivability within
international political economy. The opportunity for value creation was not
to be missed, and the social relations of capitalist competition—manifested
in ever-intensifying international pharmaceutical and biotechnology innovation—required that large-scale, programmatic infrastructural support was
highly advisable.

THE HGP AND INDUSTRIAL GROWTH

Throughout the advent and completion of the HGP, the project certainly
lived up to its expected interaction within the productive sphere of the U.S.
economy. There was, and continues to be, a continuing interrelation between the progression and completion of the HGP and forward-looking industrial growth. As such, following the initial instantiation of the project,
the HGP was developed in a manner that fostered competitive innovation
within both the biotechnology and pharmaceutical industries. As the foregoing analysis suggests, this was no coincidence: perceived industrial
growth made continuing financial and structural support for the HGP more
palatable, and the project's very existence could been legitimated through
new waves of industrial derivation. As many pointed out, the HGP would,
" . . . provide enormous commercial opportunities for the pharmaceutical
and biotechnology industries, which have been quick to realise the potential for new treatments."[98] Thus, while the originating 'moment' of the
HGP is central to understanding the forces that motivate the project, considering the manner in which its continuing historical reproduction was

legitimized in relation to capitalist accumulation can further elucidate the project's rationale.

Through the 1990s, the HGP continued to secure generous yearly U.S. Congressional appropriations. There can be little doubt that a major reason for this was that the biotechnology industry, as well as the research component of established industries, had grown quantitatively and qualitatively in step with the progression of the HGP. In quantitative terms, the biotechnology, defined by those companies with an exclusive devotion to molecular biological applications (that is, excluding pharmaceutical corporations), had grown into a multibillion-dollar industry. According to an influential report undertaken by Ernst & Young, the industry's contribution to the U.S. economy had grown to considerable proportions, despite the fact that, on the whole, it continued to absorb a net profit loss.[99] By 1999, the industry is said to have generated:

- 437 400 U.S. employment positions.
- $47 billion in revenues (although the industry continued to operate at a net loss)
- $11 billion in R&D spending.
- $10 billion in tax revenues at federal, state and local levels.

From these categories, it is difficult to ascertain how much actually represents new (surplus) value creation in the American economy. Certainly the issues of employment, revenues and R&D expenditures are critical, but without numbers that more effectively detail differing kinds of labor, revenues and expenses, definitive conclusions are impossible. That said, while not good indicators of capital accumulation, *per se,* these figures remain interesting, insofar as they point to the presence of widespread systemic effects of biotechnology production. Whether or not the industry has achieved the aspirations laid out for it in the early 1980s, there is no doubt that it had, over the course of the 1990s, entrenched itself deeply within the socio-economic fabric of the U.S.

As the HGP proceeded, there were also countless references to the qualitative results yielded in terms of biotechnology research and products. These include everything from Hood's claim that the project's objective was a "new infrastructure for biology," to Charles DeLisi's statements that the project would "produce drugs galore."[100] In fact, it is difficult to avoid the conclusion that the project's execution coincided with a stark increase in the size and productivity of the biotechnology sector.[101]

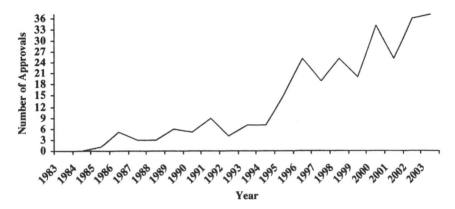

Figure 4.3. Total biotech-related drug and vaccine approvals and new indication approvals in United States by year, 1982–2003. Source: Biotechnology Industry Organization, 2004.

As Figure 4.3 indicates, there were dramatic increases in the number of biotech-related product approvals (either a new product or a new use for an existing product), which coincided rather strikingly with the progression and completion of the HGP. At the time of the project's beginnings, there had been fewer than ten biotechnology-derived products on the market, and HGP advocates asserted confidently that, even prior to the project's completion, there would be hundreds.[102] While these initial predictions may have been somewhat overdrawn, there is little denying the extraordinary effects of the HGP with respect to industry-wide productivity. It is, of course, impossible to outline in any representative way the full array of products and processes that have been spurred on by the enormous wave of investment in genome research during this period. By 2001, over 50 biotech corporations had hit a market capitalization of at least $1 billion, and their capacities to raise needed finances were considerable.[103] Biotechnology was celebrated in the 1990s as a special growth industry, and by the end of the decade it had well over 100 products on the market and approximately 500 in the late-stage development pipeline. Currently (as of 2004), there are some 370 drug products and vaccines in clinical trials.[104] Utilizing information from both the human genome and model organisms (such as the fruit fly) over 1400 corporations in the U.S. are exploring the functional components of biological pathways, and the number and diversity of R&D projects is extraordinary.

By way of example, already in the mid–1990s corporations were attempting to manipulate developmental genes in the fruit fly, in order to make comparisons with the human genome and find drugs that effect regeneration in damaged cell tissues. In this category, a number of capitals are "exploring ways to regenerate bone, muscle, and other tissue, and coax damaged brain tissue to again produce vital neurotransmitters, all to treat conditions ranging from Parkinson's disease to skin cancer."[105] What has made the HGP so important in such cases? The fastest manner to explore gene function is through comparative genomics, in which one searches in a model organism for genes that may be related to biological processes similar to those in humans. But even upon isolation of the gene in model organisms, there is no guarantee that biological pathways are similar in humans. In this sense, the availability of whole genome sequences (in human and model organisms) allows corporations to establish false or ineffective pathways at a much earlier stage. Pharmaceutical products are also being produced which are aimed directly at particular genetic sequences that have gone awry—producing a problematic biological process in the body. This 'antisense' therapy is comprised of creating antisense oligonucleotides that bind to the problem mRNA and choke off its translation into a protein. Companies such as Isis, Genta Inc., and Hybridon have "increasingly been able to exploit the technology's advantage of speed in discovering drug targets and [move] into the clinic."[106] Some corporations in this category have even taken the step of attempting to build their own versions of peptide nucleic acids (PNAs), which are stronger than natural RNA, and able to both bind more effectively and resist degradation for a longer period of time.

As only a fraction of countless possible examples, it seems more than evident that the flourishing biotechnology industry has been directly advantaged from the mapping of genomic data. An influential consulting group has recently emphasized how the public availability of the HGP has meant a wealth of opportunity for the biotechnology industry with respect to therapeutic targets, as well as substantial savings that will result from the rationalization of research and clinical development.[107] This enormous new wave of growth within the industry, however, cannot be viewed as a self-contained process. It continues to be deeply intertwined with an investment and integration process undertaken, in large part, by the pharmaceutical industry. Since the rise of the genome project, pharmaceutical capitals have demonstrated a marked confidence in investment, acquisition, alliance and various other forms of entry into genome-based research. This process gained massive momentum through the 1990s, with particularly large investment waves emerging around 1991–92, 1995–96 and 2000–01. While the first two periods raised $5.1 billion and $6.5 billion, respectively, the latter was situated around the completion of the HGP's 'rough draft' and brought a wave of commercial investment flow of over $30 billion.[108] This hardly seems surprising—it has, after all, been suggested that the likely savings on new drug development, through rationalization measures attributable to the genome project, could be as high as $300 million per successful drug.[109] The long-term trend toward investment seems unlikely to subside, as companies look to capitalize on genomic data, by aiming their research trajectories at more complicated therapeutic problems. Indeed, even the very process of genomics (the actual practice of attaining and utilizing mapping data) has itself become a commercial endeavor.

Given the large waves of commercial activity, it seems strange that so much social anxiety would have emerged over the Celera venture, announced in 1998, to produce its own human genome sequence. Venter's deal with the PE Corporation (renamed from Perkin-Elmer) made clear that he would utilize the latest in sequencing technology (conveniently produced by PE's own Applied Biosystems), at a cost between $200 and $250 million, to complete the sequence within three years—a full four years ahead of the planned completion of the HGP.[110] Following this announcement, the media overflowed with stories concerning the 'race' between the Celera/PE endeavor and the publicly funded HGP.[111] There was, in fact, a prevailing tendency to pit Venter as the 'evil genius'—the scientist that everybody loved to hate. At the time, Eric Lander of Massachusetts Institute of Technology (MIT) tapped into widely-held sentiment in the molecular biology community, when he referred, tongue-in-cheek, to the public genome project as 'the Forces of Good.'[112] While this strange characterization will be explored further below, it is important to note here that Celera was far from the first to undertake commercial genomics. In fact, companies such as Incyte and Human Genome Sciences have been working in this field for some time. Although there was a certain expression of fury over Venter's stated intention to patent between 100 and 300 significant genes, his was far from the only or most egregious of such undertakings. Not only had the above companies submitted applications for gene sequences, they had been responsible for a number of partial gene sequence (EST) submissions. In turn, established corporations have numerous existing contracts in which they get first access to patenting or exclusive licensing on patents related to potentially valuable genome research. As of 1999, "[only] half-dozen of more than 1,300 biotech companies in the U.S have gotten major drugs into the market without selling majority stakes to big Pharma."[113] One well-known deal was that between Bayer and the genomics corporation Millennium Pharmaceuticals. Under the terms of this agreement, $465 million in research support was given to the latter in return for a promise to make available 225 development 'targets' from its genomics-based research program.

Ultimately, Venter's endeavor was not as much of a challenge to the government run HGP, as it was an expression of a widespread commercial processes already underpinning genomics research. This is not to depict the endeavor as naïve or completely insignificant—it is only to dismiss its representation (then) as some kind of novel confrontation with the putatively public goals of the HGP.[114]

In fact, the explosion of commercial genomics, along with the concomitant acceleration of the federally-funded genome project, continued to build an environment in which capitals intensified their use of innovation to survive competition. In keeping with Gambardella's understanding of strategic research in the competitive health industry, maintaining the innovative advantage in the post-HGP era implies the necessity for capitals to aim at increasingly complex R&D problems. In practical terms, this will mean a move to a host of areas, at least three of which could be described as critical: single nucleotide polymorphism (SNP) and haplotype (HAP) analysis, functional genomics and 'proteomics.' In the first scenario, corporations are acquiring data on SNPs (significant nucleotide variation between individuals within given genes) and HAPs (variation between individuals across certain 'DNA neighborhoods,' in order to pursue the market possibilities of individualized therapeutic information. On this front, companies such as Rosetta Inpharmatics, Affymetrix, Incyte are working on technologies that can more effectively identify these polymorphisms and interpret their functional importance.[115] Similarly, corporations such as Genaissance and Perlegen are building clinical databases that are intended for use in 'pharmacogenomics'—the measurement and correlation of human genetic variations with individual responses to drugs.[116] The potential consequences here for capital accumulation through individualization of healthcare delivery are staggering. Functional genomics deals with the attempt to isolate genes and understand more effectively their ultimate metabolic pathways. Of course, this process has been greatly aided by the huge increase in available mapping data, as well as the relatively recent move to pay more attention to such model organisms as the fruit fly and mouse. Finally, proteomics is being billed as the wave of future research development. Proteomics involves using genomics data to better understand the sequential code and immensely complicated structural characteristics of human proteins. This is no small task—protein analysis is fraught with technological challenges at an order of magnitude higher than genome mapping.[117] Structural characteristics have a critical impact on the function of human proteins, so researchers are now engaged in efforts that both decode and determine three-dimensional form. Ultimately, this requires a bioinformatics base much more advanced than those already in existence for genomic analysis. But while the costs are considerable, so too are the systemic opportunities for capitals seeking both to 'reduce failures' and develop innovative niche areas in the market.[118] In the end, capitals have but little choice to engage with this fast-paced innovative activity. The U.S. biotechnology industry has now grown to over 1450 firms, and the market capitalization of publicly held firms in 2003 was over $300 billion.[119] Driven by the necessity of survival in a bitterly competitive structure of exploding technological investment activity, biotechnology and pharmaceutical corporations alike have fashioned their own simple systemic choice: propagate and stay abreast of innovation or face market exit.

CONCLUSION

This chapter has sought to show that, in the wake of changing circumstances within the pharmaceutical industry throughout the 1970s, the possibilities for accumulation became much greater in areas of biotechnology and, ultimately, genome research. In particular, biotechnology emerged as an industry far less as a result of any technological imperative, and far more as the consequence of the mounting pressures resulting from the pharmaceutical industry's increasing exposure to the normal logic of motion within capitalist social relations. The 'danger' that the extensive protection afforded by monopoly patents was coming due for expiry *en masse*, and that patents were, in any case, losing their *de facto* longevity, meant that capitals in this sector were less and less able to avoid standard market competition. Moreover, the re-entry of generics and the cost-cutting measures across a range of areas in health services placed further pressure on research-based pharmaceuticals to redefine and legitimize their extraordinary status. Consequently, as existing drug technologies began to be generalized, the reaction of pharmaceutical capitals was to reassert their innovative capacities.

Thus, as the fervor for biotechnology took hold in the 1980s, we see the formation of a systemic environment in which the promulgation of an HGP becomes possible, even probable. The expanding needs of industry to identify and compare increasingly large amounts of genetic material made the map an attractive proposition. Siddharta's Mukherjee's recent claim that the HGP finished 'second,' and that its problem was that most of its scientists were simply not market-oriented enough, misses the point concerning the project's close affinity to industrial needs.[120] That there was anything definitively 'public' about the HGP is certainly open to question. Moreover, the project's affinity for capitalist accumulation, expressed during the HGP's creation and its subsequent development, seems beyond doubt. Whether the results of genome research will ultimately deliver the beneficial new therapeutic products promised by pharmaceutical and biotechnology capitals remains to be seen. That, after all, is a qualitative question pertaining to use value, and capital is concerned about use value only insofar as it can be translated into commodity production and new rounds of accumulation. From the perspective of capital, the primary significance of the HGP has always been, and continues to be, the potential it creates for an ever-increasing array of commodities produced specifically for the market.

Chapter Five

The State, the HGP and Capitalist Development

While the preceding chapter argues that the promulgation of the HGP occurred directly in concert with capital's interests, it is worth recalling that the project was planned and executed almost entirely under government auspices. In fact, the federally funded nature of the HGP was used very strategically, insofar as its putative *raison d'être* could, at times, be nominally detached from any overt commercial purpose. Federal state bodies associated to genome mapping, whether the Congress, the NIH or the President's scientific advisory, were always careful to highlight the medically desirable goal of generating human health benefits. In this respect, if the state is concerned primarily with the 'public good,' particularly in matters relating to health policy, is it possible that the HGP's intersection with corporate interests was only a byproduct of—rather than a motivating force for—the project's existence? In view of the earlier theoretical positioning of the state, there is a need to examine more thoroughly the role of the U.S. state in relation to 'big science,' particularly with respect to critical technologies such as genome research.

This chapter points out the direct relevance of capitalist systemic concerns for U.S. science policy in general and genome research in particular. The HGP represented a significant attempt by the state to secure the foundations for ongoing capitalist development in biotechnology and other genome-related industrial development. Through a complex array of processes, manifested in clear instances of political struggle, the state assumed the 'socialized risk' necessary for the procurement of costly generic scientific information. As such, it placed at the disposal of capital an extremely valuable data set, which would otherwise not likely have been produced. The chapter begins with a brief introduction of the state's historical presence in scientific affairs and its pronounced expectations concerning the connection between biotechnology innovation and economic growth. Following this, it turns more specifically to the state's instantiation of the HGP, exploring the concrete reasoning behind this involvement and support. In this regard, events surrounding the U.S. Congress and its relationship to relevant agencies constituted a vital element in the state's enablement of the project. Finally, the last two sections consider the manner in which the political viability of the HGP was maintained. This required a concerted effort domestically, but also a vigorous set of foreign policies relating the ever-expanding results of genome research to international trade and property protection. Ultimately, the chapter problematizes the notion that U.S. state action or public policy in relation to genome science could be characterized as either 'neutral' or incidental to the capitalist accumulation process.

SCIENCE POLICY AND U.S. SOCIAL RELATIONS

The U.S. has always evinced a rather strong notion of technological optimism, in which the belief that increased scientific and technological research will, inevitably, lead to increasing benefits for the American population. Indeed, even when it has not at all been clear that a technological 'fix' would address national concerns, scientists have been mobilized to bring about technical solutions. For the most part, eminent scientists have tended to endorse (and secure the funds for) various challenges handed down by state-level bureaucracies. Exemplary outcomes might include the Manhattan Project or the Apollo Program, while supersonic transport and superconductivity remain somewhat less celebrated. Whatever the reality of technological benefits, there is little doubt that the state has, particularly in the post–war period, remained steadfastly generous towards the procurement of basic and applied scientific research.

While post–war state involvement in science is unique in its scale, it is not entirely unprecedented. The U.S. government's presence in scientific support has, in fact, largely paralleled the development of industrial capitalism. Nathan Rosenberg has claimed that, "in spite of continued obeisance to the idea of Yankee ingenuity, it cannot be overstressed that America in the first half of the nineteenth century was still primarily an importer of European technology."[1] This may well be true, but one should not let it obscure the unique dynamism of America's early capitalist development. The social relations of *ante bellum* America were based on a distinctive mix of petty-commodity production (based on family farms), slavery production in the South, and merchant/industrial capital in the Northeast. The manner in which petty producers gained access to the land was not by free acreage, but largely through speculators as middlemen, thus subjecting their consequent production to the law of value. High priced mortgages enforced the need for high productivity and specialization, subjecting these 'independent' farmers to commodity circulation for their sustenance.[2] This dependence would form the mainstay of the American home market, as industrial producers in the Northeast grew progressively stronger. The growth of this home market, as well as the continual influx of wage labor through European migration, meant that,

> [the] complex of industries producing farm-machinery, tools and supplies, and processing agricultural raw materials (meat-packing, leather-tanning, flour milling and baking), were at the center of the American industrial revolution. These branches were characterised by both technical innovation in their labour-process and either constituted or stimulated transformations in key branches of [farm implements and machine production].[3]

Thus, there developed a uniquely American 'system of manufactures,' with an orientation toward standardized, low-priced, and functional products aimed at the rural household. Given the centrality of the agro-industrial complex to the development of the American economy, it is not surprising that the first area in which the United States directed state funds to research was in agriculture. Bruce Smith has lamented the fact that the U.S. government "built an integrated system that included basic and applied research, agricultural experiment stations, country agents, and extensions services to support the farmer."[4] But his contention that this investment ran counter to the development of the private sector (by promoting an obsession with agricultural self-sufficiency at all costs) is ahistorical—the policy was, in fact, highly supportive of that part of the economy critical to the expansion of the U.S. home market.[5]

At the same time, the degree of state support for research remained limited until WWII, confined to directed tasks undertaken by various agencies and departments. Its other socio-economic policies, however, certainly affected the manner in which research would be directed. As American industry grew to larger-scale proportions, the use of in-house laboratories, in contact with university researchers, became more predominant. Importantly, this process was directly affected by the particular disposition of the American government towards monopoly. The Sherman Antitrust Act, put in place in the late nineteenth century, was aimed at preventing large corporations from price setting, a goal in keeping with the broadly held values of the American marketplace. But one of its earliest consequences was both to encourage a wave of corporate mergers (creating larger corporations rather than 'trusts') and the development of in-house laboratories. As Rosenberg and David Mowery point out

> [to] the extent that federal antitrust policy motivated industrial research investments by large U.S. firms before and during the interwar period, the policy paradoxically may have aided the survival of these firms and the growth of a relatively stable, oligopolistic market structure in many U.S. manufacturing industries.[6]

A particular concern for American manufacturers was the increasing industrial power of German chemical firms, and their capacity to apply scientific research to industrial ends. Thus, in-house laboratories became increasingly useful not only to identify areas for potential corporate growth, but also to monitor and often import the technologies of foreign competitors.

The legal terrain surrounding patents also constituted an area in which state policies affected the emergence of industrially oriented research. A series of Congressional and Supreme Court actions between 1898 and 1920 extended patent coverage to non-U.S. territories, made non-produced goods patentable (opening the door for defensive patents), increased patent examiners, made review procedures more efficient, and moved the patent office to an industry-friendly Commerce Department.[7] The extended utility of patents for industry provided considerable incentive to enhance research capabilities both to attain new patents and, ultimately, defend old ones. As such, in-house research, as well as the acquisition of external research, was mostly a corporate-inspired activity. It was in precisely such an environment that the philanthropic character of pre-war scientific support was able to flourish. During this pre-war period, while industrial research and philanthropy accounted for well over two-thirds of total U.S. R&D, state involvement lingered between 12 and 20 percent.[8]

Given the impact of WWII on research (see chapter 2), it is worth making clear the overall picture of post–war state involvement. During and after WWII, the state became more directly involved in the support and harnessing of basic scientific research. The majority of this support was aimed at defense purposes, an expected outcome in the context of America's participation in the war and heightened military preparedness during the Cold War. Nonetheless, considerable amounts of funding were also appropriated for 'civilian' research purposes. Smith has broken this postwar science policy down into roughly three periods. The first lasts from the war until about 1967, in which the state's science policy underwrote basic research across a range of areas. This period witnessed the creation of a system that was largely investigator-led, decentralized, and generously funded. Between 1953 and 1967, basic research funding increased by more than 350 percent.[9] In the next period, lasting roughly from 1968 until 1976, there is an overall 15 percent retrenchment in basic funding, and a prevailing wisdom that unwieldy science needs to be reigned in. Smith blames this reversal of fortune almost entirely on the widespread sense of disillusion concerning the connection between defense spending and basic research, particularly in relation to university campuses. The visibility of both the effects of basic research in the Vietnam War, as well as the protestations on American campuses over Department of Defense activities, helped to breed a environment of mistrust, in which the benefits of science could no longer be taken for granted.[10] It is worth noting that Smith's period of 'decline' coincides almost perfectly with the first postwar retraction of U.S. capitalist accumulation. Smith admits to the relevance of economic pressures in relation to policies near the end of the 1970s, but such economic processes were well under way by the second half of the 1960s, as Brenner has ably shown (see chapter 4). Beyond the notion of 'runaway science,' this may explain more feasibly why Congress, keeper of the state's purse strings, stepped in so aggressively during this period to address questions of science policy.

The third sub-period, from the Carter Administration forward, has exhibited a considerable change in the direction of science policy. Still under way, this period has witnessed President Carter—painted by his opponents as the profligate spender—passing some of the smallest deficits in years while protecting basic R&D from the imperative of fiscal stringency. In contrast, Ronald Reagan, ostensibly the fiscal conservative, sought both enormous deficits and a growing commitment to R&D throughout his two terms as president. The relative invulnerability of R&D budgets, through both thick and thin government spending, constitutes part of the context for the HGP's emergence. The tenor of state involvement in science has shifted, particularly since the 1980s, with tremendous effects for both biomedicine and molecular biology. Ultimately, the latter was viewed as a potential response to Congressional and Administrative calls to augment 'strategic' or 'critical' technologies that could feasibly give some impetus to growth in the American economy.[11]

THE STATE OF BIOTECH AND THE BIOTECH STATE

Given the shape of its development, US state intervention has generally helped to reproduce a socio-economic structure highly conducive to the emergence of 'new' areas of innovation. Unlike other advanced industrial countries, such as Germany and Japan, and to a greater extent than the

United Kingdom, the United States does not administer any overt forms of associational production relations. In other words, the state has refrained, in large part, from involved policies that explicitly guide and organize socio-economic relations. One finds no overarching associations for employers or entire labor sectors (such as can be found in Germany), few enshrined labor rights (such as 'works councils') or even traditions of long-term investment structure. On the whole, the American economy is said to be highly adaptable to market circumstances, because remarkably few obstacles stand in the way of a mobile flow of capital and an increasingly flexible labor market.[12] Capitals operating in the U.S. marketplace are said to be highly capable with respect to innovation in new production spheres, and it is notable that as a world economic 'leader,' the United States has been oriented toward short product cycles and the constant search for entirely new product innovation.

While the state has not taken an overtly organizational role, this is not to say that it has been inactive. Just the opposite: the state remains the organizational terrain in which society-wide agendas are set. At least since the late–1970s, the state has demonstrated an expressed willingness to promote the well being of capitals that are explicitly occupied with technological innovation. In relation to genome-based research, this has meant a program of political support, in which the facilitation of capitalist growth has been reinforced. In the early 1980s, the Congress had already expressed a desire to see that genetics research translated into 'useful' knowledge, subject to commercialization. In fact, it is instructive to see how easily congressional discourse during this period slid from the safety issues of the 1970s to the upcoming 'bonanza' of biotechnology.

> Now that the debate over the safety of conducting recombinant DNA, or 'genetic' engineering has subsided a bit, a new set of concerns has pushed its way into scientific and public debates. The concern arises from a new, widely shared realization of the vast commercial potential of genetic technologies, and focuses in part on what role universities and the faculties will have in this commercialization process. [13]

This newly charged commercial interest among political representatives was significant, given that the Congress is the body most clearly responsible for decisions concerning appropriations for basic research funding. It constitutes the political arena in which various forms of basic research are either secured or left to languish.

Consistent with the foregoing theoretical framework, politically constituted agendas for scientific research are not predetermined, but they remain subject to the structural boundaries of historical process. The terrain in which this agenda would be shaped in the United States was largely politico-legislative, shared between Congress, state agencies and the President's administration. If these democratic institutions and the politico-legal framework constitute the 'frontline of social struggle' over any given issue-area, then the predilections of the American state could not be clearer. Debates concerning biotechnology and genome-related innovation have largely been couched within two broad political goals: 1) that a greater degree of technology transfer between basic researchers and corporations would instantiate economic development and 2) that economic growth should be fostered, such that its benefits accrued predominantly to the United States.

With respect to the first goal, any policy 'controversy' in relation to biotechnology (such as the perception that ever tightening university-industrial relations may have a pernicious effect on academe) needs to be seen in relation to the tremendous influence of numerous legislative acts, undertaken to ensure a secure legal foundation for the commercialization of such research. In 1980, the Stevenson-Wydler Technology Transfer Act was put into effect, giving general guidance to federal agencies concerning technology transfer and mandating them to set up Offices of Research and Technology Applications (ORTA). As such, the law "acknowledged the value of technology transfer as an important economic function and legitimized grass roots efforts to transfer technology at the national laboratories."[14] Shortly thereafter, this was strongly reinforced by the Bayh-Dole Act of 1980, which allowed for private patenting on federally funded research. It mandated a comprehensive federal policy, in which universities and corporations alike could retain title to and exploit federal research. The 1981 Economic Recovery Tax Act allowed for tax credits to companies involved in R&D, whether in-house or contracted out to another firm or university.[15] Thus, while R&D was deductible from capitals' income, such firms also received a 20–25 percent tax credit. Those firms that qualified under the 1983 Orphan Drug Act, which guarantees market monopoly on compounds aimed at rare disease, gained access to a 50% tax credit.[16] Following this, the 1984 Patent Term Restoration Act and the 1986 Federal Technology Transfer Act (FTTA) were aimed squarely at the pharmaceutical and emerging biotechnology industries.[17] Under the first, corporations can apply to the Patent and Trademark Office for an official patent extension if the federal safety review process has hindered their patents' *de facto* longevity. In an industry becoming increasingly research intensive, due in large part to biotechnology-related work, this was a clear signal of structural support. The FTTA amended and strengthened the Stevenson-Wydler Act, by granting authority to federal agencies to develop Cooperative Research and Development Agreements (CRADAs) with the private sector. It mandated that a certain share of resources be devoted to each agency's ORTA, and that federal laboratories should participate with local authorities to promote technology transfer and economic development.[18] Judging by the legislative results of Congressional action, both the sanctity of academic research and any perceived dangers of commercial influence were trumped by the state's effort to capitalize on American strength in basic research.

From the outset, the political agenda to enhance technology transfer faced a certain degree of opposition, most significantly from members the scientific community who could not easily be ignored. One of the more formidable was Jonathan King, Professor of Microbiology at Massachusetts Institute of Technology. King, while not actually opposed to *some* commercial involvement in the natural sciences, had already sensed that boundaries had not been properly maintained. In some of the earliest biotechnology-related Congressional testimony, King simply refused to adopt commercialization as a panacea.

> Let me just say here that the transformation of basic research findings into useful application is a critically important process. . . . [But] we should not confuse productive and beneficial application with commercial application. They are not necessarily the same. Numerous vaccines—practical applications of basic virological research—were developed and produced by the Government, because no corporation could envisage sufficient return on investment from their marketing. Second, many marketable products—patent medicines, or some cosmetics—have very little social benefit or utility, even though they are commercially quite useful.[19]

Importantly, voices such as King's typically constituted a very small part of political discussion related to biotechnology in the 1980s. Instead, the Congressional arena accorded more weight to perspectives, which encouraged the commercialization process critiqued by King. Witnesses who offered more industry-friendly points of view were given a much stronger political voice, among them university presidents, related state agency officials, industrial interest groups and corporate representatives. The political struggle to confirm the priority of commercial transfer in basic research within the federal agenda transpired under one-sided circumstances, making a great deal more likely those legislative outcomes directly supportive of biotechnology development.

Moreover, the relation between Administrative structures and state agencies pointed unmistakably towards an agenda of accelerated commercial development and technology transfer. By the early 1980s, the NIH required little prodding to make technology transfer and commercial patent rights a priority. According to William Raub, NIH Associate Director of Extramural Research and Training, the Bayh-Dole Act effectively reproduced already-existing NIH policy.[20] But while it was one thing to have a policy in place, it was another to propagate active technology transfer. For this reason, by the mid–1980s, federal agencies (including the DOE, NIH and the Department of Commerce) were meeting with major industry representatives to investigate ways in which the federal government could bolster the development of the American biotechnology industry.[21] Additionally, the Reagan Administration insisted on utilizing national agencies more effectively, and expressed a special interest in the NIH moving away from its narrow focus on a 'disease mission,' and investing itself more heavily in the support of the biotechnology industry.[22] This position was codified with an April 1987 Presidential Executive Order, which pushed for increased technology transfer of federally funded research. The order "promoted consortium formation, exchange of research personnel between government laboratories and industrial firms, special technology transfer programmes of federally owned laboratories, and transfer of patent rights to government grantees and contractors."[23] As a critical backdrop to all of this, the Administration, in concert with Congress, shifted its policy on antitrust as a means to incite innovation. This policy "was implemented by the simple expedient of bringing fewer cases to court, especially those involving collaboration among companies in R&D and in product development."[24] Not surprisingly, by the end of the 1980s, under Congressional and Administrative pressure, both the DOE and NIH had become active at soliciting and structuring CRADAs, based on R&D funded under their auspices.[25]

The second broad political goal—enhancing the effects of biotechnology on *American* competitiveness and economic leadership—represents a more overt manifestation of political struggle. A recurring issue in genetics-related hearings, policymakers demonstrated their concern, almost obsession, with the possibility that U.S. competitiveness was suffering at the hands of its foreign competitors. An exemplary illustration of this concern lies in the 1981 controversy surrounding a newly launched venture between Massachusetts General Hospital (MGH) and the German firm Hoechst. Under the agreement, Hoechst funded the hospital with $50 million over a ten-year period for a new department in molecular biology in return for exclusive rights on any ensuing research developments. In the political aftermath, public officials raised grave concerns over the degree to which taxpayers' public research dollars were going to benefit (or subsidize) a private corporation. What was 'business as usual' in any other circumstance (other such agreements had been, or were being, formed between Harvard Medical School and both Exxon and DuPont, Monsanto and both MIT and University of Washington, Cold Spring Harbour and Exxon, Scripps and Johnson & Johnson, and University of California and Allied[26]) became, in this case, anathema to American national interests. There is no avoiding the fact that this deal's salience for U.S. policymakers was related to the involvement of a *foreign* capital. Here, we find one of the most 'testy' moments in Congressional hearings related to biomedical research, and a spectacular exchange between Senator Al Gore and Ronald Lamont-Havers of MGH is worth quoting at length. After an initial row over the availability of the actual contract (which Gore claimed they would subpoena, if necessary), Lamont-Havers made clear that MGH entered into this deal only after having previously decided to found a new department, and only in the context of a funding crunch during the mid–1970s. The Hospital was not, according to Lamont-Havers, doing anything extraordinary among American institutions. Nonetheless, Gore persisted:

> **Mr. Gore:** Let me come back to my original question. We provided $25 to $26 million a year in direct Federal aid to the Mass General. I think it's fair to say that the current biomedical research capabilities at Mass General are indebted in part to Federal support of basic biomedical research over the last 20 years. Now isn't it a little unfair to the American taxpayer after this . . . to give the cream of the results to a foreign company that gets exclusive licensing rights?
>
> **Dr. Lamont-Havers:** Let's examine that rather inflammatory statement.
>
> **Mr. Gore:** Rather what?
>
> **Dr. Lamont-Havers:** Inflammatory statement, if I may say so.
>
> **Mr. Gore:** Well, I view the agreement as inflammatory.
>
> **Dr. Lamont-Havers:** Well, I don't think you've read it very carefully, anyway.
>
> **Mr. Gore:** You haven't given it to me.
>
> **Dr. Lamont-Havers:** The executive summary is very good. Basically, you must remember the institution has a patent policy which addresses the question of the patent rights, agreements, and applies to really all of our

agreements with any company and how we treat our patents. The consulting agreement is also standard for what we expect our faculty to do. The Hoechst agreement binds the institution and Hoechst to utilise the MGH patent policy and consulting agreement. In other words, we are not treating Hoechst in any way different from any other supporter of our research—or any other industry which supports our research.

Mr. Gore: They get exclusive licensing rights; do they not?

Dr. Lamont-Havers: That's exactly the same. They are not treated any differently than Johnson & Johnson would be or any other company which would tend to support our research. And this is quite in keeping with the Federal policy, the NIH policy, there is no difference. . . . Hoechst is primarily concerned with access to new knowledge. They are not primarily concerned with the development of patents or new products. . . .

Mr. Gore: Well, why was the exclusive licensing agreement necessary then?

Dr. Lamont-Havers: If you were a company, and I would imagine the chairman of the board, you're not going to give $50 million to somebody just to get advice.

Mr. Gore: Not for nothing. They're going to get something for it.

Dr. Lamont-Havers: What they're getting is information.

Mr. Gore: What they're getting is also the exclusive right to market it.

Dr. Lamont-Havers: They're not getting anything different from anybody else that supports that research. The American taxpayer is not supporting that research. . . .

Mr. Gore: So all of the fruits of the genetic engineering portion [of research] will go to Hoechst?

Dr. Lamont-Havers: That portion which they fund.

Mr. Gore: Which is the entire department. . . .

Dr. Lamont-Havers: The molecular biology department will be funded by Hoechst. The American people in the meantime are getting the advantages of the knowledge which is coming out of that because that's going to be freely available as it would be in any other academic department. There'll be freedom of publication, there'll be freedom of

communication; so in that way the American public are in effect getting
the results of that $50 million.[27]

Following this exchange, Gore's continual 'smarting' throughout the hearing—repeatedly attempting to re-establish the credibility of his questioning
with more sympathetic witnesses—indicates quite clearly that Lamont-
Havers had carried the moment. In a rare instance, Gore stumbled, because
his concerns over the impact of commercial involvement elicited an obvious
contradiction. In any other instance, particularly those involving American
corporations, he would not have hesitated to support such contractual
terms. In fact, at a later point in the same hearing, when Daniel Steiner,
General Counsel for Harvard University, stated that the private sector in
many cases would get the benefit from publicly funded research, but that
they deserved it, because they were the ones who had 'taken risks,' Gore
agreed unequivocally.

Such hypocrisy is emblematic of the rather complicated nexus between
domestic and foreign policy, in which the state is concerned with the development of information technologies under the general rubric of free market
exchange, but simultaneously wants to maintain a superior U.S. competitive
position. In other words, the state's primary concern remained with the
preservation and advancement of America's most strategic competitive assets. During this time period, it worked diligently to expand the capacity of
capitals, large and small, to lead the United States out of its sustained productivity and profitability crisis. That such measures, in the case of biotechnology, could not always accrue benefits solely to U.S. society was, and
remains, a reflection of the internationalizing tendencies of production for
the market, rather than any deficient effort on the part of policymakers.
Ultimately, however, utilizing innovation as a segue to revitalization of the
American economy would require a more proactive intervention, in which
the state assumed a certain degree of socialized risk for the further development of biotechnology and genome-related research.

THE STATE, POLITICAL STRUGGLE AND THE HGP

The HGP is an unusual scientific program, in that its emergence was not really the result of actions undertaken by the scientific community. As Bernard
Davis has pointed out in Congressional testimony, the project,

> was not initiated by a committee of molecular geneticists with a press-
> ing need, or by the major biomedical funding agency, the NIH. Instead
> it was advanced by an administrator in the Department of Energy
> (DOE), convinced that with the powerful tools of molecular biology it

was now time to introduce centrally administered 'big science' into bio-medical research.[28]

Although some have identified the roots of the genome project in a proposal made by Robert Sinsheimer of the University of California at Santa Cruz, his efforts amounted to little, and were actually directed at an alternative use of funds originally donated for what later became the Keck Telescope.[29] Charles DeLisi, director of the DOE's Office of Health and Environmental Research (OHER) began planning a Human Genome Initiative as early as 1984, outlining a political strategy to approach Congress, and convening or taking part in three critical meetings in Alta, Utah, Santa Cruz and Sante Fe, California.[30] Once DOE's plans were known more extensively, an impressive group of molecular biologists demonstrated intense scientific interest. It is, indeed, significant that, from its earliest beginnings, the plan to map the human genome was explicitly allied to the institutional goals of a prominent state agency.

An obvious question arises here: why the DOE? Answers to this question vary, but Cook-Deegan suggests that both historical experience (with radiation experiments) and departmental mission (multidisciplinary, large-scale projects) allowed the DOE to gravitate easily toward the project. Moreover, he emphasizes that the DOE was, fortuitously, able to garner political backing from Senator Pete Domenici of New Mexico (home of a national laboratory), due to the Senator's fear that weapons and military research would soon fade from his constituency. Domenici supposedly "sought a new mission for national laboratories that did not depend on the Cold War rhetoric. . . . [and] knew that sooner or later the Reagan defense spending juggernaut would lose steam."[31] However, as Michael Fortun points out, this is a case of revisionism for which Cook-Deegan offers little substantiation. For his own part, Fortun offers up the words of Robert Moyzis, then director of the Los Alamos Laboratory, to suggest that the HGP gained momentum within the DOE as a result of scientists' excitement about it as a concept.[32] But surely this explanation does not suffice either— that a project of this magnitude would proceed merely based on the interest of those closely involved seems highly improbable. In an early workshop on genome mapping, Domenici revealed a more compelling logic, which also remains in step with the historical reality of U.S. science policy:

> Now, I know that frequently a subject as significant as this, in terms of wellness and health and diagnostic potential, and everything that goes with that, biochemical research, the pharmaceutical industry, health delivery, the delivery of health care in the future, those are all much more

frequently thought of as much more in-depth words than this word competition. But frankly, the United States Congress recently, in adopting a so-called trade bill, was engaged in a serious discussion of America's potential competitiveness in the newly integrated world market, and we were constantly talking about, let's make sure we are doing what we should to remain competitive.[33]

As Fortun is more than aware, consequential individuals only possess power insofar as they are connected to broader networks and institutions. Thus, Moyzis may well have been excited about genome mapping as an important biology project, but he could play that excitement out only in relation to the institutional structure (in the DOE) associated to DeLisi. In turn, DeLisi's actions cannot be disassociated from the wishes and goals of the wider DOE or its Congressional advocates. Thus, no matter how closely one attempts to go to the 'source' of early genome work, it remains a mistake to lose sight of the broader reasoning for its financial and structural support. In this case, the interests of Congress in reviving the competitive potential of the American economy provided the wider foundation, upon which DOE program initiatives, including the HGP, could be built.

In fact, given the abovementioned Congressional and Administrative wishes for increased competitive innovation and technology transfer in both national facilities and federally funded research, it is logical that the DOE actively sought to enable a project with a wide diversity of practical and commercial applications. OHER pursued DOE funds before securing Congressional authorization or appropriations, and by September of 1987, the Secretary of Energy had already ordered the creation of genome research centers at three national laboratories: Los Alamos, Livermore and Lawrence Berkeley.[34] However, the department's ability to undertake such initiatives stemmed from officials' awareness that Congressional discussions were already underway, led primarily by Domenici. In the Senate, Domenici demonstrated his political savvy by getting S1480, a bill sponsoring the DOE's proposed genome initiative, through hearings and onto the Senate floor within two weeks.[35] Nonetheless, this individual and departmental support would not lead to the formation of a genome project without struggle; it would be just the opposite. In fact, Hirsch's contention (see chapter 2) that state policy is never a smooth reaction to production processes speaks to the specific case of the HGP. Such political programs are always the result of intra-class struggle, which sorts out and prioritizes partial interests in relation to the general reproductive needs of American capitalism. Thus, Domenici's lightning-fast first-strike notwithstanding, contending social interests and interdepartmental friction would greatly complicate the landscape around the HGP, such that domestic political struggle would play out in at least two distinct ways: in establishing the project as an economic asset worthy of pursuit and in finalizing the project's political structure.

An Economic Priority

On one level, the struggle to bring the genome initiative to fruition must be considered in light of other contemporary projects, such as the Space Station and the Superconducting Super Collider (SSC). Particularly in the second half of the 1980s, each held its own appeal within Congress and the Reagan and Bush (Sr.) Administrations, and as late as 1990, all three were receiving support from the Congress.[36] But as finances tightened in the early 1990s, both the Space Station and the SSC came under considerable pressure. While the new Clinton administration announced its goal to increase increase the civilian share of R&D expenditures ('It's the economy, stupid.'), the Space Station project found itself increasingly "transformed into a different animal by several cost-cutting redesigns."[37] While the Space Station continued, it did so only with a ferocious effort on the part of the Bush and Clinton administrations, barely surviving in House appropriations by one vote in 1993.[38] Similarly, the life span of SSC offers an extremely interesting contrast to the HGP. According to Daniel Kevles, "the Congress . . . is selective in its economizing, tending to be tolerant of expenditures for high national purposes, especially if they are reinforced by important local political and economic interests. . . . [The] SSC failed to qualify on the national or local ground."[39] How could a project such as the SSC contend with the HGP in an expanding civilian research pie? It had no IBA or PhRMA to back it up, and even the physics community was deeply divided. When the Industrial Research Institute polled its members as to which of five major science projects (SSC, SDI, Hypersonic Airplane, Space Station, and the HGP) should receive government priority, the genome project was first with twice the votes of the second-place project.[40] In contrast to an accelerator, which only produces useful results upon its completion, "obtaining just a fraction of the human genome sequence, particularly the fraction containing genes for disease, [would] pay high scientific and medical dividends."[41] It is significant that in political disagreements around which projects could obtain or maintain funding, the central criterion for decision-making corresponded to each project's potential for 'payoffs' linked to the 'national interest.'

Recalling the Congressional disposition towards 'competition' outlined by Domenici, there is ample evidence to suggest that state actors' primary interest in making the HGP possible was the possibility of economic return. Beginning with S1480, in large part written by Jack McConnell of

Johnson & Johnson, the bill's intent could not be stated more clearly. It was, "[a] bill to improve the integration of universities and private industry into the National Laboratory system of the Department of Energy in order to speed the development of technology in areas of significant economic potential."[42] Following the failure of this bill (further discussed below), Domenici arranged a workshop on gene mapping attended by critical government officials, including DeLisi (DOE) and Ruth Kirschstein of the NIH.[43] Here, Cook-Deegan, as representative of the OTA, urged participants to think clearly about ways in which to take advantage of strengths at the NIH and DOE and think about "how to push that out into the commercially exploitable sectors, how to integrate thoughts from private companies, how to incorporate strategic planning in the corporate sense into research planning . . ."[44] Not only did DeLisi embrace Cook-Deegan's point, but he also stressed further that "the really important issues now are to get on with trying to determine how to structure this so that any innovative technologies can be transferred as efficiently and effectively as possible to the private sector and the universities."[45] For her own part, Kirschstein, who was conceptualizing any potential project as an expansion of the existing NIH grant system, implored those present to 'put the word out' that when official announcements are made, "the private sector is more than welcome to not only put in research grant applications or contract proposals or whatever, but consortium arrangements with the people from the National Labs, people from universities, any setup that one wants."[46]

The economic logic of the HGP was also not lost on the Congress in early hearings related to the project's emergence. In a 1988 House hearing dealing with the release of a much anticipated OTA report, Chair John Dingell reminded the subcommittee that "[if] NIH does not proceed with the mapping of the human genome, American science and U.S. industries will fall behind, perhaps permanently in the quest to better understand human disease."[47] In a Senate hearing the following year dealing with appropriations and ethics, chaired by Al Gore, Domenici himself was invited to testify. In fact, he was given the opening testimony, and asserted in relation to the HGP that Congress' aim should be to "get this American economy where its productivity and growth is occurring and continuing and reliable enough where these kind of exciting programs can be afforded."[48] Within this testimony, there were also clear references to the basic scientific priorities, around which the entire Congressional struggle was oriented.

> We may not be able to afford that much random science. . . . Some scientists do not like to hear it, but . . . while we want most of them to be random and doing their thing, we might have to ask some what is the

commercial value and are you working with the private sector and are you working with the National Laboratories, the National Institutes of Health to an end that is discernable that would have some kind of marketplace value in the fields of health care, wellness, biomedicine or the like.[49]

In the same hearing, both Senators Bryan and Kerry admonish Robert Wood of OHER (who had replaced Charles DeLisi) for the DOE's track record on technology transfer, which was generally not considered to be as strong as the NIH. The implications here were clear: if the DOE wished to receive continuing political (and possibly financial) support for such projects, it would need to step up its capacities to commercialize the basic science under its auspices. One can point to such moments *ad inifinitum*, in which government officials and Congressional representatives highlight the need for the HGP based on the potential 'shot in the arm' it would give to U.S. competitiveness. In this way, the HGP gained ascendancy primarily because, at almost every turn, its advocates in the administration, the Congress, industry and the scientific community tapped into a general governmental desire to promote U.S. competitive advantage. Thus, in analyzing the HGP's emergence, Fortun (whose work is not concerned with political economy) states quite correctly that it "had a strong economic identity, and that was very important to Congress. Perhaps more than any other identity, it is the one that . . . has been most obscured in conventional accounts, and which deserves to be restored to some prominence."[50]

Finalizing Structure

In addition to the fight for the HGP's credentials *vis-à-vis* American capitalism, it is possible to identify another level of political struggle. This requires a step back to the DOE's early presence in genome project planning. From as early as 1987, all did not proceed the way that either the DOE or Domenici had originally planned. S1480 never attained the political support necessary for its survival in the Senate. But why in a legislative body, where most had become convinced of the politico-economic purpose and value of the genome project, would Domenici's bill 'hit the skids'? There were early signs of trouble for S1480 in its first hearings, in which alternative visions surfaced as to how such a project could be administered. Most significantly, NIH Director James Wyngaarden, clearly hoping the NIH could eventually mount a better project strategy, tried subtly to stall the bill's ascent to the floor.[51] Politically, the DOE would need the NIH on side if its genome initiative were to gain authorization and appropriations in the Congress. But with no NIH plan yet developed, Wyngaarden could only hope to evade Domenici's contrivances for a 'lead agency' (namely the DOE), by insisting that this research could be done under existing NIH and DOE structures:

> Domenici: If Congress wants to do it, how do we do it? Just give the NIH more money under their existing program and give DOE some more money . . .
>
> Wyngaarden: I think that is a very good way to do it.
>
> Domenici: And would it get done?
>
> Wyngaarden: Yes.
>
> Domenici: Without any changes in the law?
>
> Wyngaarden: I think so.
>
> Domenici: Where would you get the direction to do the mapping? It is not around. You just told me there is no national policy and no statutory direction to do the mapping.
>
> Wyngaarden: I think most of the things that we have accomplished in biomedical science are without a state national policy. They are done by providing resources to the scientists capable of doing the work. With guidance from Congress as to priorities, and we respond to that.[52]

Wyngaarden carefully understated his opposition, by claiming that while the NIH "agree[d] with the intent of S1480 to highlight the importance of understanding the genetic basis of living organisms, [it did] not feel that the bill as originally described represent[ed] the optimal route toward obtaining these objectives."[53] Domenici's skill in committees prevailed in getting the bill to the floor, but Wyngaarden's move was representative of a wider struggle related to the upcoming direction and management of the project. Behind the scenes, key figures of the scientific community, politicians and industrial organizations reconsidered the shape and structure of the project. In particular, a major problem was identified in the distribution of roles between the NIH and the DOE. The DOE apparently had the political upper hand, because it had 'stepped up to bat,' but many felt that the NIH, although its involvement was never in question, was more appropriate to lead such a project.

Was this merely a case of an inter-departmental 'turf war'? Although this depiction always captures a certain element of ministerial politics, the struggle between the DOE and the NIH amounted to something more significant. The NIH, quite logically, was the major supporter of research related to any potential genome project. By 1986, it was already involved in over 3000 investigator-initiated grants that supported projects related to mapping and sequencing. As Table 5.1 points out, the NIH's combined budget for these activities was approaching $300 million, spread across various institutes. At the same time, as Kirschstein reminded participants at the summer workshop of 1987, it was also imperative to keep in mind that "almost every molecular biologist at a university throughout the United states, and indeed the scientists working on the NIH campus, government scientists, now have developed interrelationships with the small and sometimes large biotechnology industrial components all over the country."[54] In other words, the NIH's interconnections to industry in this research area were already both large and varied. Taking note of this advantageous web between the NIH and the wider biotechnology community, influential reports weighed in subtly for a central role on the part of the NIH. The 1987 IBA survey made explicit mention of the issue, stating its member companies to be in favor of the NIH as the lead agency by a factor of over three to one.[55] The 1988 OTA report veered way from explicit recommendations, fearing that to do so could potentially interrupt research done at either agency. However, it did state squarely that if "Congress finds that the advantages of a lead agency outweigh the disadvantages, then NIH is the natural choice for lead agency."[56] In the end, the NIH's capacity to direct basic genetic research in a manner which was consistent with the broad interests of Congress, assuring technology transfer and economic development, was far more advanced than the DOE's.

This posturing of the NIH in relation to its wider biomedical and industrial constituents was simultaneously augmented by the immediate political struggle inside the Congress. Domenici's bill would not receive the smooth ride which he had likely anticipated, as Florida Senator Lawton Chiles, chair of the critical appropriations subcommittee and interested in the development of biotechnology (apparently in relation to his home state's orange crops), effectively blocked it in 1987. According to most accounts, both Chiles and Edward Kennedy, whose home state contains an enormously strong regional cluster of biotechnology capitals, were busy soliciting opinions and receiving 'storms of protest' over any potential DOE lead.[57] Chiles refused to sign onto Domenici's bill, a move that reportedly infuriated Domenici. There is a close tie-in between Congressional action and the machinations of the NIH. As Kevles points out, while both Kennedy and Chiles were soliciting advice, they were also the object of mobilization

Table 5.1 NIH Funding for Gene Mapping and Sequencing, 1986
($ millions)

National Institute	Human Research	Nonhuman Research	Total
Institute of General Medical Sciences (NIGMS)	12.4	99.6	112.0
Cancer Institute (NCI)	18.3	24.2	42.5
Institute of Allergy and Infectious Diseases (NIAID)	6.0	28.0	34.0
Institute of Child Health and Human Development (NICHE)	11.8	18.2	30.0
Institute of Neurological and Communicative Disorders and Stroke (NINCDS)	10.7	10.6	21.3
Library of Medicine (NLM) and Other Institutes	31.9	22.1	54.0
Total	**91.1**	**203.0**	**294.0**

Source: U.N. Congress, OTA, Mapping Our Genes, p.94.

on behalf of Wyngaarden's staff and a host of prominent molecular biologists. The latter, "insisted that the NIH should get into the game, not least to take the principal control of it away from the DOE."[58]

The result of this back-and-forth was the introduction by Chiles and Kennedy of S1966, the Biotechnology Science Coordination and Competitiveness Act. In its final committee form, the Act literally adopts the text of the Commerce Department in explaining its underlying purpose, by referring to the need for sound monetary and fiscal policy with an eye toward the importance of basic research. It further emphasizes that, in order to fulfill the goal of converting science into commercialized products, the government "must also provide incentives, remove policy barriers, provide information and, where appropriate, supply catalytic services that individual businesses cannot supply for themselves."[59] Institutionally, the Act recommends a national advisory panel set up by Congress and composed of a number of 'stakeholders,' most of which would be appointed by the President.[60] This, to some extent, forced the hand of NIH to find a measure of accommodation with the DOE, which it did by signing a Memorandum of Understanding on interdepartmental cooperation in late–1988. While the NIH and a large portion of its constituents had effectively undermined any lead status for the DOE (by scuttling S1840), an advisory body imposed by Congress was equally unappealing. Instead, both departments agreed to create a joint NIH-DOE committee created from each department's own advisory committees.[61]

With the need for an imposed solution made redundant, it might appear that NIH had 'come up short' in the overall struggle for predominance in genome mapping. However, in October of 1988, Wyngaarden continued to act strategically, by creating the Office of Human Genome Research (OHGR), giving NIH research an independent base of power.[62] As had been Wyngaarden's apparent intention from the start, the NIH sought authorization to create a new national institute out of the OHGR. This was accomplished in less than year, giving rise to the National Center for Human Genome Research (NCHGR).[63] The NIH's share of the project now had a power base independent of the DOE, and it was authorized to spend funds directly, rather than under the authority of the National Institute of General Medical Sciences (NIGMS).[64] Thus, ultimately, although the DOE had started the process with a budget appropriation in 1987, by the end of 1988, the NIH had set up an autonomous structure and, with the help of a Congressional visit by James Watson and David Baltimore, secured an appropriation of $18 million (compared to $12 million for the DOE). To top off the NIH's *de facto* victory, Watson, co-discoverer of DNA structure, would become the Director of NCHGR, giving it a future legitimacy and centrality in genome research unmatched by the DOE. That the NIH was able to prevail is evident in the direction of Congressional appropriations over the course of the project, as demonstrated in Table 5.2. The growing dominance of the NIH over HGP funds amounted to far more than just a cunning departmental appropriations strategy. It was the end result of concerted political struggle, in which multiple actors coalesced and settled the extent of the state's commitment, the parties it was intended to benefit, and the most effective structure to bring about those benefits.

Overall, the complexity rendered by these two levels of political struggle reveals an important point—that the historical outcome of state policy is neither random nor predetermined. Building a strategic coalition also meant working politically against the possibility of 'random' outcomes or hindrances. It should not come as a surprise, for instance, that those opposed to genome mapping were unable to make the slightest dent in state policy, largely because their arguments were sidelined and not allowed to progress beyond academic concerns. At the same time, for the HGP to be assembled as a state project under NIH auspices, a very particular—not inevitable—combination of factors needed to coalesce at a unique historical juncture, including Congressional and Administrative attempts to 'boost' the economy through innovation, the ever-present effects of biotechnology and

Table 5.2 Human Genome Project Funding by Government Department
($ Millions)

FY	DOE	NIH	U.S. Total
1988	10.7	17.2	27.9
1989	18.5	28.2	46.7
1990	27.2	59.5	86.7
1991	47.4	87.4	134.8
1992	59.4	104.8	164.2
1993	63.0	106.1	169.1
1994	63.3	127.0	190.3
1995	68.7	153.8	222.5
1996	73.9	169.3	243.2
1997	77.9	188.9	266.8
1998	85.5	218.3	303.8
1999	89.9	225.7	315.6
2000	88.9	271.7	360.6
2001	86.4	308.4	394.8

Source: U.S. Department of Energy

pharmaceutical lobbies, and the increasingly market-friendly testimony and
persuasion of scientific and institutional experts.

ENSURING ACCUMULATION

Looking beyond its formative years, the struggle over the shape and effect of
the HGP continued to preoccupy state actors throughout the project's lifespan. It would not have been enough to mount a major scientific project, and
then merely hope that its effects would be conducive to greater U.S. technological innovation and new areas of value accumulation. Rather, various elements of the state needed to ensure that innovative research, having been
placed under its auspices, could find some market-oriented outlet. More
specifically in relation to this study, without the state's continuing facilitation of commercialization in biotechnology research, there would no *inevitable* translation of the genome project into economic development. As
such, after the initial politicking to make the HGP a part of the state's
agenda, as well as the rancor over its institutional structure, the running of
the project and the fulfillment of its intended tasks remained a highly politicized activity. Just as the originating moments of the HGP tell us something
about the state's intentions and its role in the capital accumulation process,
so too do instances of 'crisis,' in which the program underwent criticism. In

these historic moments, the project's structures become highly visible, as its day-to-day proceedings become the subject of analysis, explanation or justification. A closer consideration of two such moments renders insights into the purposes of state participation: the controversy over the NIH's attempt to secure patents on expressed sequence tags (ESTs) and, as referred to briefly above, the difficulties surrounding the emergence of a corporate effort to sequence the human genome.

NIH and Patenting ESTs

Even prior to the enactment of the FTTA in 1986, the NIH had been active in industrial relations and had visibly sought out cooperative relationships (CRADAs) with private industry. By the end of 1993, the NIH had signed well over 100 CRADAs with private companies. This trend suggests that NIH policy had already catered to the needs of private industry over public well being, and, if anything, this was reinforced in relation to the HGP.[65] In June of 1991, then NIH scientist Craig Venter mentioned in a speech that a patent application would be submitted to the PTO on 1000 ESTs resulting from his research. A standard way of isolating the genetic sequence of particular proteins is to isolate its corresponding mRNA and convert it back into a strand of complementary DNA (cDNA). Libraries of cDNA (propagated and stored in bacteria) are kept as standard practice in molecular biology as representative samples of active genes for particular cell types (brain, muscle, liver, etc.). While these libraries were generally used to identify the particular cDNA clones that matched particular genes already under investigation, Venter proposed to reverse the process and create a large series of partially sequenced (200–300 bases) 'tags' from each cDNA, which could then be used to identify genes. ESTs could be used to compare with known gene collections of other species and draw inferences with respect to the candidate gene's function in the human organism. The EST itself, however, remained merely an incomplete sequence of a candidate gene, about which the investigator, at least initially, knows neither the full structure nor function—and therein lies the controversy.

As of June 1991, and then again in February 1992, the NIH sought patents on the full range of ESTs elaborated by Venter on cDNA libraries produced from human brain cells. The requests on the part of Venter and the NIH sought wide subsequent control for a relatively small scientific intervention. Initially, the patent application requested coverage of the ESTs themselves, the genes from which they were taken, the proteins for which their corresponding genes code, antibodies related to the gene, and the process for producing cDNAs.[66] This proposal brought considerable scorn from the scientific community at large. Even James Watson, then Director of the NIH's genome effort, stated publicly that the scheme was 'sheer lunacy' and that it was a scientific project which 'could be run by monkeys.'[67] Several more scientific figures weighed in with negative evaluations of the scheme. Nobel laureate Paul Berg claimed that it "makes a mockery of what most people feel is the right way to do the genome project."[68] And David Botstein (of RFLP mapping fame) suggested that "[no] one benefits from this, not science, not the biotech industry, not American competitiveness."[69]

The intensity of these public reactions relates both to the apparent ease of the scientific procedure and the stage at which patent protection was being sought. In order to gain a patent, the product or process must meet three conditions: it must be novel, it must be non-obvious and it must have a utility. While no one had explicitly used the EST approach in the past, some references had been made to it in the literature.[70] Moreover, many argued that the knowledge of the importance of cDNA libraries made this process obvious to anybody 'trained in the art' of molecular biology. It is also debatable whether the ESTs had a justifiable use that could be cited in the application. Since the sequence tags' matching genes were unknown, the NIH cited their possible usages as genetic markers, in forensic tests, and tissue typing. Strictly on a legal level, successful patent applications require only a minimum 'threshold' utility, not all of the utilities for which the patent may ultimately apply.[71] Whether the patent applications were ultimately viable is open to contention; more interesting for the purposes of this work was the state agency's rationale for pursuing them, as well as the nature of the debate surrounding this pursuit.

Although Venter would ultimately become the scientist that everybody 'loves to hate,' helped on by the media, the EST patenting endeavor was not really his own doing. Rather, Max Hensley, a patent attorney for Genentech, heard about Venter's undertaking and contacted Reid Adler in the NIH's technology transfer office, in order to convince the NIH to consider a patent application. According to Rebecca Eisenberg, there were two major reasons for seeking the patents: 1) that the NIH should seek broad patent rights so that they could, through licensing, guarantee firms a wide enough monopoly incentive on commercial development and 2) that unless the NIH pursued patents immediately, material in the public domain would not entice firms to invest, due to the weak basis for monopoly.[72] Additionally, Adler himself published a long article in *Science* defending the NIH's actions. In it, he states that,

> [once] a programmatic decision was made to characterise the human
> genome through a large-scale structural (in other words, sequence-based)

approach, the present debate became inevitable. Wide dissemination of sequence data will encourage research, but due consideration must be given to protecting the market exclusivity necessary for the private sector to risk enormous sums of money in product development efforts. The biotechnology industry is critically dependent upon patent protection to maintain its threatened leadership in highly competitive world markets.[73]

In this, Adler was supported vigorously by then NIH Director Bernadine Healy, who made clear that "the rationale is not to make money, but rather to promote and encourage the development and commercialization of products to benefit the public and to do so in a socially responsible way."[74] By the time the request reached Venter, he "[was] told that if [they] did not patent, [they] risked greatly undercutting the U.S. biotech effort."[75] The importance of the application to NIH officials in relation to what they viewed as broad industrial concerns seems unmistakable. Indeed, the rejection of the initial application by the PTO, on the grounds that its justifications of novelty, non-obviousness and utility were "vague, indefinite . . . incomplete, inaccurate, and incomprehensible," did not seem to deter the NIH, which launched an appeal.

Meanwhile, industry officials themselves were not unanimously amenable to the NIH's actions. Industrial trade organizations with interests in the genome project were publicly split over the issue. The Association of Biotechnology Companies supported the move, on the basis that it would avoid novelty problems down the road and secure profit expectations of licensees. The IBA and the Pharmaceutical Manufacturers Association, however, opposed the NIH's actions, viewing it as improper that the NIH should have patent control over genes of unknown utility. The latter, in a letter to the Secretary of Health and Human Services, insisted that "a governmental policy of ownership and licensing of gene sequences would inevitably impede the research and development of new medicines."[76] Some within the biotechnology industry went so far as to argue that this was an attempt on the part of the NIH to extend a dubious, widespread practice in which companies seek to control research and methods far removed from any visible product. Ostensibly, through such practices, there are greater possibilities to profit from a wider range of resulting products and any commercial value they may accrue.[77] The amount of corporate disagreement over this issue renders a crucial question: why were NIH policies—clearly intended to support commercialization—not supported by the capitals that it was ostensibly aiming to serve?

The dissension over the NIH patent applications points again in the direction of political struggle. Even though the HGP's existence was already on secure footing, the relationship between this state-based project and corporate needs required active reproduction. At issue was how best to satisfy the goals set out for the state's involvement in the first place: technology development for the expressed purpose of capitalist economic development. In keeping with the technology transfer legislation of the 1980s, this meant that a substantial institutional effort needed to be devoted towards securing the conditions for commodification. However, while the trajectory of capital accumulation typically helps to supply the historical parameters in which the state issues science and technology policies, there is no single, 'correct' reaction to be undertaken by state institutions. In this case, a state agency's patent policy to advance the valorization of capital may have, from the perspective of particular capitals, overshot its mark. Patents are generally used within industry to hinder 'excessive' competition, but the possibility that NIH patents on such fundamental research material could rather obviously result in so-called 'blocking' patents or 'stacking' licenses was unpalatable to industry.[78] As such, the IBA's position paper on this topic asserted that in the face of the NIH's proposed patents, companies would be encouraged "to abandon current research efforts that are aimed at product development in favor of routine genetic sequencing for the purpose of staking claims to as much of the genome as possible."[79] It would be quite wrong to conclude from this that such actors are not well disposed toward gene patenting. Indeed, the biotechnology and pharmaceutical industries generally demonstrate a clear preference for a strong patent system. But while pharmaceutical and biotech capitals regularly and forcibly argue on behalf of patent protected commodification, the degree of 'upstream' monopoly control immanent in the NIH's policy ventured too far from the *general* conditions necessary for sectoral prosperity.

Still, while industry's reaction fits as part of a general struggle endemic to state patenting policies, the question remains: why, even in the face of industrial and scientific resistance, did the NIH continue to push its EST patenting application? The answer leads us back to the issue of political conflict on an interdepartmental terrain. The extent of HGP advocates' support for guaranteed patent protection was matched by their concern over the concomitant mounting difficulties within the PTO's biotechnology division.[80] There is no doubt that industry had been making its displeasure known for some time concerning both the uncertainty and increasing amount of time involved in genome-related patents. By the end of 1987, the total backlog in the PTO's biotechnology division had already reached 6907 applications, and companies were waiting on average of over four years before their application would receive a ruling.[81] By 1991, pending applications had risen to 18,600, and biotechnology industry officials complained bitterly about the quality of decision making, claiming that "when major patent decisions do come down . . . they are often murky, narrow, and wrapped in an impenetrable legal jargon."[82] Within the NIH, this problem was considered closely with respect to the data issuing from the human genome project. Watson's attention to the issue in a 1989 Senatorial hearing is instructive in relation to the NIH's concerns over the PTO's breadth and depth, but it is also revealing as to how strategic commentary can enforce or renew specific political agendas:

> **Senator Kerry:** I met with a group of our biotech companies in Massachusetts recently, and one of the things that they complained about was how long it takes to move patents through the system now. They said that there is a real bottleneck and as a consequence nobody really knows who may have the rights to some particular process. Is that accurate, and is there any way to do something about that?
>
> **Dr. Watson:** You have to speed up the patent process.
>
> **Senator Kerry:** How do we do that?
>
> **Dr. Watson:** Probably more examiners.
>
> **Senatory Kerry:** Are there enough examiners qualified to understand this area?
>
> **Dr. Watson:** No.
>
> **Senator Kerry:** So what do we do?
>
> **Dr. Watson:** Commercially, you would say raise their salary and more people will go into it, but I do not know quite how to do this within the. . . .
>
> **Senator Gore:** If I could interject. . . . This is one of the main bottlenecks, and we really have to solve it. I would be delighted to join with my colleagues on this subcommittee in initiating communication with the sister committees that have jurisdiction over the Patent Office to advise them that in our investigation in this matter we have once again identified this as a major concern and attempt to speed up a solution to it.
>
> **Senator Kerry:** I agree, and I will join in the effort with others. . . . This is a real problem to them and it is slowing down the process of commercializing. Thus it is one more instance in which we seem to shoot ourselves in the foot with respect to our own productivity and commercialization.[83]

In the long run, the HGP's voluminous flow of valuable information gave rise to a foreseeable problem, in that much of it would enter the patent process in one form or another. From the position of the NIH, charged by Congress and the Administration with the responsibility of proactive technology transfer, the backlog and lack of clarity at the PTO represented a major institutional hindrance.

Given this situation, it is reasonable to postulate another level of complexity in the NIH's unpopular attempts to patent.[84] What should we make of the fact that Hensley himself poses serious questions about the patents' tenability: "[if] it was 10 or 50 genes a year, I could make that fly. But when you start talking about 20,000 genes, a buzzer goes off and you wonder, how will I get that by a judge?"[85] Early on in the debate, an intervention by Rebecca Eisenberg emphasized that the NIH's actions, regardless of their standing among individual scientists and industrial actors, were significant because they would force the PTO's hand. Eisenberg observed that

> sooner or later the PTO will have to decide how to treat these or similar interventions under the patent laws, and judicial review of its decision is virtually inevitable. Given the high profile of the Human Genome Project, congressional attention to these issues is also a distinct possibility. How should these institutions think about patent rights in these inventions?[86]

In the use of patents as a vehicle towards extraordinary value accumulation, clarity is golden while 'murkiness' and delay are clear disadvantages. If we take seriously the NIH's insistence that EST patents applications constituted an 'interim policy,' it seems reasonable to suggest that the agency's goals were, in large part, about accelerating policy clarity on the part of the PTO. Indeed, Reid Adler's 'defense' of the NIH's actions produces as many arguments about the motivation of the application as it does the viability of the applications *per se*. The issue for Adler seemed to be about prodding the PTO, such that it not only had to pronounce some policy position, but also recognize its own weaknesses *vis-à-vis* genetic patenting questions. He was aware of the high likelihood of initial rejection by the PTO (a standard practice, according to him), but argued that this would give rise to an important dialogue between applicant and PTO, based on technical and legal guidelines. Thus, for Adler, "the initial PTO decision on the . . . cDNA patent application . . . undoubtedly [would] argue that the claimed sequences are unpatentable but [would also] provide minimal policy guidance."[87]

Needless to say, while the NIH could instigate the process, it could not in any way control all of its parameters. Following the NIH's cue, genomics companies such as Incyte and Human Genome Sciences deluged the PTO with applications for tens of thousands of partial cDNA sequences. Thus, the NIH's actions may have led to, but were never really part of, a large-scale attempt to appropriate gene and partial gene sequence material. While the NIH may not have intended added pressure in this form, the ensuing effects of the original applications matched perfectly with Adler and Healy's stated intentions. Not only was the PTO forced to take notice of its incapacity to deal effectively with the quantitative demands related to biotechnology and genome research, but industry actors were also motivated to address qualitative shortcomings in the PTO's approach. Even as application review time appeared to be dropping, industry officials complained that the process within biotechnology remained "confused, unpredictable, and governed by intramural rules that aren't made public."[88] Over the course of the 1990s, the PTO was pressured by several quarters, including the Congress, industry and government departments, to undertake a policy of guideline clarification, in order to elucidate the 'novelty' and 'patentability' status of EST applications. Ultimately, in its attempts to draft guidelines, the PTO took extensive consultations with industry officials and trade organizations, and was able to promulgate regulations to the satisfaction of most interested capitals.[89] The guidelines, aimed especially at 'upstream' patents (on genes or partial genes), insist on a clear, substantial and specific utility for each application.[90] The EST patenting crisis demonstrates, above all, that with projects such as the HGP, securing resources and project control are only part of the equation. Rather than the conventional notion of a 'turf war,' the EST struggle revolved around shaping principles of state conduct outside the immediate rubric of science and technology policy. In such cases, state agencies charged with a particular task could utilize the means at their disposal to effect a wider state disposition—one which was more amenable to accumulation among those capitals with which the agency had established and long-standing relations.

The HGP and Private Mapping

Paradoxically, as the HGP came closer to its eventual goals, the legitimacy of its existence seemed to become less certain. One result of the NIH patenting controversy, viewed with less concern at the time, was the departure of Venter from the NIH. Venter had been turned down by the NIH in his grant application to attain large quantities of partial gene sequences utilizing the EST process. At the same time, he was receiving offers from the corporate sector to undertake his work in partnership with industry. In July of 1992, Venter decided to leave the NIH and involve himself in a quasi-private arrangement to undertake large-scale EST analysis. The resulting non-profit organization, The Institute for Genomic Research (TIGR), would be funded by a private corporation, Human Genome Sciences (HGS), with $70 million over the course of 10 years. TIGR laboratory proved exceptionally productive, doubling the amount of available sequenced genes through EST analysis within months. Venter was never able to attain a frictionless relationship with the wider scientific community, many members of which characterized his work as little more than a 'scaling-up' that, in itself, lacked originality. Simultaneously, Venter had disagreements with HGS over the speed with which its EST data should be made publicly available. While Venter was in favor of rapid release, the corporation continued to insist on a longer exclusivity period in which it could evaluate and secure commercially valuable data. In 1997, Venter discontinued the TIGR-HGS contract and surrendered the remaining $38 million in funding, an immediate consequence of which was the public release of very large amounts of EST sequencing data to the scientific community.[91]

Venter's decision was also based on the decision to reorient the goals of his scientific work, and his chance came in 1998, when he was approached by PE Corporation to undertake mass sequencing along the lines of his previously used method: mass shotgun sequencing. Venter's initial reaction is said to have been disbelief, but by May of 1998, he announced plans in cooperation with PE Corporation and Applied Biosystems (a subsidiary of *PE*) to undertake massive sequencing of the whole human genome.[92] By that summer, Venter had formed Celera Corporation and was testing his sequencing methods on increasingly complex organisms.[93] Without a doubt, the announcement dropped like a bomb on the participants of the HGP. Although there was an initial 'honeymoon,' in which all sequencers evinced their desire for broad cooperation, participants responsible for the federally funded HGP also reacted with a certain degree of alarm. At a summer meeting of sequencers at Cold Spring Harbour, there was widespread sense that the HGP's effort should be stepped up. Indeed, the Wellcome Trust's (the foundation funding British mapping efforts) reinforced financial commitment to the project was publicly pronounced at this meeting, to a standing ovation from participants.[94] The reaction hardly stopped there: by fall of the same year, the NIH had announced an accelerated plan to create a 'rough draft' of the genome by 2001, and the 'gold standard' sequence by 2003. The schedule for this draft-version would, soon afterwards, be pushed forward to the spring of 2000. Strangely, however, when the relationship between the Celera endeavor and the HGP came (somewhat accurately) to be depicted as a 'race,' those closest to the project reacted with considerable dismay.[95] Given the inconsistencies of this institutional reaction, it is useful to unpack the state's intentions in the context of this 'crisis,' with an eye towards understanding the motivations of state science policy in relation to technology transfer and increased capital accumulation.

Beyond the media fury over 'public' redundancy, it is worth considering the degree to which Celera's efforts actually put the legitimacy of the HGP in question. In the scientific community, the tension between the two sequencing efforts was quite palpable. Maynard Olson, a leading HGP scientist from the University of Washington, asserted that Celera's methods were akin to 'science by press release,' and that the quality of data would remain an extremely critical issue.[96] Other prominent scientists joined in, with John Sulston and Robert Waterston taking rather acerbic positions concerning the probable quality of Venter's results.[97] There was certainly tension between the NIH and Venter, a degree of bitterness plainly evident in Venter's Congressional testimony.[98]

> [One] of the questions I get asked most often is why we didn't just apply to the Federal Government for funds to do this new strategy. Well, I think it's clear, Maynard Olson is the Chairman of that review committee and I think you've heard the comments. I think if we went and asked for $300 million to do this new project, that they might get some good chuckles out of it, but it's not the way new initiatives can be made.[99]

This antagonistic dynamic can, in part, be chalked up to the question of scientific prestige—Venter is viewed by many as having accumulated far more status than the quality of his work merits. This should not imply that those associated to the HGP failed to take Venter's work seriously; in fact, the federal project's hastily rescheduled sequencing goals signal precisely the opposite. In fact, confirming the likelihood of Venter's success, both sides attempted to meet in order to work out some form of cooperation. Even Celera's chief scientific advisor admitted that "[it] would not be good if the public effort [were] seen to lose."[100] Is it then merited to characterize this confusing dynamic as a product of mere scientific animosity and the need to preserve the image of U.S. science policy?

An appropriate answer to this question would highlight the fact that the HGP's reaction to the Celera endeavor reproduced inconsistencies already contained in U.S. science policy, oriented as it was around technology transfer and capital accumulation. In a Congressional hearing called to address the effects of Celera's scientific program on the HGP, Tim Roemer, Ranking Minority Member, demonstrated a perspective common among policymakers with respect to the role of corporately developed innovation. Emphasizing the centrality of the Congressional *mantra* of 'faster, cheaper, better,' he positioned the Celera development as a "golden possibility, of a private-public partnership that could result in phenomenal return for science and in phenomenal return for the taxpayer."[101] Despite some rivalry and baiting among scientific and institutional figures, the strong majority of participants central to the HGP were quick to echo such a perspective, particularly when in the realm of policymakers. Thus, in the abovementioned hearings, Francis Collins (Watson's successor) emphasized that "[p]artnership with the private sector is both necessary and desirable and we welcome this new initiative . . . In fact, such public/private partnerships have characterized the genome project from the outset."[102] Aristides Patrinos of the DOE echoed those sentiments, by stating that from "the very beginning the [HGP] has focused on developing technologies and resources that would advance the utility . . . of the information contained in the human genome and it is in that vein that we welcome the . . . initiatives . . . announced by Dr. Venter and Perkin-Elmer."[103] There was little doubt among HGP participants as to the appropriate underlying priority of the state: first and foremost, to accommodate the growth of industry. Similarly, Congressional representatives waxed euphorically about the more pronounced entry of the private sector into genomics, because it was the logical extension of that body's most closely cherished goal concerning scientific funding.

As a result, in the face of corporate competition, defending the viability of the HGP required a skillful negotiation between criticism and appreciation of capital's presence. In keeping with the abovementioned theoretical rendition of the state, a major goal of U.S. science policy can be summarized as an attempt to reproduce and improve the general conditions necessary for capital accumulation, while also maintaining a nominal politico-legal neutrality. In precisely this manner, those fronting the HGP's reaction to Celera's presence utilized an effective mix of public conflict, detached scientific 'objectivity' and capital-friendly logic. Collins, for instance, defended the HGP in terms of its service to industry *as a whole:*

> [The] sequence of the human genome is of such profound importance, that I think a scenario where large quantities of it were only available within the database of single private entity might be a rather unstable situation. If business demands were to change or personnel were to change or the stockholders were to decide it's not such a good thing to be giving this all away anymore, one would not want to see a circumstance where the publicly-funded effort was suddenly found to have dropped the ball.[104]

Here, Collins is able to differentiate quite clearly between the state's wish to promote cooperative technology transfer and the conditions under which such cooperation should obtain. While capital's endorsement of genomics was seen as a positive development, the state needed to be positioned in a manner that detached its interests from any particular capital or group of capitals. In the case of Celera's efforts, since the scientific outcome was not yet known, Collins craftily engaged the benefits of private sector involvement while effectively warning against an abandonment of the *general* interests of capital. In a similar vein, when Ken Calvert, Chairman of the House Subcommittee on Energy and the Environment, asked Collins about his opinion of William Haseltine's (CEO of *HGS*) assertion that the federal effort at sequencing should be discontinued, his answer was unequivocal. According to Collins, Haseltine's was a 'fringe opinion,' representing "an individual who has a transparent financial conflict of interest in making . . . genome projects of all sorts, public or private, [cease] to exist."[105] By differentiating between capital and capitals, advocates of the HGP could easily reconcile the project's continuing existence with events in the corporate world, regardless of the wishes of particular capitals. Venter himself recognized the prevailing currency of such logic and, despite his personal difficulties with the federal project, urged Congress not to cut the HGP's funding in any way. Ultimately, the HGP's 'survival' was only superficially a question of public relations. Similar to the case of EST patenting, the justifications for continued federal involvement reveal the centrality of state institutions in maintaining a perceived balance between public support for the improved conditions for accumulation and a capitulation to the accumulation of certain capitals.[106]

INTERNATIONAL STRUGGLE

Having shown how the HGP contributed to the general conditions for capital accumulation in health-related industries, it would be remiss not to examine the wider international parameters of U.S. activity in this area. While U.S. international policy directly related to the HGP was not especially visible, policies aimed at an accommodation of American high-tech industries accorded very closely with the HGP's goals. Recall that the policies, legislation and infrastructure associated to the HGP have generally had the objective of technology transfer and *American* economic development. While policymakers and HGP proponents are supportive of bringing research and technology to the marketplace, the intention was to create conditions that, to the greatest possible degree, favored American capitals. This, in turn, required the active shaping of an environment amenable to capital far beyond U.S. jurisdiction.

As much of the foregoing material has made clear, the international political issue dearest to U.S. biotechnology and pharmaceutical capitals was (and remains) related to the securing of political protection offered through intellectual property regimes. Throughout the period in which biotechnology and a restructured pharmaceutical industry came to the fore, the U.S. state shifted its policies, taking an increasingly aggressive international stance on intellectual property. Originally, U.S. copyright law protected only American citizens, with little adherence to international reciprocity. The instantiation of reciprocity grew over the course of time, allowing for the President to negotiate bilateral treaties to establish such relationships. The creation of the 1883 Paris and 1886 Berne Conventions signified the first international efforts to set up regimes for, respectively, patents and copyrights.[107] But the United States was never official party to the Berne Convention. Thus, it never played a decision-making role in that convention's secretariat, the World Intellectual Property Organization (WIPO), and continued, instead, to exercise enormous degrees of national sovereignty.[108] In fact, the United States not only expressed frustration with WIPO, but it even withdrew in 1984 from the United Nations Educational, Scientific and Cultural Organization (UNESCO), the secretariat of the international agreement to which WIPO had become attached, the Universal Copyright Convention.

The early 1980s witnessed a critical shift in U.S. policy on matters of intellectual property. As large American corporations came to see their accumulation interests converge around high-tech innovation, they called on the Federal Government to consider intellectual property as an agenda item in the next round of international trade talks. The initial reaction to this was negative—given the one-country/one-vote structure of the WIPO, government officials informed major corporations that the political constituency for such a move was non-existent. This state of affairs was, in large part, altered by the creation of the Intellectual Property Committee (IPC), a coalition of thirteen corporations dedicated to the inclusion of intellectual property rights in the General Agreements on Tariffs and Trade (GATT).[109] Importantly for this work, major American pharmaceutical corporations formed the sectoral majority within the IPC. In his own writing, the lead lobbyist of this group of capitals, Jacques Gorlin, made clear that in the summer prior to the opening stages of the GATT rounds in Uruguay, "representatives of these industries went abroad to convince their private-sector counterparts in other developed countries that the GATT negotiations on intellectual property would provide a significant opportunity to improve the current protection accorded intellectual property."[110] This exercise in constituency creation yielded solid results, manifested directly in the policies of other regional organizations—the Union of Industrial and Employers' Confederations of Europe (UNICE) and the Japanese Federation of Economic Organizations (*keidanren*). Their mutual interaction created a common framework, presented to participants of the Uruguay round in 1988, which included the need for minimum standards on intellectual property, national enforcement procedures, border measures against counterfeited goods, and international standards mechanisms.[111] This report, however, was mere reinforcement for the American government, which had long since taken its cue and established a negotiating position that included the relocation of intellectual property issues under GATT.[112]

In the 1980s, then, U.S. multilateral policy became reflective of this political struggle on at least three fronts, with advantageous outcomes facilitated through an additional set of unilateral, executive powers. The first involved the concerted effort to transform the discourse surrounding intellectual property into a trade issue. In this effort, it was the task of U.S. negotiators, in keeping with the wishes of the IPC, to redefine the circumstances surrounding intellectual property such that they could be seen as a prevailing *barrier to trade*. This was largely accomplished by depicting weak intellectual property laws as an effective trade 'distortion.' Thus, in addition to its national role in accelerating technology transfer and accumulation, innovation would now require an international political framework offering adequate protection for property rights. In the absence (or weak presence) of such a framework, those in the international economy offering such protection could legitimately be seen to suffer trade disadvantages. In this, the evolution of discourse was very particular: Western companies were represented in terms of their 'lost' or 'pirated' profits, regardless of whether they had actually ever established meaningful markets in the regions in question.[113] As such, "when the United States used the term 'trade distortions,' it was referring to the putative loss of comparative advantage resulting from lack of protection for intellectual property rights in certain countries."[114] Once negotiators made clear that the mere existence of 'piracy' and counterfeiting constitutes evidence of lost markets, one commentator went so far as to connect such processes directly with the United States' new status as a debtor nation.[115] This problematic terminology positioned U.S. negotiators in such a way that they appeared to be merely defending the impinged-upon rights of Western (particularly American-based) capitals. This went some distance toward driving the initial wedge for an acceptance of intellectual property principles. After all, how could any country position itself in favor of 'piracy' or 'theft'?

The link between new U.S. demands with respect to intellectual property and genome research and biotechnological development could not have been clearer. According to Gail Evans,

> The effective legal protection of intellectual property during the ultimate phase of its commercial exploitation ensures a return to those who invest in R&D. . . . The need to combat counterfeiting and piracy becomes all the more urgent in light of the fact that the level of R&D necessary to develop new products has increased, particularly in certain high-technology industries.[116]

With this urgency in mind, a second front was necessary in order to establish an advantageous venue, in which advanced industrial countries could address trade 'distortions' related to intellectual property. Conventionally, much of this had been undertaken through the WIPO, but its one-country/one-vote decision making procedure dismayed U.S. and other Western negotiators. GATT, in contrast, had always proceeded on a consensus basis, largely avoiding the need for formal voting, and heavily dominated by the United States and other OECD countries. Until 1990, prominent third world states, especially India, Brazil and Argentina, directly challenged the prospect of intellectual property being included under GATT, preferring to keep it within the jurisdiction of the WIPO. Not only did they fear the dominance of Western countries within GATT structures, but they also feared the reinforcement of Western countries' utilization of legal monopoly to maintain advantages *vis-à-vis* innovative technologies. As the Uruguay round of GATT inched toward a conclusion, however, this resistance would give way to an acceptance of the largely U.S. motivated intellectual property framework. With the help of various instances of unilateral pressure—discussed below—the United States and other Western states were able to insert a framework into the GATT, containing almost exactly the parameters desired by the IPC. From the Uruguay round was born both the World Trade Organization (WTO), a structure oriented around the maintenance and enforcement of GATT regulations and procedures, and, more importantly for the purposes of this work, the agreement on Trade-Related Aspects of Intellectual Property (TRIPs).

The accomplishment of bringing intellectual property under international trade structures, as well as the content of TRIPs itself, enabled a third and external level of political struggle for the United States. The TRIPs agreement established various conditions for member-states' approach to intellectual property:

1. The GATT principles of 'national treatment' and 'most-favored nation' must be applied in the area of intellectual property protection.
2. Member states agree to substantive obligations with respect to the protection of six types of property protection: copyright, trademarks, geographical indicators, industrial design, patents and design of integrated circuits.
3. Member states agree to procedures within domestic law that will address the violation of intellectual property laws.
4. Patent protection is to be provided for 20 years.
5. Remuneration will be provided to those who are subjected to compulsory licensing or government use of patents.[117]

These legal parameters are not fully secured within a number of states that are signatories to TRIPs. The reasons for this are varied, but they can range from pressure emanating from domestic capitalist lobbies inside the given member state to critical health crises, which make TRIPs enforcement a harsh prospect.[118] The critical point, however, is that the United States carried the terrain of struggle into the domestic political environments of foreign countries affected by TRIPs. In this sense, the political activity necessary to bolster the development of accumulation related to genome research extended far beyond the U.S. border. In the same way that the U.S. state chose to bolster the interests of particular sectors for an enhanced overall accumulation effect, it also indirectly waged a struggle against foreign (particularly generic drug) producers abroad. In doing so, it not only secured the 'rights' of U.S. and Western capitals, but also expanded the viable marketplace in which genome-related products could feasibly be sold. After all, in much of the non-Western world, it is not so much a matter of regaining a 'lost market,' but of ensuring that new, innovative commodities—under stringent patent protection—are able to permeate as many markets as possible.

Due to the fact that the TRIPs negotiations were embedded in the GATT process, participating states were also subject to the negotiating pressures of trade 'linkages.' In other words, Western states' capacity to achieve an intellectual property agreement conducive to advanced industrial interests could not be detached from the extraordinary power which they wielded in international trade issues. However, even beyond 'linkage' dynamics internal to the TRIPs process, the U.S. foreign policy establishment possessed a more compelling weapon. In both the 1984 Trade and Tariff Act and 1988

Omnibus Trade and Competitiveness Act, the U.S. Congress extended the 'section 301' elements of the 1974 Trade Act to intellectual property. This gave the U.S. President power, under the advice of the U.S. Trade Representative (USTR), to "swiftly retaliate with trade sanctions in the event that targeted countries fail adequately to protect its intellectual property."[119] The use of 'special 301' (especially related to intellectual property rights) was made open to any U.S. capital or lobby group, requiring that they submit a formal request to the USTR, who can categorize the offending country along the lines of three increasingly severe lists: 'watch list,' 'priority watch list' or 'priority foreign country.' Under the latter category, the USTR *must* initiate a 'fast track' section 301 investigation and bilateral negotiations with the 'offending' state. In the case that the offending policies remain in place, the USTR is authorized to enact trade retaliation by way of duties, import restriction or exclusion from the General System of Preferences.[120]

The unilateral use of 'special 301' by the U.S. government has been extensive, before, during and after the TRIPs agreement. In fact, major countries opposing the agreement, such as Brazil, Argentina and India, grudgingly opted in only as an alternative to the intense pressure being maintained by the U.S. government through 'special 301.' It should come as no surprise that, along with the International Intellectual Property Alliance, the most frequent applicant to the USTR on delinquent countries is the PhRMA. From the second half of the 1980s forward, the pharmaceutical sector was extremely active in submitting complaints to the USTR with respect to inadequate protection for multinational pharmaceutical concerns. Particularly critical incidents included the 1987 PMA case against Brazil (resulting in $39 million in tariffs on Brazilian drug exports), the 1988 case against Argentina, and the 1991 case against India (with the threatened $60 million withdrawal of GSP benefits). With these and other cases, the U.S. was able to exert an enormous degree of pressure, such that an international agreement under the decision-making mechanisms of GATT would seem the lesser of two evils, insofar as it was nominally subject to multilateral, rather than unilateral, control. Since the inception of TRIPs, however, foreign countries have received little respite from 'special 301.' As Susan Sell has rightly pointed out, the United States has continued to use this domestic trade clause in tandem with sure-win cases in the TRIPs Council (the mechanism for dispute settlement), such that member states view it increasingly in their interests to abide by the agreement's parameters.[121]

Thus, the United States has been able to effect particular changes in the multinational arena with the added 'incentive' of unilateral trade policy. Since many countries' dependency on the U.S. market is considerable, the costs of resisting TRIPs became far too high. Similarly, the continuing presence of 301 made enforcement of TRIPs-friendly domestic law part of an ongoing struggle for member national governments. As Sell points out, "[the] spread of hegemonic norms alters domestic political incentives," and the tenability of TRIPs-friendly arrangements in developing countries "will depend on both the emergence of politically powerful domestic constituencies committed to the new direction and the ability of interested private parties to mobilize these constituencies to uphold and enforce these policies.[122] There is little doubt that as corporations continue to invest heavily in biotechnology and genome-related innovation, their advocacy for, and utilization of, national and international governance mechanisms will only intensify. In this sense, it is useful to view the U.S. state's support for the general conditions of innovation-related accumulation as a multi-level process, with ongoing political struggle at every level. While infrastructural programs such as the HGP are critical, the pharmaceutical and biotechnology sectors continuously press for, and receive, the greatest possible security in terms of political conditions, both nationally and internationally. This, in turn, makes the prosecution of the U.S. genome project seem all the more vital, as the international environment for innovation, patent protection and market-oriented competition and trade become increasingly prevalent.

CONCLUSION

From the historical materialist perspective, the state cannot be seen as a unidirectional mechanism that automatically reacts in a servile manner to the interests of capital. Rather it constitutes the political domain in which those interests are achieved through strife and maneuver. Ensuring the conditions of accumulation for high-tech, innovative industrial sectors in the U.S. economy has been made a priority of the state since at least the late 1970s. As such, those sectors which could be identified as 'pioneers' of innovative accumulation have both fought for and received a great deal of structural and regulatory backing. In the case of the HGP, the state's historical role has been complex, having been formulated through a complicated set of influential groups, including state agencies, corporate lobbies, legislative actors and the Executive Office of the President. The project forms a critical part of a generalized set of measures, put in place to intensify the processes of widespread innovative change, particularly in the biotechnology and pharmaceutical sectors. Seen as leaders (or, in the case of biotech, a potential leader) in U.S. capital accumulation, sectoral actors have utilized state terrain to legitimize publicly their interests, ensure that institutional arrangements for their realization are optimized, and influence a foreign policy suitable to enhanced international profitability. None of this occurred seamlessly (objecting parties and resistance are always present), but the capacity of dominant capital interests to prevail throughout the overwhelming majority of policy issues remains striking. Ultimately, the state's openness to 'socialized risk' as a means to bolster capital accumulation makes problematic any depiction of the HGP as a purely 'public' endeavor. State goals cannot be *equated* with any one industrial actor, but there is a conspicuous prevalence of policy outcomes that facilitate the general conditions of the capitalist economy. As will be seen in the following chapter, these aims take hold at more than just the national and international levels. Those involved in the actual production of biotechnology and genome knowledge—the scientific community—also underwent their own social rearrangement, as the systemic necessity of capitalist innovation became the cause of popular and institutional celebration.

Chapter Six

Science and Labor: Changing Norms, Discipline and the HGP

Understanding the HGP in relation to capitalist social relations requires an investigation into a third and vital issue: scientific labor. If the emphasis placed on both capital and the state is to have significance, it is necessary to explore the manner in which scientific practice might be interpreted as productive labor, and how such a scenario could have emerged. The problem of producers is a complex one in the case of the HGP, mostly because it is difficult to view the obvious candidates—practicing scientists—as 'workers' or 'wage-laborers.' It should be apparent from the preceding chapters that it is by no means easy to discern a relationship of animosity or antagonism between scientists and their source of funding, be it capital or the state. As they are portrayed in relation to biotechnology, publicly visible scientists seem positively 'entrepreneurial' and far removed from a role in which they are the objects of labor-based value extraction.

Nonetheless, there are discernible shifts in the scientific community which signal changes in practice—changes that bring about or contribute to the enhanced productive value of scientific knowledge. Explaining these processes presents a challenge, because, on the surface, they appear as the product of neither explicit political coercion nor economic necessity. Scientists, especially within academe, are typically understood to enjoy an autonomy and freedom not typical of laborers, and their involvement in either the HGP or genome science is by no means an *automatic* consequence of incursions by capital or the state. Still, their ultimate *en masse* acceptance (passive or otherwise) of market-based purposes, toward which genome research has been directed, presents a notable contrast to the Asilomar process of the mid–1970s (see chapter 2). Recall during that process how the scientific community, in part for reasons of preserving its own autonomy, engaged in a *self-imposed* moratorium and intra-communal debate. Within the current dynamics of biotechnology and genome research, it seems unlikely that a process of this scale and quality could take place in the United States. But without an understanding of the specifically capitalist incursion into scientific practice, participants in the HGP could, at best, be characterized as a mere 'bystanders,' naïve to the processes of accumulation and profit.

In contrast to such a depiction, this chapter demonstrates both an ongoing transformation of scientific practice integral to the explosion in biotechnology and genome research and, more importantly, the historical role that the construction of the HGP played in this transformation. In relation to this, three questions are pertinent. First, to what extent have scientific practices within molecular biology undergone alteration? Second, what circumstances explain such an alteration? Finally, what is the historical relationship between these circumstances and the HGP? The chapter points to the important discontinuities that molecular biology exhibits with its own past, and marks the HGP as a historical process, around which these changes were strategically rearranged, and even finalized. In attempting to elucidate these processes, the Marxist treatment of capital-labor relations is augmented with the theoretical suggestions of Michel Foucault. Foucault's attention to disciplinary rearrangement positions his theoretical approach as a useful complement to the Marxist explanation of power relations. The chapter begins by suggesting the central components of change in the scientific community, pointing to a well-documented set of practices resident within the life sciences. Utilizing Foucault, it then turns to an explanation of plausible mechanisms and conditions by which these disciplinary practices have been fostered. Finally, it positions the HGP within this process, suggesting its historical importance in the redrawing of the professional scientific landscape.

SCIENTIFIC PRACTICE, THEN AND NOW

In the last three decades, there have been dramatic changes afoot in the biological sciences. Institutional and scientific practices are becoming constituted by an altered set of permissible behaviors. The second chapter of this work reviewed the early emergence of molecular biology and genetic science, drawing the clear lesson that molecular biology has never been disassociated from societal interests (science never is). Nonetheless, there did exist a certain degree of scientific autonomy, which molecular biology community members had been willing to defend against all comers (the public, the state, corporations). Thus, while one can discern a number of interesting historical continuities with the current scientific practices of molecular biologists (such as competition between scientists), there are also reoriented practices that offer a startling historical contrast. In getting from the past to the present, it would be difficult to demarcate any exact point of 'transition'—transitions are always murky processes, difficult to isolate within particular events or moments. But for purposes of comparison, it is worth elucidating some of the marked changes in individual and institutional behavior that would have been largely unthinkable only 25 years ago.

If not entirely in practice, then at least ideally, there has been a self-perception among molecular biologists mostly along Mertonian lines. There was a conception that the 'pure science' undertaken within the community needed to be free from overt external influence, because such influence could disrupt an established procedural objectivity and the innovative discoveries resulting from scientists' autonomy.[1] For example, the internal mobilization of the scientific community in reaction to the rDNA debate in the late 1970s was motivated by a desire to maintain the self-direction and regulation internal to the scientific endeavor. 'Whimsical' local regulation or overbearing Congressional interference in the affairs of molecular biology was seen as a major threat by scientists. While this external defensiveness may not have been entirely admirable, it was certainly a manifestation of scientists' perception of their own work as autonomous, fulfilling an important public role. It was also largely in line with a self-reported set of 'norms,' involving an ethos in which, " . . . a scientist is supposed to respect the collaborative nature of the process: credit is to be shared appropriately; the findings of others—even from competing labs—are to be cited; students are to be treated generously; materials and data are to be shared freely."[2] These, along with other values attributable to collegiality and openness, are representative of an ideal that was probably never attainable in the post-war competitive grant system of American life sciences. But while the ideal was subject to various counter-examples, its circulation through the discourse and practice of the community did maintain a certain behavioral tendency, typically associated to the traditional notion of the academic.[3]

Much appears to have changed since the late 1970s, when biotechnology-related research began to emerge as a 'hot' area of study. At this point, an especially immense array of possibilities for value accumulation emerged through research in molecular biology, and this was already being associated to changes in scientific work. Jonathan King made one of the first critical suggestions of this during the 1981 Congressional hearing dealing with commercialization in the academic biomedical research community. His forceful statements alluded to the issue of 'patenting' in academic culture, where he noted a changing environment that, in his opinion, already constituted a substantial threat to academic values and practice.

> Once patenting becomes the mode, then individuals have a vested interest in keeping strains and techniques secret until the patent is granted. This may be up to a year; but even if less, it establishes a destructive element in scientific relations, secrecy and barriers to information flow, which retard overall biomedical progress. I will tell you that the atmosphere around biology department coffee pots has changed in the last few years. It is clear this is a new element coming in there.[4]

King's reference to patents as a (then) new and significant factor in the actions of the scientific community constitutes a useful starting point for analysis, because it highlights the contrast between corporate expectations (manifest in patenting processes) and the normative designs of scientific practice. Concomitant with the legislation discussed in the previous chapter (such as the Bayh-Dole and Federal Technology Transfer Acts), the volume of university-based patents, specifically those related to the life sciences, has risen dramatically.[5] As Table 6.1 points out, these developments are a recent process, and are heavily weighted toward the life sciences. The top three areas in university patenting, each closely related to molecular biology, have increased at an astounding rate. While the total patenting increase in the United States between 1965 and 1992 was only 50 percent, there was a growth in patenting related to university life sciences of well over 1100 percent.[6] Moreover, the number of U.S. universities engaged in the patenting process grew rapidly in the 1980s and 1990s, with 173 universities receiving patents in 1998 (up from 111 in 1985 and 28 in 1965).[7]

Table 6.1 Patents Granted to U.S. Universities and Colleges in Top Five Utility Classes, 1969–1980 & 1991–1990

Utility Class		Number of Patents	
		1969–1980	1991–1999
435	Chemistry: Molecular Biology, Microbiology	146	2377
514	Drug, bio-affecting, body treating compositions	163	1598
424	Drug, bio-affecting, body treating compositions	126	1101
530	Chemistry: natural resins, derivatives	25	469
600	Surgery	100	475

Source: National Science Board, *Science & Engineering Indicators—2000*.

The value of patents for capitals, including those attained through university research, has already been elaborated, but it remains to be seen whether scientists behave differently as a result of patent utilization. On this front, a forceful argument can be made concerning a distinct contradiction between the demands of patenting and scientific practice—that is, between the needs of a proprietary regime (geared toward accumulation) and the free exchange of scientific data. Conventionally, the advancement of scientific knowledge has been understood as a long-term, cumulative, and communal process. In keeping with this understanding, investigators contribute minute but important elements, always relying extensively on the work of myriad others. For this reason, progress in the field has always been closely connected to data sharing, open publication, and broad scientific recognition (through multiple authorship and extensive citation). Given that patents are essentially intended to regulate and control the use of knowledge, their increased presence throws into relief some of the more fundamental questions concerning the inner social relations of contemporary basic scientific research.

In this regard, Kathryn Packer and Andrew Webster have spelled out a suggestive and empirically grounded thesis, claiming that scientists must now negotiate and move effectively between the very different social worlds of academic science and intellectual property law.[8] They refer to complex problems negotiated by practicing scientists, including those related to publication content and intellectual credit, restriction of knowledge circulation, and scientific prestige. On the first issue, the entire point of academic publication is to disperse information to scientific colleagues as soon as it has been legitimately verified. This constitutes the main vehicle whereby scientists contribute to the incremental, broadly based construction of scientific knowledge. In order to properly understand and utilize new information, academic publication has generally demanded appropriate intellectual credit for the many previous insights contributing to any 'discovery.' In this sense, Packer and Webster's study documents a belief among practicing scientists in the

> gradual advancement of knowledge in small steps and . . . not . . . simply in terms of the march of intellectual history. New genes were sequenced, novel strains of bacteria were isolated from newly acquired samples, improved and ingenious methodologies were developed, and reviews of previous work led to more perceptive theoretical insights. Although some advances were seen as more significant than others . . . they were all considered novel and contributing to progress in the field.[9]

This conception does not square easily with the notion of invention associated with the patenting process, in which 'novelty,' 'non-obviousness' and an 'inventive step' must be demonstrated. Whereas citations are both a means both to distribute credit and buttress the legitimacy of an academic publication, they are an effective liability in patent application. Within the patenting process, citation of others diminishes the non-obvious character of the work in question. According to Packer and Webster, citation is used in scientifically derived patents only to recognize work that patent examiners are likely to know, ensuring not to suggest any close relation between the research presented and works cited. What the authors call 'constructing non-obviousness' is a practice perhaps most at odds with the communal understanding of scientific practice.[10] The degree to which scientists are able to keep the 'non-obvious' element of patenting separate from the legitimate need to accord recognition to others remains an unanswered question. There are, to be sure, a surprising number of 'flare ups' within the bio-medical field oriented around precisely this contradiction.

On the issue of information restriction, contrary to a host of rhetorical assertions by the pharmaceutical and biotechnology industries, the application of a patent is intended to block or regulate the use of developed knowledge. Recalling the previous discussion of patenting by capitals, this seems an obvious statement, but it is important to highlight this process at the level of scientific practice. Patentees are legally obliged to provide disclosure of their inventions, but in the case of molecular biology, such information does not necessarily lead to possibilities for reproduction of the work. Packer and Webster point out that patents tend to be intentionally obscure, oriented toward preventing reproduction. Indeed, they cite several scientists on the issue, making clear that patents often contain 'claims that resist translation' and frequently describe a chain of causation in a way which is 'over the top' in terms of believability.[11] This is because patents are not used to enroll colleagues, but to 'stake a claim' and keep them away. The problem is particularly acute in relation to how publication and laboratory practices affect the increasingly pronounced desire for patenting. In various court cases, non-obviousness has taken on a meaning very different from that in the scientific world. Indeed, for something to be considered 'obvious,' "it must be spelled in very complete terms and *in one place* (for example, in one scientific publication)."[12] This means that in the face of patent litigation, the gradual building of knowledge through exchange of scientific information has a diminished currency. If patents are increasingly critical, laboratory practice and publication must, if they are to survive potential patent litigation, adhere increasingly to the parameters of commercial production practices. This means, additionally, that the withholding of research until it is in a 'complete' and defensible form will become increasingly important for molecular biology.[13]

For their own part, credit, prestige and reward represent important elements of the 'social glue' that binds the scientific community together. As James Darnell of Rockefeller University puts, "credit is coming to matter more and more as we get deeper into this insanely competitive phase of science."[14] The degree to which a connection has existed between publication and professional recognition has been vital to open exchange within science. For instance, it is certainly true that competition existed in science before the advent of biotechnology, as it is true that information or materials would sometimes be withheld from competitors.[15] But this process could always, to an extent, be held in check by the possibility that withholding publication or vital materials would mean either that somebody might publish first or that one's credibility within the community would be damaged. If patenting involves the withholding of information until it is in completed form, and serious rewards are being accrued to scientists through patenting, the possible infringement on scientific practice is considerable. Packer and Webster make very clear that scientists within the molecular biology community are increasingly using patents as a tool of prestige and credibility. There is certainly the question of individual payoff, but beyond this

> [scientists] use patents to initiate and maintain connections with outside bodies such as companies; they use patents to further their position within university hierarchies; and they use them in their own laboratories to help in writing their own patents. Scientists do not necessarily see patents as the vehicle for technology transfer, but they use patents to great effect to enable them to carry on with their academic research programs.[16]

As is so often the case with social relations, changes occur rarely because of an overt drive towards something new, but because individuals or groups are trying to preserve their present situation by whatever means necessary. Thus, scientists act as agents within the confines of an institutional and systemic set of parameters, not entirely of their own making. The important point here is not to hold up the prospect of widespread patenting, point to a conflicting set of practices, and insist that a passive scientific community is being annexed into a new legal and cultural terrain. Rather, scientists accentuate some, and disregard other, conventional behaviors in a manner that helps them navigate their surrounding institutional and politico-economic context. Patents are themselves a function of that context, and scientists are increasingly obliged to take them into account in both the day-to-day processes and the reward structure of their profession.

The problems raised by patenting are illustrative but difficult to track in relation to their systemic influence. However, this is not to say that no systematic information exists concerning the contemporary behavior of scientists within the life sciences. In terms of industry affiliation, legitimate concerns have arisen over apparent changes in scientific practice, as it has been subjected to commercial influence. An indication of this has been provided within studies that deal with the correlation between industry involvement in life science and individual scientific behavior. Starting in 1986, David Blumenthal, et al. set out to consider some of the possible effects of industrial affiliation on questions of trade secrecy and research influence.[17] The results were somewhat striking: by the mid–1980s, already 23 percent of biotechnology-related faculty were receiving support from industry, 28 percent of whom had over 50 percent of their budget underwritten through industrial affiliations. Faculty connected with industry were more than twice as likely to commercialize a product from their work, and were four times as likely to have trade secrecy result from their research. Among those with industrial affiliation, 24 percent reported having research that could not be subject to publication without the consent of an industrial sponsor. Finally, and perhaps most importantly, those with industrial support were over four times as likely to report that industrial considerations had influenced their research to some or a great extent. When asked whether industrial considerations were receiving an excessive emphasis within academic science, both industrially affiliated and unaffiliated scientists agreed to a large extent (70 and 78 percent, respectively).[18]

In an accompanying study, Blumenthal, et al. observed the extent of industry support from the corporate side of the equation.[19] They found that over half of biotechnology firms had relationships to university research, and that there was "evidence that UIRRs [University-Industry Research Relationships] pose risks to traditional university values and practices."[20] For surveyed biotechnology firms, university research resulted in 23 percent of patent applications, and 41 percent of these firms had derived at least one trade secret from university scientific work. The authors found that 21 percent of non-Fortune 500 firms surveyed reported funding faculty holding significant equity in the firm. Even companies "expressed concern that this situation would create strong incentives for faculty to design their research to serve the narrow commercial interests of the firm rather than the broader goals of basic science."[21] Finally, 32 percent of firms reported that they directly fund the university training of graduate students or postdoctoral fellows, and one-third of these reported that students are obliged to work on problems defined by company interests. Both studies rendered a cautionary note for universities: the increased industrial support of life sciences was unlikely to be trouble-free and, in particular, the pedagogical effects of higher industrial support could have consequences unpalatable to society.

In a further study dealing with industrial affiliations among academic scientists, Sheldon Krimsky, James G. Ennis, and Robert Weissman, examining data from 1985–88, argued that the links between U.S. biologists and industry were widespread.[22] Their work supplies quantitative evidence, without relying on self-reports by university faculty. They checked the ratio of dual-affiliation biotechnology scientists (DABS) to the total number of faculty in various universities, and found that industry affiliation is both strong and highly concentrated in prestigious institutions. By checking against a list of 'elite' scientists in the National Academy of Sciences (NAS), they found similar results. The top ten universities range from MIT (31.1 percent affiliation) to Yale (11.1 percent), while total affiliation among NAS (biological or biomedical) scientists was estimated at 37 percent.[23] To this, the authors added an interesting finding regarding peer review. By investigating National Science Foundation lists, they determined that 49 percent of those on referee lists were industrially affiliated. If these latter figures seem incidental, or of little consequence, one only needs to consider that peer reviews, for both grant applications and publication

> are locked into the way [scientists] distribute recognition, money, hierarchical position, and power in science in the United States. Crucial to that system, both are methods evolved to protect the autonomy and self-regulation of the sciences. . . . [Peer] review and refereeing . . . are both under pressure for several reasons, of which the most basic is the contradiction that makes peer review possible at all. The fact is, of course, that the persons most qualified to judge the worth of a scientist's grant proposal or the merit of a submitted research paper are precisely those who are that scientist's closest competitors.[24]

While scientific contributions have conventionally been seen as 'inputs' into the progress of the field, under the increasing pressure of commercial influence, contributions are more likely to be evaluated with respect to research 'outcomes' as they relate to industrial utility.[25] The authors argue, convincingly, that the location and status of those most heavily involved with industry also matters. Their findings indicate not that dual-affiliation is merely limited to certain institutions (and is, therefore, of limited importance), but rather that the location of this activity makes its consequences all the more profound. As the authors state it, these universities, "not only are the well-spring of future path-breaking discoveries, they also are vital as the training grounds of the next generation of leading scientists and faculty."[26] Therefore, as a structural model for the entire system, the magnification of university-industry linkages through the dispersal mechanism of scientific prestige is likely only to increase their significance as the norm.

The above research applies to periods prior to the advent of the HGP, and it could reasonably be questioned whether it still has a great deal of applicability. For instance, it was the expectation that the biotechnology and pharmaceutical industries would remain dependent on basic research institutions in the early phases of industrial development, but such dependency would wane as extensive private in-house capacities grew through the late 1980s and 1990s (recall that private industry now spends more on life science R&D than the federal government). This, according to 1996 follow-up studies by Blumenthal, et al., has not been the case.[27] In the first study, the authors again measured industry connections to university programs and found that over 90 percent of life science corporations now had ties to university research. These included consultancy (88 percent), direct research report (59 percent) and support of students and fellows (38 percent). The possibility of declining involvement was largely ruled out by respondents, as two-thirds of corporations expected to increase their research support greatly or somewhat over the next five years. Much of this support was for contracts of shorter duration, which suggested a focus on applied rather than basic research.[28] Most interestingly, the authors measured the extent to which corporate actors contribute to a withholding of information within academic research. Over half (56 percent) of surveyed firms said that they had required universities to keep material confidential longer than is necessary to secure a patent application. 58 percent made clear that they typically required universities to withhold materials for longer than six months (30–60 days being the 'reasonable' period recommended by the NIH). The most damaging conditions may, in fact, be directed at graduate students and postdoctoral fellows. Here, 57 percent of corporations reported that, "confidential, proprietary information sometimes or often emerges from their sponsorship of graduate students and postdoctoral fellows; 88% reported that their arrangements require students and fellows to keep such information confidential."[29] Ultimately, the presence and influence of corporations within 'basic' research facilities seem to be increasing rather than declining.

From the academic side of the equation, the 1996 companion study considered the participation of faculty in industry relationships.[30] Here, the degree of enrolment among faculty had not reversed but increased to 28 percent. While these faculty members tended to be more 'productive' in terms of publication and service activities,[31] they were also much more likely to report restrictions on their research. Of those supported, 14.5 percent reported having trade secrets result from their work, while 35 percent said that their choice of research was influenced by commercial considerations.[32] Two additional, more refined studies deal with the withholding of research and industrial 'gifts' directed at academics. Interestingly, because of the funding sources for these studies, they included a particular investigative category for scientists with research directly related to the HGP. The data from this latter category, however, will be considered in the specific discussion of the HGP below. In the first of these studies, the authors suggest that the withholding of research has clearly affected a very significant portion of faculty in the life sciences.[33] While the NIH's guidelines of 30–60 days as a reasonable withholding period are clearly disregarded by industry, almost 20 percent of faculty reported having delayed publications for more than six months, and almost 9 percent reported explicitly refusing to share research results in the last three years. If the latter number seems harmless, the authors balanced it against the number of scientists who reported having been denied access to research results and products—a number which totaled 34 percent.[34] Clearly, the inconsistency between these numbers suggests that the refusal to share has become a significant factor within academic science.

Moreover, a compelling study by Eric Campbell, et al. concerning the prevalence of industrial 'gifts' aimed at academic researchers suggests another level of potential influence.[35] Gifts from industry to faculty are generally not subject to regulation by university institutions, because they are aimed at single researchers without the necessity of a contract. As such, they are less formal and incorporate a wider array of activities than strict affiliation or university-industrial linkage.[36] The authors discovered that 43 percent of faculty members in the life sciences receive gifts, the most frequent of which were biomaterials and discretionary funds. Critically, for the purposes of this work, 71 percent of preclinical researchers reported that these gifts were 'important,' 'very important' or 'essential' to their ongoing research. Moreover, the authors concluded that this industrial 'philanthropy' could, "be associated with a variety of restrictions and expectations of returns."[37] These include expected acknowledgement (63 percent), restricted handling *vis-à-vis* third parties (60 percent), restricted use (59 percent), prepublication review of articles or reports (32 percent), future consulting considerations (20 percent), and ownership of all derived patentable results (19 percent). These results are suggestive, in that they go beyond formal associations and indicate that academic-industry interchange is even more extensive and subject to conditions than the initial Blumenthal et al. studies suggested.[38]

Taken together, such studies clearly point to a change in practice in the biosciences, signaling a modification in the meaning and object of scientific work. This modification is, however, obscured by the tendency to depict eminent scientists as entirely representative of their field. In the case of molecular biology, individuals such as Paul Berg, Leroy Hood, or David Baltimore command enormous influence, and they elicit broad support, if not open advocacy, for commercial involvement. As Bruce Alberts, President of the National Academy of Sciences, suggests with respect to corporate involvement, "[good] science is roaring along, and people are talking about it. First rate people don't let things get in the way."[39] Along these lines, it is a myth to interpret molecular biology as having moved very far away from its conventional norms of science. Admittedly, according to a recent study of life scientists' self-perception of their fields' ethical norms, Alberts' understanding holds partly true. The study's authors presented a large sample of molecular and cellular biologists and university administrators with multiple scenarios, in which they were asked to determine their ethical reaction, by according a 'malfeasance rating' between 1 and 10.[40] The participants exhibited a rather uncompromising reaction to problems such as fabrication, falsification, plagiarism, misleading information, and failure to give proper attribution. Nonetheless, even here both 'conflicts of interest' and 'failure to share research results' elicited less serious reactions from participants. This apparent shortfall from Mertonian values may, in fact, point to one way in which an alteration in scientific work is discernible: an accentuation of the contradictions already resident in scientific practice.

In this regard, the competitive flavor of scientific practice in the postwar era has always fit uncomfortably with the communal values of free scientific exchange and openness. The latter values have persisted in science because of an ostensibly common desire to see knowledge progress for its own sake—in more suggestive terms, knowledge had a value not typically subject to quantification or exchange value. This overriding norm crossed with, but almost certainly held in check, the competitive drive for scientific prestige and reward. Situating the value of scientific work in knowledge *per se* meant that overt actions to block the latter's development had met, in large part, with moral opprobrium. However, according a *measurable* value to scientific knowledge—the quantitative value inherent in the systemic pressure towards technology transfer and commercialization—means that scientists account for new factors in their relation to conventional scientific norms. As such, Rebecca Eisenberg is partially correct to claim that, "[although] there are signs of tension over adherence to the norms, commercial pressures appear to be only a new aggravation of a familiar problem."[41] It does not, however, suffice to analyze this rise in competitiveness by stating glibly, as one prominent scientist has, that "[there] have been bastards in science from the beginning."[42] Specifically, transitions in historical structure are very often a function of attempts to reproduce existing conditions that, as a result of internal and external pressures, effect certain qualitative changes. It thus seems likely that the shift in professional practice within the life sciences represents more than just a competitive upswing; rather, it signals the reprioritization of specific social relations between scientists, such that they are increasingly organized around the economic and quantifiable value derivable from their work.

In addition to the intensification of internal contradictions, however, it is important to note both the ever-relaxing attitude within biological sciences towards 'conflict-of-commitment' and the 'contract' character of university-industrial relations. Through the post-war period, many American universities gradually had come to follow the lead of MIT with respect to faculty's involvement within industry. The 'one-fifth' rule stipulated that faculty could spend no more than one day in the week devoted to their industrial commitments.[43] However, the onslaught of short-term funding projects (one to two years)—oriented predominantly around applied research topics, consulting and product testing—makes clear that this rule has come under considerable pressure. Little wonder that Blumenthal et al. warn that short-lived and targeted research "may not generally be conducive to maintaining the level of excellence of fundamental academic research in those fields."[44] It is certainly true that the time and complexity of corporate affiliations is drawing non-corporate researchers increasingly away from their institutional commitments.[45] In fact, Henry Etzkowitz has stated that the Blumenthal et al. and Krimsky studies

> likely underestimate the extent of faculty involvement, especially in molecular biology. For example, in the biology department at MIT where surveys identified half the faculty as industrially involved in the late 1980s, an informant could identify only one department member as uninvolved at the time. In the succeeding years, a complex web of relationships has grown up among university organized start-ups in emerging industries and older and larger firms in traditional industries. Often the same academic scientists are involved with both types of firms, managing a diversified portfolio of industrial interactions.[46]

Even assuming that leading researchers are able to balance effectively their institutional and industrial commitments (and this is a big 'if'), this says little about the many post-doctoral fellows, graduate students, and technicians who do large amounts of the 'legwork' integral to research. The one-fifth rule (or any derivation from it) for prominent faculty may nominally record time spent on industrial activities, but it does not seriously monitor actual research performed, and there are no restrictions concerning the industrial content (or applicability) of research output. On this count, the studies of Blumenthal et al. and Campbell et al. are telling in terms of the extent to which industrial presence is changing the object of young researchers' work. The typical "graduate student role has expanded from its feudal format of acolyte to incorporate teaching, research, and invention activities. Pay and status have lagged behind the reinvention of the role."[47] The character of faculty prestige and reward structures prove critical, because they determine the distribution of both commercial and non-commercial funds, enabling, in turn, the ongoing support of post-doctorals and graduate students who 'make the lab run.' As such, although universities may nominally regulate leading scientists' connection to commercial structures, the content of university-industry agreements are usually put into motion through the productive work of the laboratory, conducted by individuals largely invisible to either scientific or commercial reward systems.

The focus here has been predominantly on academic researchers, because their conventional autonomy and prestige have made them difficult to consider as laborers. Of course, looking to the corporate sphere, autonomy and research control are very often not in the hands of individual investigators, and scientific practice is easier to delineate as labor in the Marxist sense.[48] But since most basic science has been performed in universities or non-profit institutions, such settings constitute a more informative 'baseline' as to the state of scientific practice. As this baseline applies to the molecular biology community, the evidence points to both quantitative and qualitative changes that render scientific practice more closely attuned to the capital-labor relationship. Not only have scientists acquiesced to the use of their work in value accumulation, itself a function of this social relationship, but they have also progressively reshaped their work environment, such that it corresponds to a production of 'outputs.' Nobel Laureate Paul Berg has recently summoned up nostalgia for the Asilomar process: "[the] recombinant DNA controversy arose from the ranks of science . . . [and] there were lots of kudos to the scientists for raising it and deciding to deal with it."[49] But in the wake of the rise of biotechnology and extensive university-industry relationships, it is questionable, "whether it's possible for [scientists] to still exhibit the sort of self-restraint they did a quarter century ago, or whether caution gets lost in the heat of ambition and the thundering of the hooves."[50]

THE CONDITIONS OF CHANGE

The closer 'fit' between scientific work and the capital-labor relationship renders a difficult question: under what conditions has this set of changes been possible? The overbearing power and influence of capital certainly provides considerable explanation, but academic research has, historically, demonstrated some capability to resist such influence. Similarly, the reliance on individually motivated 'commercial payoff' explanations proves somewhat weak. As Etzkowitz points out, "opportunities for commercial utilization of scientific research has often been available to scientists in the past, such as Marie and Pierre Curie and Pasteur, who did not believe in crossing the boundary between science and business themselves, even though they evinced a strong interest in the practical application of their findings."[51] As a starting point for analysis, it is worth reflecting on the main thread of this work's explanatory approach—historical materialism.

In analyzing the conversion of labor practices, Marx devoted a significant part of *Capital* to understanding the 'so-called primitive accumulation of capital.' In this, he set out to demonstrate some of the political imperatives put in force to bring labor into line with a transformed (now capitalist) social reality. More specifically, he was concerned with the social and political processes undertaken to *create* the wage-laborer—processes which he in no way understood as only 'enforcement.' On the one hand, he was clear that the genesis of wage-labor requires direct political intervention. As such, "[the] bourgeoisie, at its rise, wants and uses the power of the state to 'regulate' wages, i.e. to force them within the limits suitable for surplus-value making, to lengthen the working-day and to keep the laborer himself in the normal degree of dependence."[52] Toward this end, the state plays a critical role, and Marx highlighted multiple examples of legislative/state acts that secure low wages and criminalize that section of the population failing to respond to the new work imperative. In the context of the present discussion, there is little use in simplistically *equating* Marx's historical description with the new conditions of work in molecular biology.[53] It is, however, worth reemphasizing critical historical moments, in which the intervention of the state has aimed directly at changing the practices of those working in science. As previously detailed, legislative acts such as Bayh-Dole or the Federal Technology Transfer Act clearly encouraged—indeed, made obligatory—a reassessment of the scientist's role *vis-à-vis* productive behavior. The notion that researchers in the life sciences carry a 'responsibility' to report *any* socially 'beneficial' (read: patentable) results to their institutional affiliation was given widespread political currency in the United States through such legislation.

Marx also depicted the complicated nature of the wage-laborer's agency as social relations take hold. Beyond the stultification of labor's capacity to resist the imposition of capital, it is appropriate to invoke a prior question posed by Marx: "why this free labourer confronts [the capitalist] in the market . . . ?"[54] His answer suggests that once the laws of motion of capitalism take hold, force becomes increasingly unnecessary due to the self-reproducing effects of production conditions.

> It is not enough that the conditions of labour are concentrated in a mass, in the shape of capital, at the one pole society, while at the other are grouped masses of men, who have nothing to sell but their labour-power. Neither is it enough that they are compelled to sell it voluntarily. The advance of capitalist production develops a working-class, which by education, tradition, habit, looks upon the conditions of that mode of production as self-evident laws of nature. The organization of the capitalist process of production, once fully developed, breaks down all resistance . . . The dull compulsion of economic relations completes the subjection of the labourer to the capitalist. Direct force, outside economic conditions, is of course still used, but only exceptionally. In the ordinary run of things, the labourer can be left to the 'natural laws of production,' i.e., to his dependence on capital, a dependence springing form, and guaranteed in perpetuity by, the conditions of production themselves.[55]

As the laborer becomes increasingly more disposed to the capitalist labor market, the question remains how widely Marx intended the concept of 'conditions' to be interpreted. His own elaboration made enormous strides toward understanding prevailing production relations, state legislative power, and the wretched (dependent) condition of the working classes. But it does seem reasonable to augment this analysis by exploring the manner in which social institutions—separate from either capitals or the state—adapt and contribute to a new capitalist terrain.

In the context of contemporary scientific practice, it is useful to supplement the theoretical framework provided by Marx with that of Michel Foucault. Foucault's starting point is different from that of Marx, as he asks us to *assume* the imposition of larger political and economic imperatives (although he most definitely maintains their importance throughout his work) and directs our attention to an " . . . 'economy' of power, that is to say, procedures which allowed the effects of power to circulate in a manner at once continuous, uninterrupted, adapted, and 'individualised' throughout the entire social body."[56] It is—at the risk of being provocative—useful to position Foucault in a more amiable relation to the intellectual trajectory of historical materialism.[57] This is neither to assert that Foucault's thinking constituted a superior 'progression' from Marx nor that the former was, in reality, a 'closet Marxist.' Rather, it is to utilize Foucault's exploration of *how* power relations take hold as a rough guide to consider changes in contemporary scientific practice. Foucault was in no way the only intellect to undertake this task, but his particular interest in the instantiation of 'discipline,' institutional rearrangement, and what he called the 'microphysics of power' makes his work particularly relevant to the discussion of contemporary molecular biology.

The bulk of Foucault's work is concerned with the process of historical change, in which very particular social practices emerge and help constitute new 'truths' that are amenable to, and productive for, the wider politico-economic context. In this sense, all of Foucault's 'historical' studies of madness, medical practice, criminality and sexuality contributed to an attempt to understand how particular social institutions, architectures and discourses could be redirected, in order to better serve a changing political economy of 'work.'[58] He was concerned with the manner in which 'disciplines' are used to arrange what he figuratively referred to as 'docile bodies' within the machinery of power. For Foucault, discipline " . . . increases the forces of the body (in economic terms of utility) and diminishes these same forces (in political terms of obedience)."[59] In general terms, Foucault's notion of discipline incorporates a compellation of ordering techniques effectively serving three functions. First, disciplines exercise power at the lowest possible political and economic costs, keeping outward enforcement unnecessary and suppressing instability through a particular 'normalizing' discourse. Second, they intensify the effects of social power, by carrying them into a wider of human experience. Third, they link economic exploitation with a series of critical 'apparatuses,' embodied in prisons, educational institutions, hospitals, and the military.[60]

For Foucault, the emergence of discipline was not a spontaneous but rather a distinctly historical happening. As such, he understands them only in relation to over-arching power strategies:

> No 'local center,' no 'pattern of transformation' could function if, through a series of sequences, it did not eventually enter into an overall strategy. And, inversely, no strategy could achieve comprehensive effects if it did not gain support from precise and tenuous relations serving, not as its point of application or final outcome, but as its prop and anchor point . . . one must conceive of the double conditioning of a strategy by the specificity of possible tactics, and of tactics by the strategic envelope that makes them work.[61]

There is no doubt which 'overall strategy' Foucault is ultimately naming, by stating emphatically that "[the] *growth of a capitalist economy* gave rise to the specific modality of disciplinary power, whose general formulas, techniques of submitting forces and bodies, in short, 'political anatomy,' could be operated in the most diverse political regimes, apparatuses or institutions."[62] He pointed out only that 'discipline'—a process he later termed 'bio-power'—involves an invaluable (from the perspective of capital) investment in the calculated management of an increasing number of social spheres. As such, the " . . . adjustment of the accumulation of men to that of capital, the joining of the growth of human groups to the expansion of productive forces and the differential allocation of profit, were made possible *in part* by the exercise of bio-power in its many forms and modes of application. The investment of the body, its valorization, and the distributive management of its forces were . . . indispensable."[63]

In pointing to the 'microphysics' of power circulation, Foucault directs our attention to two major areas of concern: 1) institutional structure and relations and 2) circulating discourse. On the first issue, the very setup of institutional structures—architecturally, hierarchically, or even in relation to other institutions—can have dramatic effects in the manner in which power is channeled. This relates to a pressing question within this work: what are the conditions under which given institutions have been able to channel predominant power relations within the molecular biology community in a manner increasingly conducive to the interests of capital? While tracking the behavior of scientists under university-industry linkages illustrates the presence of change, it is necessary to understand the architectural parameters within which that change has occurred. How has the university extended the double conditioning of power, such that scientific practice could be increasingly optimized into scientific labor? If the abovementioned capital restructuring and state/legislative activity can be taken as representative of predominant power relations, then the university (along with the federal laboratory) can very legitimately be understood as an effective nodal point of disciplinary power. On this point, there are multiple ways in which institutional designs have complemented with the assertion of capitalist power relations from below.

It is difficult to say where the assertion of power through capitals and the federal state ends and institutional response begins. Nor does it seem entirely necessary to demarcate such a clear division between the two. Starting from the *mezzanine* level of state governments, their historically passive reception of federal funds for the purpose of education in the sciences changed dramatically in the 1980s. In the investment fever of that decade, state governments, legislatures, and governors began to position themselves proactively in relation to their rediscovered 'assets': universities and research institutions. At the same time, a move on the part of capital to organize production processes in horizontal 'networks' meant that opportunities abounded for local policymakers and institutional actors to promote the vitality of their research resources. Much has been made of the 'network' model itself as a *cause* of industrial and technological change.[64] But a more convincing argument relates network-oriented production to a 'survival' strategy among capitals. As a class, capital has driven the range of technological specializations necessary for production to a level which no single capital can possibly engage alone. Thus,

> [r]ecognition of this change in the location and organization of expertise means that it is inappropriate and misleading to focus only on changes in the organization of universities, without examining how changes in universities dovetail with simultaneous changes in private sector R&D, federal policy, and the evolving structure of science. In short, we must view cutting-edge science as the product of a coevolutionary system of interlinked institutions.[65]

At a local level, then, alliances, consulting, outsourcing, CRADAs, 'cottage' and entrepreneurial industries have become a prevailing organizational edict. In relation to biotechnology, this disposition has proven quite meaningful, as local governments, in cooperation with university political structures, seek to create their own version of 'silicon valley' or the San Francisco Bay Area. Already by 1988, there were thirty-three states with biotechnology development programs, with plans in six other states to do the same. As such, the conventional role of local government was " . . . expanded to include state grants and subsidies to particular projects, institutes, or consortia in particular scientific labs thought to hold the keys to the industries and jobs of the future."[66] The goal has been an intensification of regional desires for beneficial 'resource' utilization, wrapped up in an inter-governmental competition to win in what some have called a 'rent-seeking' environment.[67]

In this environment, universities have 'dovetailed' their structures in such a way that the social relations of capitalist accumulation can better permeate institutional processes, increasing the prevalence and necessity of productive behavior among practicing scientists. Indeed, within the 'network' environment, universities have adapted their own 'coping' strategy, possibly spurred on by a perceived claw-back in federal support structures.[68] Interestingly, Etzkowitz and Webster have argued that this is no less than a

shift away from mediaeval structures which traditionally characterized—
and, to a certain degree, sheltered—the university, even through the twentieth century. This shift involves, fundamentally, " . . . the translation of
research findings into intellectual property, a marketable commodity, and
economic development."[69] While universities had, for some time, been involved in various linkages with industry, they tended to do so in a manner
that preserved a distance between product development and their own ap-
prentice-based knowledge pursuit. Particularly in the life sciences, however,
there has been a rather sudden and aggressive move to align the university
much more closely with the network production structures utilized by capital. A central issue in university policy, as well as regional economic development, has been to "create conditions to produce a self-sustaining chain
reactions of high technology firms . . . linking universities to firm formation
through private and state venture capital."[70] Institutionally, this has meant
a proliferation of research parks that can, by virtue of proximity, make interaction between faculty and industry personnel increasingly likely. Indeed,
these are often built in collaboration with industry, such that the latter's personnel are guaranteed physical access to the academic research environment.
Throughout the university system, patenting offices and technology transfer
offices have either been set up anew or intensified. In fact, a 1992 survey by
the U.S. General Accounting Office determined that 34 of 35 surveyed universities had substantially enhanced their institutional capacities for patenting and licensing, as well as established technology transfer offices.[71]

The reality is that the most financially lucrative effects of patenting
and technology transfer have been limited to prestigious institutions. But as
a consequence of these successes (exemplified by institutions such as MIT,
Stanford, or the University of California), there has been a demonstrable
'mimetic isomorphism,' building on an already uniquely competitive inter-
university dynamic in the United States. Moreover, as Irwin Feller has quite
rightly pointed out, the issue is not that university patents to date "have
yielded so little in the way of commercial innovations. Rather, it is that to
purposively attempt to change these outcomes requires an explicit change in
the determination of academic research priorities."[72] Beyond infrastructural
adjustments, universities have moved into 'active technology transfer' by
spreading their endowment funds into high-risk equity investments and encouraged increasingly extensive university-firm research agreements. Along
with funding organizations, there is clear encouragement of 'team' research
leading to innovation. The image of a few struggling graduate students bol-
stering a professor's laboratory increasingly does not pertain to molecular
biology. This rearrangement has placed science faculty in charge of large

interdisciplinary teams, composed of BAs, MAs, doctoral students, post-doctorals, research associates, technicians, and computer and bioinformatics specialists. There is a great deal of truth in Etzkowitz and Webster's claim that faculty are increasingly positioned in a managerial role, making their professional crossover to 'entrepreneurial' activity increasingly viable.[73] In this sense, the range of roles in the large-scale academic research environment is both varied and hierarchal. But while the 'entrepreneurial' role of lead scientists involves less outwardly productive behavior than, say, a technician, even the former's organizational activity can be characterized as productive behavior.[74]

Organizational behavior and infrastructural arrangements matter, because they serve to alter or reinforce particular power distributions within scientific research. There has always been a uniquely competitive environment within U.S. biological research community. It is no coincidence that in the country with the strongest market-oriented social organization, research has been spread out geographically, combined graduate teaching with research, and assigned grants largely on the basis of an investigator-led competitive basis.[75] Indeed,

> [g]overnments in some countries, especially the United States and the United Kingdom, have sought to promote this growth in the commercialization of academia as a surrogate for the introduction of a formal industrial policy where national planning for science and technology and innovation more generally is regarded as politically unacceptable, contrary to the principles of the 'free-market' economy.[76]

Thus, while the structural changes in U.S. universities introduce a new architecture for research scientists to navigate, this has also involved the utilization and reinforcement of existing organizational characteristics. As indicated above, any attempt to understand historical shifts, always uncovers elements of the 'old' in the 'new.'[77] But the fact that certain structures, such as technology transfer offices, have some history within certain U.S. universities does not make their sudden numerical upswing, intensification, and active investment into the practices of faculty any less significant. In terms of disciplinary behavior, the amplification and proliferation of commercially oriented structures reaches deeply into the prevailing value sphere of the research community. From a Foucauldian perspective, universities have been actively rebuilding their own edifice, such that labor activities fit into the normal parameters of institutional operations.

The second area of concern for Foucault, circulating discourse, operates simultaneously with these altered institutional arrangements. For

Foucault, discourses play an immense role in shaping regimes of behavior, especially those involving labor, because they are at once caught up in a 'normalizing' function. Circulating discourse carries out the effects of oppressive and exploitative power (the existence of which Foucault freely admits), by regulating the distribution of norms at countless pressure points (for example, schools, prisons, healthcare). This normalizing process need not be constituted by a redevelopment of content in circulating statements, but rather, "is a question of what *governs* statements, and the way in which they *govern* each other . . ."[78] In other words, the basis upon which statements are evaluated cannot but effect behavioral proclivities within a given social grouping, insofar as it concretizes power by making it functional.

> If power were never anything but repressive, if it never did anything but say no, do you really think one would be brought to obey it? What makes power hold good, what makes it accepted, is simply the fact that it doesn't *only* weigh on us as a force that says no, but that it traverses and produces things, it induces pleasure, forms knowledge, produces discourse.[79]

This demands an examination of the manner in which structural institutional change has been conducive to an altered, more 'productive,' set of norms. As Feller points out, the process of structural change must necessarily effect a new distribution of norms within the university. Such change, "entails socializing an organization's members to a new set of precepts, in part through a formal recasting of modes of compensation (salary) and status, but also through tacit but nevertheless widely understood (and shared) conclusions about those types of behaviors considered either appropriate or beyond the pale."[80] Emergent norms now embedding themselves in the discourse of the life sciences point to an 'ethos' in which commercial linkage is not only being seen as increasingly desirable but even necessary. These do not emerge out of 'thin air' (contrary to the often-heard charge that Foucault simply sees power everywhere); rather, like state policy terrain, discursive regimes can also be an active site of political struggle. In different periods, different standards of judgement and criteria will 'govern statements' circulating in the university as a whole, but also within particular disciplines.

In a somewhat provocative piece, Jonathan R. Cole has referred to this conflictual process as an attempt to gain 'control of the null.' A 'null hypothesis' in statistical analysis sets up a standard of zero difference or equality, the point of which is to disprove through the identification of statistical deviations from the hypothesized 'norm.' According to Cole, "[as] any social scientist can attest, it is extremely difficult to accumulate enough acceptable evidence to reject, or overturn, the null hypothesis . . . Therefore, whoever controls, or 'owns,' the definition of the null is apt to preserve it against attacks based on existing evidence. The formulation of the null also determines who bears the burden of proof."[81] In the life sciences, particularly in molecular biology, subtle shifts in the 'null hypothesis' are expressed within a contemporary discourse that has abandoned the assumption that commercial activity is inimical to the basic sciences. In fact, it is fair to say that American research universities, along with the life scientists who help populate them, have seized the opportunity to define the trajectory of academic-commercial relations as mutually beneficial. Whereas, prior to the emergence of the biotechnology industry, scientists 'going corporate' carried the burden of evidence concerning their own good standing with the university, today that burden rests squarely on those who would assert anything other than compatibility (albeit asymmetrical) between university and corporate goals. The discursive shift witnessed during the 1980s and 1990s can be brought together under at least three general trends: the re-evaluation of academic and corporate culture; the degradation of the applied-basic dichotomy in scientific research; and the reformulation of science's (and scientists') public responsibility.

The evaluation of academic culture within the life sciences has clearly witnessed changes over the last two decades. It is interesting to note that in 1982, Harvard University, then known for its resistance to extensive commercial ties, declined involvement in formally assisting its professors' business interests. Then President Derek Bok, stated that "[all] in all . . . the financial advantages to the university appear more speculative than heretofore supposed, while the dangers to academic science from participating in these ventures seems real and severe."[82] The criteria governing Bok's statement prioritized both the sanctity of academic culture, wherein the 'burden of proof' rested with those who would challenge this sanctity.[83] However, during the 1980s, this was hardly the dominant discursive trend in major American research universities. Testifying before Congress, then President of MIT Paul Gray referred specifically to the uniqueness of academic culture as a 'secret weapon.' The university's capacity to compete with industry was said to be " . . . infused in particular with the kind of enthusiasm, vigor, and stream of new ideas which young people bring to it . . . a most unusual environment . . . which enables [it] to outperform in terms of research the kind of results that arise in other settings."[84] Seen in relation to the extension of large laboratories, this discourse takes on an especially ominous tone, in which research is discursively represented as a 'strategic asset,' heralded by administrators and faculty alike.

Moreover, a comparative discourse has emerged that makes the commercial element of organized science increasingly attractive for scientists. Contrasted to the slow, bureaucratized and cautious support systems that are said to typify the academic research culture, commercial involvement accords access to resources 'without all the fuss.' In fact, a 1989 study indicated that over 50 percent of life scientists agreed that industrial research culture involved better access to resources and less 'red tape.'[85] All of this is reinforced by an increasingly positive image of corporately based biology research. Along these lines, the leading journal *Science* has made substantial efforts to persuade its readership concerning the benefits of corporate involvement.[86] Claims made concerning the life of corporate scientists may constitute the most palpable example of the 'productive' element of Foucault's disciplinary power. In interviews with young scientists, *Science* emphasizes the positive, citing one new PhD concerning " . . . how easy it is to do science here [in a corporation]. There's no money trouble . . . and there is a large support staff to make your life easy . . . It feels like I'm going to be a postdoc forever . . . which some people may describe as heaven."[87] In this environment, the representation of the university culture itself has been nudged (or has nudged itself) into a discursive shift. Universities continue to avow their goal of autonomous, innovative research, but such goals have been more closely aligned with those of industry, such that scientists and the academic community feel more comfortable with an interchange between the two cultures.

Prior to the late 1970s and early 1980s, discursive rules concerning the separation between basic and applied science remained dominant in the life sciences. The basic research done at universities was regularly differentiated from the applied research undertaken in corporate laboratories. Scientists, the university community, industry and the media, have eroded this differentiation, as a result of alterations in the representation of current scientific practice. This is not to downplay the reality of material changes in the structural connection between university research and product development. Systemically, any effective analysis must come to terms with the difficulty of separating these spheres in the present context of molecular biology and biotechnology. Nonetheless, it is worth pointing out that the constant barrage of information—with little or no accompanying explanation—concerning the blurred lines between 'pure science' and 'applied technology' has made the shift to industrial linkage appear all the more inevitable and 'natural.' Even critical analysis rehearses a discursive assumption that biotechnology has " . . . largely collapsed the distinction between basic and applied science: fundamental new discoveries, such as gene therapy or the identification of a fat gene, have immediate scientific and medical importance as well as enormous commercial relevance."[88] To this technological explanation is added the notion that scientists wishing to remain on the 'cutting-edge' of research must necessarily connect to industry. In a complicated discursive affirmation of this, corporate actors insist that their needs would be poorly served by the loss of basic science in universities. Although this appears to deny a collapsing of basic and applied research, it actually fulfills the opposite goal. Regardless of the degree to which targeted research is undertaken by faculty, the association of pure innovation to coincidental company needs makes scientists' corporate linkages seem irrelevant to the 'basic' character of their work. As such, when arguing for university linkages to capital, the pure/applied division in molecular biology can be held up by universities as an irrelevant artifact of the past, while much of corporate discourse helps preserve an image of 'autonomous' faculty research that is, nonetheless, immediately applied. Under this discursive regime, researchers and research institutions can maintain both that these are 'different times' *and* that their research plays to no one else's tune.

A third discursive shift involves a rearticulated concept of public responsibility among scientists. In a model not unlike customer-service relations, scientists are viewed less and less as servants of an abstract 'public good'; rather, they are increasingly understood as the specific servants of taxpayers, a scenario in which they are required to 'deliver the goods.' Especially following the procurement of the Bayh-Dole Act, the life-sciences community has sharpened its public alertness to the obligation of repaying taxpayers, primarily through the mechanisms of technology transfer. Indeed, despite Al Gore's disgruntlement with regard to Ronald Lamont-Havers and the Hoechst-MGH deal (see chapter 5), that Congressional flare-up revealed a good deal about how early and widespread such norms were being established. In fact, by 1994, Leroy Hood could confidently proclaim that

> [we] scientists have a major obligation not only to discover things but, where possible, to put them to use in society . . . You can transfer knowledge in the form of an instrument or technology or patents, or alternatively you can transfer knowledge in the manner of creating companies. We owe society an obligation because society is paying for science, and this is an obligation that scientists are just starting to take seriously.[89]

Discourse of this variety, rampant in Congressional testimony, effectively serves to fuse central ethical obligations of scientists with corporate productive goals. In other words, the public duties of scientists have been repositioned, such that their research is now deeply entwined with individual and institutional practices that effectively serve a clear functional purpose within the social relations of production. Here, the 'public interest' model blends into that of 'commercial utility,' as the conditions of value extraction, derived from mental labor, are adopted further and further up the R&D chain.

Overall, a combination of structural rearrangement and discursive modification has governed a reevaluation of scientific practice. According to Etzkowitz, "[once] the university accepted firm-formation and assistance to the local economy as an academic objective, the issue of boundary maintenance was seen in a new light."[90] In this sense, Martin Kenney was, early in the years of biotechnology's emergence, absolutely correct to identify the 'conflict of interest' problem for what it was: a 'scapegoat' mechanism that unfairly individualized a wider structural set of problems.[91] The changing work conditions of scientific practice can only, to a minimal extent, be attributed to the putative 'entrepreneurial' and sometimes 'greedy' behavior of prominent scientists. Utilizing a Foucauldian framework to further our understanding of the local and institutional conditions that funnel scientific labor, it is necessary to make note of scientists' changing 'scenery': from regional governments, to their own campus, to intra-scientific gatherings. In step with the explicit federal state policy and the large-scale entry of capital, these 'micro-institutions' have adjusted the terrain upon which science is now practiced and evaluated. Scientists, of course, still make choices, but those choices are circumscribed within a new version of 'directed autonomy,' to a considerable extent affected by the 'external' imperatives of value accumulation.

THE HGP—GALVANIZING A LABOR FRAMEWORK

Over the two decades in which connections between life sciences and economic development witnessed a meteoric rise, the HGP's historical role in relation to scientific practice should not be overlooked. It would clearly be an exaggeration to claim that the HGP was *the* deciding factor with respect to changes in the practice of molecular biology. However, the project did serve to accelerate and normalize many commercially related activities, and it could not fail to have its effects on participating scientists. It was, in fact, hardly surprising that, " . . . the technologies and information needs of the Human Genome Project . . . led to a recent rash in academic-based firm formation, or firms whose principal executives were key players in the genetics research community."[92] This was especially prevalent in the explosion of specific genomics oriented companies in the 1990s.[93] Ultimately, the widespread and galvanizing effects of the project on molecular biologists make it a difficult factor to overlook in relation to changing scientific practice.

Beyond its mark on the 'biotech boom,' more specific effects of the HGP have been suggested in the later studies undertaken by Blumenthal et al. In these studies, the authors included a sub-category of researchers who were receiving funding from the HGP. In doing so, they found that HGP-related researchers were significantly more likely to have withheld research results and twice as likely to cite 'preserving their lead' as a motive for refusing to share. The authors speculated that this was a result of the highly competitive nature of genetics as a field of study. They suggested that " . . . the prevailing attitudes or culture among genetics researchers may be more tolerant of data withholding," and that there was a " . . . need for attention to the acculturation of geneticists."[94] Given the foregoing analysis, such results may not seem especially surprising. The question remains, however, whether the HGP had a decisive or special effect on the changing practices within molecular biology.

On the question of the scientific work itself, fears were expressed at an early point in the project's construction, closely related to the potential for significant shifts in labor conditions. Recalling the initial opposition directed at the project from within the scientific community, it is worth examining more closely the most prominent criticisms, and how they were handled throughout the project's emergence. The assertions that researchers would be "wading through a sea of drivel," or that a genome project threatened to change "the structure of science in such a way as to indenture [biologists], especially the young people," need to be considered not only as scientific arguments but as an explicit questioning of how scientists understand their own work environment.[95] Even the optimistic James Watson admitted very early on that " . . . everyone else at Cold Spring Harbour was against [the project]," because they were young and " . . . scared that if sequencing goes ahead there will be few funds available for research."[96] Here, whether intentional or not, the textual differentiation of 'research' from 'sequencing' went straight to the heart of the matter: whether the HGP contained goals which were consistent with the post-war investigator-led structure of U.S. biological sciences.

Among two prominent sources of controversy during the HGP's emergence, the first was a set of letter-writing campaigns initiated by Martin Rechsteiner (University of Utah) and Michael Syvanen (University of California at Davis), in which the authors expressed their objections to an all-out sequencing effort. Their resistance was concerned with the diversion of valuable research funds away from 'small' biology and the likelihood that such an effort would lead to " . . . mediocre, mind-numbing work unfit for training young scientists . . . concentrating the effort in few big centers instead of spreading the wealth."[97] In a later interview, Rechsteiner emphasized the role of less established scientists:

> [f]undamentally, I got interested in the project because I got angry. And I got angry because I had young faculty that had been recruited who were having trouble getting grants. And while I was sitting here seeing talented young investigators struggling, I was reading about the millions of dollars that were going to well-established investigators, or at least seemed to be targeted on them.[98]

There is more to Rechsteiner's difficulties than the question of how funds are to be distributed. Laced throughout his concerns was the notion that "the 'project' would provide 'little useful training and no intellectual stimulation to young scientists,' and it would be 'divisive' to the biomedical research community with its 'big science versus little science' implications."[99] This amounted to a questioning of how labor within molecular biology was to be structured, with both Rechsteiner's and Syvanen's letters raising the possibility that eminent scientists would gain even greater control over state funds while young researchers' contribution would become, in terms of scientific recognition, increasingly meaningless. These thoughts would later be asserted forcefully in Rechsteiner's submission to Congressional hearings. After making clear that the HGP's proposed yearly budget could buy 1000 R01 investigator-led grants, offering a diverse and beneficial environment for graduate students and post-doctoral fellows, he warned that " . . . HGP centers will result in armies of technicians skilled only at obtaining DNA sequences and entering the results in computer data bases."[100] Importantly, R01 grants are the central mechanism through which decentralized, competitive health research funding had been maintained in the United States. But they were also the main vehicles through which scientists, both junior and senior, could achieve an (albeit short-term) autonomy to pursue their research interests. In Rechsteiner's thinking, the genome project constituted an altered mode of research autonomy, which would have a profoundly differential impact on the scientific community.

The second prominent source of controversy was found within criticism from Bernard Davis of Harvard—criticism that also found its way to Congressional hearings. Davis insisted that he spoke on behalf of a 'clear majority' in his department (Microbiology and Molecular Biology), and implied that he had the sympathy of large sections of the biomedical community. Similar to Rechsteiner and Syvanen, he voiced concerns in relation to whether the diversion of funds to a genome project was necessary or fair in a period of 'belt-tightening.' Davis argued that, "many people in biomedical science feel that this project needs serious reevaluation. The mapping is a repetitious, quasi-industrial program, which may indeed benefit from and need central organization. But whether it deserves the scale of funding that it now has, in competition with other things, is not so clear."[101] Again, the question of how labor in future biological research could be properly envisioned took center stage. It would not, ultimately, be Davis, Watson, Hood, or any other prominent biologist actually performing the bulk of labor necessary to complete the genome project. It was, however, precisely the impeccable credentials of Davis that make his public wariness and criticism so compelling for analysis. His public appearance meant that project advocates, if they were to downplay the weight of his criticisms (which were not entirely new in biology circles), would need to engage him politically and discursively, neutralizing his significance.

The most interesting element of the Davis testimony is an exchange between Senator Pete Domenici and Davis; the latter's political and professional isolation by Watson and Hood; and Davis' (professionally necessary) attempt to recover. Following Davis' initial remarks, Domenici, clearly having been briefed by the NIH, launched a surprisingly visceral attack at the HGP critic. After providing some counter-figures concerning funding cuts, asserting that the numbers of grants are down but that their size has grown considerably, Domenici proceeded to deliver a devastating political blow.

> [It] is very difficult, Dr. Davis, for me to explain how you can blame the genome initiative for the drop in the number of grants when last year with genome at $60 million it made up less than 1 percent of the entire $7.5 billion at NIH . . . But I am thoroughly amazed, Doctor, at how the biomedical community could oppose this project. I mean the obvious interdisciplinary requirements for capitalizing on technology and other science, when you merge them, is, for me essential . . . I cannot believe that you are going to insist on business as usual in this field. It is beyond my comprehension, I repeat, beyond my comprehension . . . [You] cannot sit here and tell me that in all of the research that is going on . . . that there is not more than $200 million, that if we even asked you to go look, you would say probably went for naught.[102]

Davis, for his own part, stood firm, insisting on the relevance of his claims and continuing with a somewhat less-than-total critique of the HGP.

> The problem is . . . if I were only presenting my own idiosyncratic point of view, I would feel properly chastened, but I would urge you not to underestimate the extent of unhappiness in the biomedical community over this issue . . . The members of the Public Affairs Advisory Committee of the American Society of Biochemistry endorse this

statement. And virtually all the members of my department and the faculty, endorse the statement that is going to appear in *Science* in a couple of weeks that is virtually identical with my written offering. There is great uneasiness over aspects of this program, and the notion that it somehow deserves to be a crash program, very generously funded, at a time when there is famine in other parts . . . There is also the failure to be convinced that from the sequence will emerge all these beautiful things that are promised. And that is why my last recommendation was that this be reevaluated by a committee involving leaders in a variety of areas that are using molecular genetics to advance their field . . .[103]

Following this, in a clear attempt to direct the outcome of debate, Domenici broke etiquette and gave the floor to Watson (who had already completed his testimony), soliciting a response to Davis' comments. Watson, an 'old friend' for whom Davis explicitly highlighted his 'highest respect,' offered a less than flattering opinion.

The genome project has been evaluated by several groups. One evaluation was conducted by the National Academy of Sciences. Maybe Dr. Davis can say it was biased. The National Academy that appointed a first-class committee, which came out with a unanimous opinion. Now, you can say do another evaluation and I would be willing, but I just have to say that I have listened for years to biochemists disliking DNA, and now I am hearing them say it again. In the case of Dr. Davis' department, I suspect it is a case of political orientation . . . I think if you put some things to a vote of people who are not trying to do things, they will often vote against you . . . [If] you expect to get a majority of people to try and do something new, they are going to say no. They are going to want to continue just going with the status quo.[104]

There is much in Watson's dismissal worth noting, especially his reduction of critics' concerns to petty jealousy and political orientation. In Davis' written supplemental, he refers to a petition, protesting the growth of the HGP, from the full faculty in Biochemistry/Biophysics and Biology at Texas A&M, which he notes is hardly, " . . . a hotbed of left-wing agitation."[105] Moreover, the capacity of Watson—as *the* American senior statesman of science—to reduce reasonably articulated criticism to a determined mediocrity, vested in self-satisfaction with the *status quo,* strategically spoke volumes to the experience of Washington-weathered Congressional members.

Certainly some of the most politically effective arguments being leveled at Davis were debatable. For instance, it remained unmentioned that the three committees invoked by Watson were deeply overlapping, containing a majority of elite scientists who were already proponents of the project.

Leroy Hood, who weighed in after Watson, claimed that the NAS committee had three committee members who were initially 'opposed' but came to support the project. As Michael Fortun points out, however, the meaning and significance of the term 'opposed' in this context remained unexplained. After all, Davis' own criticism stopped short of condemning the project's merits. And even if opposing members of the committee were thorough critics of the project (which they were not), " . . . that left twelve 'in favour'; four to one odds (with powerful figures like Watson and Hood among the majority) must have seemed pretty comfortable in those circumstances. Little wonder that the 'debating process' worked."[106] The asymmetrical power balance within the committee review process carried over to Congressional hearings, and, as the meeting was being closed by Domenici (who said point blank that he would do 'everything in his power' to make sure the project would be earmarked for funding), Davis almost certainly must have realized that the 'game was up.'

> May I make one more statement. I would not want it to appear on the record that I am opposing the program. I have questioned how its scale should be evaluated relative to the scale of other biomedical research and the fiscal problems that face us. But I stated plainly that every one of the goals of the project is something about which I am enthusiastic.[107]

Fortun interprets this final statement as a 'whimper,' but it is much more than that. The degree of power wielded by even this limited collection of eminent scientists and Congressional figures could not have escaped Davis' understanding. As the exchange made clear, individuals such as Rechsteiner and Davis could never mount the political effort of Watson or Hood, because they were not connected to structures of power in the same way. The latter could mobilize massive institutional affiliations (for example, the NIH) and extremely well placed figures of power (for example, Pete Domenici, Edward Kennedy, or James Wyngaarden) to their cause. Thus, in the closing moments of a highly visible meeting, as an eminent scientist also reliant on power structures for support, Davis literally could not *afford* to find himself publicly characterized as an HGP 'foe' (to say nothing of his likely considerations concerning the characterization and well being of his academic department).

The Davis testimony proves particularly interesting, because it represents a moment in which the dominant power of the state and disciplinary power (described by Foucault) worked in almost perfect rhythm. It is noteworthy that the overlapping imposition of this power—through a dismissal of the project's most significant scientific critic—revolved, in large part around the question of labor. On the level of state imposition, the process can be understood in the context of 'earmarking,' an increasingly popular legislative and budgetary procedure. Congressional 'earmarking' refers to a process by which scientific research funds are distributed such that they bypass peer review. The use of such funds has most certainly been on the rise, a trend beginning almost simultaneously with the emergence of biotechnology. Between 1980 and 1992, earmarking increased from $11 million to $708 million.[108] Traditionally, these were monies intended for building projects, but by 1992 a full 42 percent (a figure representing $300 million) was directed at research.[109] For its own part, not only did the genome project represent a more directed manner of distributing research funds, but it also supplied an outlet for the well-known Congressional frustration with the peer-review system.[110] For some, the frustration over the rise in this targeted research, as well as the large-scale characteristics of the HGP itself combined to present an image of state authorities and structures slowly reigning in, and wresting control of, the post-war academic scientific enterprise.

On a disciplinary level, scientists like Watson and Hood invoked a complementary use of discursive power to ensure that the contours of the HGP's design were not whittled away by criticism. Although proponents insisted that the project was neither heavily centralized nor 'big science,' the decision to bypass the structures of the R01 (peer-reviewed) grant system, while opting for an increasingly centralized and large research team approach, tended to squarely contradict these claims. In bureaucratic circles, Watson had already gone to battle with Ruth Kirschstein, Director of the NIGMS, over conflicting views on centralization. Kirschstein's support for a project oriented around an expansion of the existing R01 system was logical, in that individual grant holders in genetic research were her main political constituency. However

> [the] constituency favoring the genome project was, in contrast, many senior and powerful opinion leaders in molecular biology. Kirschstein's positions were cold comfort for them. The position that NIH was already committing hundreds of millions on genome research and the implied failure to distinguish gene hunting from global genome mapping undermined support for NIH leadership. . . . Kirschstein's position was aimed at preserving a strong base for undirected research. This put her in conflict with those, such as Watson, who argued that genetics now demanded a more deliberately planned and coordinated approach, with attention to technology development and completion of maps.[111]

In this aspect of project planning, Watson (helped by Walter Gilbert and Paul Berg) prevailed over Kirschstein. The grant system, they argued, simply would not coalesce into an organized and effective effort to map and sequence. On behalf of 'powerful opinion leaders,' Watson insisted that " . . . we have to build up around ten research centers, each with specific objectives, if we want to do this project in a reasonable period of time."[112] While at other moments advocates would have gladly praised the decentralized nature of the NIH's funding system, particularly when trying to play down any 'big science' conception of the HGP, the project critics' utilization of the same logic could not go unanswered. Thus, at a press conference six months after the Davis testimony, when Don Brown of Carnegie Institution criticized the HGP by emphasizing the time-honored and proven track record of R01 grants, Watson aggressively asserted that Brown should stop being, " . . . mystical about R01s. Most of them aren't that great anyway."[113] Such sideswipes of opponents went directly to the focal point of how future scientific labor was envisioned by project advocates, and they defused through professional discipline any serious political consideration of the concerns registered by Davis, Rechsteiner or Syvanen.

Overall, the role of the HGP in helping to reformulate acceptable notions of scientific work cannot be overlooked. Genome centers, modeled largely on the national laboratories run by the DOE, ultimately realized some of the critics' concerns. Early on in the planning process, Dr. George Bell of Los Alamos National Laboratories referred to the need for what he called " . . . sequencing factories, that is, places where the business in life is to determine sequences . . ."[114] More interestingly, he outlined a conventional approach to graduate student training in his laboratory:

> We employ six to eight graduate students, typically, for a year or two at a time, and they come and if they know something about computers, then they learn something about molecular biology in order to apply computer technology to organization of the data base. If they know something about biology, then they learn about computers. And when they return to graduate school or medical school or wherever they're going, they're very much in *demand as resources* who are familiar with the GenBank data base.[115]

Interpreting such a statement does not necessitate that we assume the conversion of promising students into mere automatons for data entry—that would be bald exaggeration. However, there is something poignant about the emphasis on training graduate students, such that their services would be 'in demand.' To be clear: it is not that their labor (at the moment or in the future) inherently lacked challenge, but rather it is to note the compatibility of such a system to widespread and circulating scientific service labor in numerous large public and corporate laboratories. In the case of the HGP, the developing normalization of such a laboratory structure intensified as the project proceeded. Particularly large centers were consolidated during the much-publicized 'race' with Celera and Craig Venter, as funding, centralization and output was streamlined into five prominent and productive centers (aptly named the 'G-5'). To offer one example, Eric Lander's Whitehead Institute Genome Center became" . . . the flagship of the U.S. genome effort, with Lander supervising an army of more than two hundred researchers and technicians."[116] Reinforced by the successful completion of the genome project, large research teams, under the management of prominent scientists, are now a well entrenched organizational dynamic. Recalling that complex mapping and data analysis projects, such as SNP analysis and 'proteomics,' are considered 'hot' research domains of the future, the increasing call for productive scientific labor is unlikely to subside.

CONCLUSION

In the context of molecular biology's emergence during the first half of the twentieth century, it would stretch credulity to claim that contemporary practice has not undergone distinct alterations. However, it would be simplistic to claim that the HGP alone has occasioned an atmosphere significantly different from that which produced the Asilomar process. Instead, the capacity for the molecular biology community to engage in self-regulation and, to a certain extent, self-critique (such as that during the 1970s) depended crucially on the unfettered and free circulation of scientific information. It also depended, to a certain extent, on the nominally disinterested position of most participating community members. As a matter of somewhat straightforward observation, available evidence concerning academic-industrial interaction leads to a conclusion that the 'playing field' for biologists has been considerably modified. The upper strata of prestigious scientists, those who have sizeable control over the distribution of both funds and credit in molecular biology, are increasingly interconnected in complex ways with capital, as well as other capital-friendly structures. Not only are their practices more likely to adapt to the social relations of contemporary capitalist production needs, but those with whom they interact must necessarily feel the imposition of that adaptation. As such, while Etzkowitz, Webster and Healy have asserted that there is an effective break from the mediaeval character of the university, they are careful also to state that ". . .the graduate student-professor relationship has yet to be revised from its feudal format, which extends virtually absolute faculty power over the student across the multiplicity of tasks that the latter's role has accrued, including generation of intellectual property."[117] The entrenched power relations between research professors and his/her 'apprentices' seems to have been reinforced in a manner which makes possible the effective use of 'old' structures for the satisfaction of new research goals.

This changed set of relations has *not* emerged merely *as a result of* the all-too-frequently mentioned 'entrepreneurial professor.' Yes, research scientists have become heavily involved in capital relations, but this has not happened in a neutral institutional or structural space. Instead, as the second section of this chapter has made clear, structures and discourse have been altered in such a way that the accumulative value of basic research, as well as practices which exploit that value, have been explicitly championed. Along the lines of Foucault's disciplinary scenario, commercially-related structures have been subjected to an evaluative shift in the domain of biology—no longer taboo, university departments fit neatly into new trajectories aimed at increasing institutional self-financing through value accumulation, nestled in a package of regional economic development. In the same vein, the HGP must be interpreted as part of the process whereby the alteration of 'macro' and 'micro' structures was affirmed. As a model of productivity in relation to basic (now valuable) scientific data, it was exemplary. It both reflected and enhanced changes in the character of scientific labor, through the encouragement of commercial linkages, centralization, and the productive use of non-economic (predominantly student-professor) research relationships. Tellingly, at least within the scientific community, it is increasingly difficult to exercise serious criticism of the now extensive genome research apparatus. To borrow terminology from Etzkowitz, Webster and Healy, the genome project constituted a set of endeavors that 'bridged the gap' between state/corporate economic goals and disciplinary rearrangements, and that allowed capitalist power relations to flow more freely at the scientific and institutional level.

Chapter Seven
Conclusion

There have been considerable efforts on the part of many HGP advocates to represent the project as both benign and clear-cut in its origins. When prompted by Michael Fortun, David Botstein simply could not contain his technologically deterministic understanding of genome science.

> [S]cientists for the most part, you see, are pragmatists. Science is driven completely by technology. Science is actually very rarely driven by abstract ideas . . . [The] genome project is also driven by technology. It's driven by the DNA sequencing—the DNA sequencing and the recombinant techniques made all biology possible—biology in the sense that the genes do things.[1]

Such offerings may serve the scientific community as a kind of shorthand history, but they function as only as a trivial form of historical analysis. There is, of course, no shortage of such off-handed analyses concerning contemporary biology, contributing to a prevailing discourse that accepts at face value the explanatory value of 'technological revolutions' or 'information societies.' They reproduce a peculiar image of technological inevitability, not as a product of social relationships, but as a natural outlet of human existence. As such, in attempting to *explain* the emergence of any current science or technology, such discourse often relies on the causal effects of some antecedent technological event. Intended or not, such circular and naturalizing explanations of scientific and technological advancement render a historical understanding that is effectively devoid of human agency.

On a general level, the burden of this work has been to contribute to a body of research that subjects science and technology to political and historical analysis. It builds on the critical work of authors such as Edward Yoxen, Martin Kenney, Sheldon Krimsky, Susan Wright, and Michael Fortun. In this regard, the HGP as a historical process proves to be a valuable study, because it demands an understanding of social relations between a broad range of actors, including scientists, pharmaceutical corporations, biotech firms, state agencies, legislative bodies, universities and, ultimately, citizens. The analysis of this work, grounded in political economy, has necessitated a historical appraisal of these predominant social actors, as well as the manner in which their interaction gave rise to the 'need' for a genome map in the first place. As such, it has situated rapid contemporary scientific and technological advance in its appropriate social setting, the drive by capital to find innovative, monopoly-protected shelter from the chronic pressure of capitalist competition. At a more specific level, the work has focused separately on three critical social components associated to the rise of the HGP: capital, the state, and the research community.

In the context of capital's behavior, the HGP must be seen as a constituent part of a general historical movement among interrelated capitals, especially those in the pharmaceutical and biotechnology sectors (agricultural and chemical sectors also play a visible but less significant role). Just as biotechnology development must be seen as a function of corporate needs among large research-based firms, so too was the HGP an instrumental springboard for both small and large capitals. Not only did the genome project greatly enhance their prospects and capacity for value accumulation, but it also provided a wealth of potential (monopoly-based) innovative outlets from the ravages of competitive capitalist developments. In this sense, the social relations giving rise to the HGP must be understood as fundamentally political. The pronounced interests of capitals as social agents, coalescing around both the HGP and the general development of biotechnology and genome-based science, related directly to a re-orientation of production systems and value distribution. Capitals did not merely 'react' to an emerging set of scientific and technological practices—they acted with intention, as effective social agents, operating politically within the historical parameters of capitalism. While many fascinating developments emerged (and will continue to emerge) from the HGP, these particular effects should not be confused with the underlying historical drive of the project: competitive capitals' need to enhance their potential for profit and strengthen their position within the contemporary expression of capitalism.

Importantly, capitals' agency to affect outcomes could occur only within the systemic features unique to capitalism. While a nominal political-economic divide constitutes one such feature, the necessity of political structures that *ultimately* ensure the reproduction and well being of economic relations remains ever-present. As chapter 5 made clear, extensive governmental involvement in the promulgation of the HGP cannot be interpreted as 'neutral' government policy, because it was deeply entwined with the state's historically shaped role as a facilitator of capital's needs. Importantly, the form of this facilitation was not predetermined, suggesting that the state constituted a space of active political struggle. The question of *whether* the HGP could emerge became deeply intertwined with struggles between potential controlling parties and the vested interests to which they were associated. The state constituted, in this regard, a political terrain open to contestation, but historically structured in a manner that was weighted in favor of capital's interests. An array of politically significant actors exhibited a capacity to steer state policy along lines conducive to innovation-based economic development while balancing these general concerns against the interests of specific capitals. Debates surrounding institutional responsibility (the NIH or the DOE?) were indicative of the struggle to ensure infrastructural support in a manner that optimally ensured capital's development. Similarly, moments of policy crisis, in which the viability of the HGP seemed subject to questioning, ultimately revealed a heightened awareness among relevant agencies concerning the need for a proactive state role. In both instances of policy controversy, state behavior was strategically directed toward ensuring the commercial value of the HGP for the broadest possible cross-section of capital. Similarly, this strategic orientation was (and continues to be) reproduced at the international level. Prominent capitals were actively able to shape an agenda concerning intellectual property that ensured the potential for an expanding worldwide market in monopoly protected biomedical (and other high-tech) commodities.

Finally, the social relations of the research community, as well as the institutional structures in which it operates, also conditioned the emergence of the HGP. Here, the utilization of Foucault's analysis, particularly in relation to political economy, highlights the fact that neither biotechnology nor genome research can be solely understood as a top-down extension of capital and state interests. At the same time, it would be equally misleading to understand them as the product of putatively selfish scientists. Rather, institutional structure and professional discipline has helped to mould behavior more conducive to the 'productive' elements of the HGP, as well as biotechnology more generally. A changing institutional environment—particularly at the university level—has enabled the reformation of molecular biology into large research teams, which are increasingly connected to supportive capitals. The altered scientific practice that has resulted, so well attested to in empirical studies, helps to frame the particular character of the HGP as a collection of scientific undertakings. The struggle to mount the project, in part, revolved around the issue of exactly what constituted legitimate, productive, and challenging scientific practice. Tellingly, criticism of the HGP, particularly concerning its effects on scientific labor, in no way seriously affected the political outcome. The formulation and goals of the HGP, supported both within political institutions (Congress, the NIH, the DOE) and among senior scientists (Watson, Berg, Gilbert, Hood, etc.), were defended and enforced structurally and discursively in the face of any meaningful challenge.

Drawing these areas of concern together, the conclusion of this work must be two-fold. First, however innocently or even as a matter of shorthand, *it is misleading and problematic to refer to the HGP as a project stemming out of either the necessary progression of knowledge or existing technological imperatives.* While these factors may indeed play a role, their causal invocation, very often without explanatory context, obscures our understanding the HGP's emergence, allowing for little more than reactionary historical and political analysis. Second, and more significantly, a historical understanding should properly situate the HGP as *a project necessitated by a historically specific expression of capitalist social relations, reflective of a particular logic of motion and operative within corporate, state and institutional terrains.* To some, this may seem an all-encompassing explanation rooted in so-called economic determinism. However, this would amount to a seriously flawed rendition of Marxist historical analysis. In fact, the very concept of "economy" cannot be disassociated from a range of political and institutional *struggles* that bring about material outcomes, mostly—but not always—beneficial for current, historically-bound, structures of capitalist value accumulation. Along these lines, history cannot be understood to proceed mechanically, but rather as a 'structured process'—at every stage, structure is susceptible in one way or another to both contestation and support. Nonetheless, it is difficult to overlook the shape of the current historical juncture, in which capitalist structures and those agents who support them possess enormous staying power. The historical tenacity of capitalist social relations must, at least in part, be attributed to a systemic tendency to continuously find 'outlets' in which the accumulation process can regenerate and grow. The burden of this work has been to point out that the HGP's emergence in the United States is directly embedded in—indeed, it is a product of—this systemic tendency.

Given its historical and explanatory understanding of *why* and *how* the HGP emerged, this work most certainly gives rise a range of critical implications. Areas of concern might include the questionable benefits and motives of corporately driven genome research; the degree of responsibility of attributable to scientists; and the efficacy of bioethical criticism. This discussion does not purport to be the final word on these issues but, instead, is intended to segue future analysis.

It has been aim of this work to explain the not-so-obvious connections between actors and structures within industrial, state and institutional spheres, and how they can be understood within the logic of motion of capitalism. An important implication of this is the underlying support for critical evaluations of the tightly knit dynamics between capital, biotechnology and genome research. It cannot be emphasized enough that capital urges on the need for publicly supported research, such as that offered through the HGP, while contending that the ever-spiraling price of resulting commodities remains justified, due to the exorbitant current costs (and 'risk') of R&D. The push for patenting monopoly on genetic material is bolstered by precisely this logic—the beneficial effects of which on the delivery of healthcare are in no way clear.[2] In this regard, even if one were to put aside the fact that these corporations spend twice the overhead on marketing that they do on R&D, it remains a fact that

> [t]he ten American pharmaceutical companies in the Fortune 500 list [in 2001] ranked far above all other American industries in average net return, whether as a percentage of revenues (18.5 percent), of assets (16.3 percent) or of shareholder's equity (33.2 percent). (For comparison, the median net return for other industries was only 3.3 percent of revenues.) And this has generally been the case for the past two decades. A business consistently this profitable cannot by any stretch of language be described as 'risky' or as needing special protection of its revenues.[3]

There is, moreover, a strong argument to be made that the pharmaceutical and biotechnology industries greatly exaggerate both the cost and medical significance of their research and development. On the former, the reported cost estimates between $800 million and $1 billion per successful drug are highly contestable. These figures are dependent on estimations evaluated with very high 'opportunity costs of capital'; do not account for the fact that many successful drugs are researched in the non-profit sector, before corporations ever invest anything; and leave aside the many tax benefits, government clinical sponsorship, and 'fast-track' approval methods placed on 'orphan drugs' (approximately half the drugs in the R&D pipeline).[4]

In the face of this extraordinary growth and overestimated cost within the health industry, it remains anything but clear that the intensive investment in genome research will bring about the expected degree of biomedical benefits. These potential benefits formed one of the principal justifications for the HGP (and biotechnology more generally), and the results of genome research have been widely touted as the doorway to a health 'revolution.' And yet with the increasing weight of the health industry comes the concomitant observation that market mechanisms do not always effectively differentiate between medical need and commodity exchange. In this sense, the commercial explosion supported by the HGP may indeed be driving research in a direction that is less than optimal from the standpoint of medical progress. It is worth restating the fact that

> . . . only 12 of the 348 drugs introduced by the twenty-five largest pharmaceuticals between 1981 and 1991 were considered therapeutic advances by the FDA. The vast majority—84 percent—were viewed as having little or no potential for advances in treatment. In stark contrast, 70 percent of the drugs that have substantial therapeutic gain are produced with government involvement and up to half of the most promising AIDS and cancer drugs are concocted in government or university labs.[5]

Even in the wake of the HGP, this trend appears to have continued.

> Over the twelve-year period beginning in 1990, 1,035 drugs were approved, and of these only 23 percent were classified as likely to be a 'significant improvement' on products already on the market. (In our own judgment as physicians, even many of these drugs would be more accurately described as modest, incremental improvements.) All the others were classified as appearing to have 'therapeutic qualities similar to those of one or more already marketed drugs.' Moreover, just 15 percent of the approved drugs were classified as both a significant improvement and an NME [new molecular entity]. Last year, the FDA approved 66 drugs for the entire drug industry. The agency classified only ten as a significant improvement, and only seven of these were NMEs. So the already small percentage of newly marketed drug products that are really novel and important seems to be dropping still further, with me-too's [sic] becoming the rule.[6]

The advances in genome research have undoubtedly contributed, and will continue to contribute, to the development of these commercial (applied) research trajectories. Systemically, the health industry depends for its livelihood on the illness 'market,' and is predominantly inspired to privilege treatment over cure. This is not to say that medically beneficial products will disappear, but industry's overwhelming focus on 'me-too' products within already existing therapeutic classes will almost certainly not deliver the much-heralded 'gold mine' of therapeutically new drugs ostensibly made possible through genome research. In line with the logic of capitalist production, the pharmaceutical and biotechnology industries engage in the production of therapeutic advances only insofar as the latter can be reasonably expected to serve profitability. As the cases of human growth hormone, human insulin and tissue plasminogen activator demonstrate, 'advance' can be defined in very problematic ways.

Here, political economy serves as a foundation toward a more complete evaluative framework. Without a critical assessment of the widespread, socially derived pressure toward innovation resident in capitalist societies, such evaluations fail to register some of the factors that drive genome research in the first place. Similarly, to effect serious change in the trajectory of genome research would require that we rethink far more than just 'regulation' of ongoing events in the biomedical sphere. In the case of U.S. genome research, such change would mean that the benevolent nature of capitalist production in relation to biomedical goods should not be assumed—that is, the trajectory of science and technology would need to be re-subjected to an explicitly political (and social) agenda. Unfortunately, such a radical reorientation of American (or any advanced industrial) political culture seems, in the post-HGP period, extremely unlikely.

Nonetheless, given the unlikelihood of such a process, political economy can still tell us something about the social values that advanced industrial societies might be prepared to alter. Along the lines of critical political economy, 'demand' reveals little about why genome research has accelerated systemically over the last two decades, but it may speak volumes as to why, socially, it would prove very difficult to disengage. There is a legitimate argument that advanced capitalist societies have become overly medicalized cultures, and that access (however unequal) to innovative biomedical products is now highly cherished.[7] Indeed, a notion of health has come to prevail, in which the *purpose of* and *justification for* biomedical commodification is almost automatically assumed to be human wellness. But as one eminent molecular biologist, Erwin Chargaff, recently bristled, "[w]e've turned into such outrageous whiners. Just as humans are not born to be rich, they're not born to be healthy. Health is nice, but it's not an argument. People live longer now, but how do they live longer? And why?"[8] The identification of biomedical research practices, which are both therapeutically significant and *socially valuable* (in a 'use value' sense), turns out to be no easy task. Although political economy can point to both blatant and subtle contradictions between societal needs and basic research as a tool of economic development, it cannot easily delineate where the legitimate concern for individual and public health ends and the systemic imperative for value accumulation begins. However, if we track the core capitalist, state and institutional dynamics that infuse genome research, we gain at least a chance of further understanding how and where exchange value becomes the predominant motivator for resulting therapeutic trajectories. As such, we may come one step closer to differentiating socially significant research from the capitalist imperative of value accumulation, and genuine healthcare from the 'healthcare industry.'

Political economy is also useful for constructively steering us away from problematic social criticism related to genome research. One such form of social criticism has been aimed directly at the scientific community. Since the rise of biotechnology in the early 1980s, there has been a suggestion—sometimes subtle, sometimes explicit—that scientists bear a special moral responsibility to inhibit any dangerous or reckless uses of scientific knowledge. Whether aimed at scientists as a collective body or especially visible individuals, such criticism usually calls on researchers to pay special attention to the content and consequences of their practice.[9] UNESCO's much publicized *Science Agenda—Framework for Action,* for instance, emphasized that the sciences " . . . must be put to work for sustainable peace and development in a progressively responsive and democratic framework," and that scientists " . . . must correspondingly recognize their ethical, social and political responsibilities."[10] It is certainly fair to emphasize that scientists should consider the consequences of their work. However, with regard to the dominant set of social relations affecting biotechnology and genome research, it is deeply problematic to place an undue degree of ethical responsibility for the consequences of fast-paced, innovative science only the shoulders of scientists. American (and other) genome researchers operate under the same broad set of social parameters as any other member of a capitalist society. To expect scientists to extract themselves from this set of relations, and somehow establish a special moral horizon, while other members of society thrive off and exacerbate the tremendous productive power of capitalism is unrealistic, unfair and not very fruitful.

Similarly, given the privileged position it held in relation to the genome project (through creation of ELSI), there is a need to query the efficacy of 'bioethics' as an independent means of social commentary *vis-à-vis* either biotechnology or genome research. There are, of course, differences among various bioethical positions, ranging from conventionally understood bioethical perspectives to somewhat more critical variants. The former largely assume the progressive introduction of scientific and technological goals into society and are concerned with how to understand and regulate their consequences. As one prominent bioethicist states with respect to the HGP, the " . . . ethical debate must focus on how to use the new information, rather than on whether to discover it, if for no other reason than inevitability. It is pointless to bury our heads in the sand, as the knowledge will come . . . The question is how to use it properly."[11] There is a grain of truth in this perspective—the rapid progress of genome research will clearly demand society's forethought in relation its widespread uses. Nonetheless, it is a weakly conceived ethical position not so much because of its specter of inevitability, but because it exhibits a naïve understanding of how knowledge operates in society. At least in western societies, where health is becoming a dominant focal point for personal and social identity, emerging genome knowledge will have its own regulatory effect on individual and social expectation. Wrapped up intricately with the powerful social relations associated to capitalist production, it is highly likely that individuals will feel an increasing pressure to 'know themselves,' demand genome-based information in multiple areas of concern, and act on it in the name of their own health and identity. Under these circumstances, ethical perspectives and conceptions of the 'permissible' are not a stable 'given'—rather, they are constantly subject to the pressures of capital's production and market goals and the subsequent reinforcement of highly medicalized social expectations.

More critical bioethical approaches are less ambivalent about the progressive nature of science and technology, but they still tend to leave fundamental interrogations of genome science, and particularly its economic functions, out of the picture. It is important to note that this literature is successful in pointing to numerous social, ethical and legal conundrums associated to either real or potential scientific practices.[12] However, much of this has been "the domain of ethicists and lawyers whose theoretical and conceptual frameworks comes from their own disciplines . . . Its tone is reasoned, scholarly and largely, although not entirely, apolitical."[13] Without any systematic analysis of how to characterize the major determinants that underpin the progression of genome science, such perspectives remain reactionary and conjectural in scope, both intellectually and politically. Here, even sophisticated understandings of the connection between the social world and the potential effects of genetic knowledge can lead to simplistic solutions. One commentator notes, in relation to the diagnostic knowledge already being garnered by the HGP, that primary care providers will now be 'gatekeepers' of socially-sensitive knowledge, and that they must be " . . . prepared to 'close the gate' on genetic testing that is inappropriate or misused."[14] While this thinking minimally turns away from the notion of 'inevitability,' the unrealistic degree to which it places disinterestedness and restraint on the shoulders of primary workers is striking. This individualized, after-the-fact 'solution' reinforces the notion that "[b]ioethics is an excuse to allow everything that is unethical," and it is fails to pay heed to the socially constructed aspect of bioethical positions.[15] Here, a failure to address directly the socially pervasive and dramatic effects of capitalist underpinnings in genome science translates into perspectives that overlook major factors effecting and altering ethical boundaries—even for healthcare providers. Indeed, as recent events have indicated, the activities and judgement of bioethicists have, due to their heightened role stemming from the HGP, been vulnerable to extraordinary social pressure and influence.[16]

The manner in which the HGP is historicized—on both an intellectual and a political level—will almost certainly manifest itself in the social effects associated to the project's existence. Prevailing explanations of its purpose and goals as primarily biomedical (and altruistic) in nature will, undoubtedly, give rise to passive social acceptance of the majority of ensuing (and related) biomedical technologies. In contrast, an explanation of the project grounded in political economy constitutes a valuable first step in the path toward a more complete analysis of 'health' in advanced industrial societies. Such analysis will estimate, more systematically, the purposes for which genome research is likely to be engaged by predominant social actors (state, capital, institutions), as well as the historical trajectories that could conceivably follow. The demonstration that genome research is intricately tied to the systemic imperatives of value accumulation, resident in capitalism, places in serious doubt any blanket explanation of such research as immanently virtuous. Similarly, analyses that examine the political effects of genome research on personal identity, healthcare culture and any future regulatory structures will need to be continuously cognizant of the manner in which capitalist social relations permeate these other spheres.[17] A range of new genome-based medical choices (in the way of treatments) will not necessarily be synonymous with an enhancement of the human condition, individual health or the well being of societies. Political economy should, therefore, play a vital role in attempting to extricate the most genuinely useful set of practices from those that are based on overtly non-medical imperatives. It must remain front and center in our historical understanding of the HGP, in order to sift through future ethical and political decisions in a manner that depends on a realistic and socially based set of criteria.

Notes

NOTES TO CHAPTER ONE

1. A mere sliver of the reaction and commentary includes: Daniel E. Koshland, "Sequences and consequences of the human genome," *Science* 246, no.4927 (1989): 189; Leslie Roberts, "Report card on the genome project," *Science* 253, no.5018 (1991): 376; Robert Bohrer, "Future Fall-Out From The Genetic Revolution," *Futures* 24 (1992): 681–8; "The proper study of mankind," *Economist,* September 14, 1996, 19–21; Anne Gearan, "Clinton finds inspiration in Human Genome Project," *Globe and Mail,* December 25, 1999, A1; Margaret Munro, "The moon walk of medicine," *National Post,* March 13, 2000, www.nationalpost.com/content/features/genome/0313001.html; Andy Coghlan, "Land of Opportunity," *New Scientists* 168, no.2263 (2000): 30.
2. James D. Watson, "The human genome project: past, present and future," *Science* 248, no.4951 (1990): 45.
3. Here we might consider, additionally, large-scale projects that have been unable to proceed, such as Supersonic Transport and NASA's proposed mission to Mars.
4. In relation to genome science, some examples would include: Thomas Lee, *Gene Future: The Promise and Peril of the New Biology* (New York: Plenum, 1993); Jerry E. Bishop and Michael Waldholz, *Genome: The Story of the Most Astonishing Scientific Adventure of Our Time—The Attempt to Map All the Genes in the Human Body* (New York: Simon and Schuster, 1990); Jeff Lyon and Peter Gorner, *Altered Fates: Gene Therapy and the Retooling of Human Life* (New York: W.W. Norton, 1996).
5. R.K. Merton, *The Sociology of Science: theoretical and empirical investigations* (Chicago: University of Chicago Press, 1973). On a glaring contradiction of Mertonian norms in relation to the hydrogen bomb, see William J. Broad, "Who Built the H-Bomb? Debate Revives," *New York Times,* April 24, 2001, F1.
6. Examples of this might include: Andrew Kimbrell, *The Human Body Shop: The Engineering and Marketing of Life* (San Francisco: Harper Collins); Jeremy Rifkin, *The Biotech Century: Harnessing the Gene and Remaking the World* (New York: Putnam, 1998).
7. Rifkin, *The Biotech Century,* p.1.

8. Robert Cook-Deegan, *The Gene Wars: Science, Politics, and the Human Genome* (New York: W.W. Norton & Company, 1995).

9. Cook-Deegan, *The Gene Wars*, p.11, emphasis added.

10. Cook-Deegan's analysis might best be compatible with the explanatory framework suggested by Bruno Latour. In Latour's thinking, explaining the emergence of science and technology requires only the description of all possible linkages between its deployment and social agents. In attempting to understand the *why* of technological development, " . . . we have no need to look for additional causes. The explanation emerges once the description is saturated. . . . If something is missing it is because the description is not complete." See Bruno Latour, "Technology is society made durable," in *A Sociology of Monsters: Essays on Power, Technology and Domination*, ed. John Law (London: Routledge, 1991), 129–30; see also *Science in Action* (Cambridge, MA: Harvard University Press, 1987).

11. Other authors in this category might include: Stephanie Yanchinski, *Setting Genes to Work: The Industrial Era of Biotechnology* (New York: Viking Penguin, 1985); Michael Fortun, "The Human Genome Project and the Acceleration of Biotechnology," in *Private Science: Biotechnology and the Rise of the Molecular Sciences*, ed. Arnold Thackray (Philadelphia: University of Pennsylvania Press, 1998), 182–201.

12. Besides Krimsky and Kenney, other authors in this group might include: Evelyn Fox Keller, *Refiguring Life: Metaphors of Twentieth-Century Biology* (New York: Columbia University Press, 1995); Jonathan King, "The Biotechnology Revolution: Self-Replicating Factories and the Ownership of Life Forms," in *Cutting Edge: Technology, Information, Capitalism and Social Revolution*, eds. Jim Davis, Thomas Hirschl and Michael Stack (London: Verso, 1997), 145–56; Frederick Buttel, "Biotechnology: An Epoch-Making Technology," in *The Biotechnology Revolution?* eds. Martin Fransman, Gerd Junne and Annemieke Roobeek (Oxford: Blackwell, 1995), 25–45. Of special importance is also Michael Fortun's unpublished dissertation on the HGP. However, while it provides a considerable degree of information (see particularly chapters 5 and 6), it is more concerned with the problem of 'historical narrative' than any historical account of the HGP's primary motivating forces. See Michael Fortun, "Mapping and making genes and histories: The genomics project in the United States, 1980–1990," (Ph.D. diss., Harvard University, 1993).

13. Given the frequent references to rDNA research methods below, it is worth supplying the reader with a basic description. Recombinant DNA research involves the splicing of foreign DNA into an organism's local DNA. The intent is to achieve the expression of the foreign DNA within the organism's molecular mechanisms. For example, the organism may begin to produce a specifically desired protein, which it would otherwise not produce naturally.

14. Sheldon Krimsky, *Biotechnics and Society: The Rise of Industrial Genetics* (New York: Praeger, 1991), 23. For Krimsky's earlier work, which is of substantial importance in the next chapter, see *Genetic Alchemy: The Social History of the Recombinant DNA Controversy* (Cambridge, MA: MIT University Press, 1982).

15. Despite his own exploration of the blurred boundaries between research institutions, state programs and corporate industrialization, Krimsky determines that commercial exploitation can be regulated by the mere rearticulation of state and institutional policies. He conveys his " . . . belief that industrial America, through its experience with the atomic age, hazardous chemicals, ecological degradation, and occupational hazards, can draw upon the collective wisdom of largely well-intentioned people and guide biotechnology through a path safer than that of previous technological revolutions of a similar transforming character." At the heart of this is Krimsky's problematic separation of institutional-political regulation and economic processes. Within this conceptualization, the latter sphere is invaded by the reality of genome research while the norms of the former are then reconfigured accordingly. In other words, the more realistic possibility that three kinds of activity—scientific, economic and political/regulatory— are exerted in mutually constitutive and enforcing ways loses its tenability. See Krimsky, *Biotechnics and Society,* p.16.

16. Martin Kenney, *Biotechnology: The University-Industrial Complex* (New Haven: Yale University Press, 1986), 3.

17. For samples of both, see Joseph Schumpeter, *Business Cycles: A Theoretical, Historical and Statistical Analysis of the Capitalist Process* (New York: McGraw-Hill, 1939); Ernest Mandel, *Late Capitalism* (London: Verso, 1978).

18. For instance, a later paper by Kenney posits knowledge-innovation strategies as an expression of capitalist value-appropriation. Unfortunately, this paper never explicitly applies such a framework to genome science, and a subsequent paper on biotechnology seems to revert back to an Schumpeterian perspective. See Martin Kenney, "Value Creation in the Late Twentieth Century: the Rise of the Knowledge Worker" in *Cutting Edge: Technology, Information, Capitalism and Social Revolution,* eds. Jim Davis, Thomas Hirschl And Michael Stack (London: Verso, 1997), 87–102; "Biotechnology and a New Economic Space," in *Private Science: Biotechnology and the Rise of the Molecular Sciences,* ed. Arnold Thackray (Philadelphia: University of Pennsylvania Press, 1998), 131–43.

19. Kenney, *Biotechnology,* p.7.

20. Jordan Mejias, "Research Always Runs the Risk of Getting Out of Control (Interview with Erwin Chargaff)," *Frankfurter Allgemeine Zeitung* (English ed.), June 4, 2001, www.faz.com.

NOTES TO CHAPTER TWO

1. There are, of course, exceptions to this rule, particularly in the areas of bioethics, science, technology and society, and legal studies.

2. In setting up her work on the industrial utilization of genetic research, Stephanie Yanchinski selects the rediscovery of Mendel's research as the moment that " . . . was to verify scientifically that the transmission of inherited traits rests on discrete units we now call genes, and that the process is predictable." This is followed up by a string of scientific accomplishments,

which make the move to recombinant DNA research possible in the early 1970s. See Stephanie Yanchinski, *Setting Genes to Work: The Industrial Era of Biotechnology* (New York: Viking Penguin, 1985), 30–44.

3. Lily Kay, "Problematizing Basic Research in Molecular Biology," in *Private Science: Biotechnology and the Rise of the Molecular Sciences,* ed. Arnold Thackray (Philadelphia: University of Pennsylvania Press, 1998), 21.

4. Particularly good in this regard are works by Robert E. Kohler, "The Management of Science: The Experience of Warren Weaver and the Rockefeller Foundation Programme in Molecular Biology," *Minerva* 14 (1976): 279–306; Edward Yoxen, "Life as a Productive Force: Capitalising the Science and Technology of Molecular Biology," in *Science, Technology and the Labor Process*, eds. Les Levidow and Bob Young (London: CSE Books, 1981): 66–102; Angela Creager, "Biotechnology and Blood: Edwin Cohn's Plasma Fractionation Project, 1940–1953," in *Private Science: Biotechnology and the Rise of the Molecular Sciences,* ed. Arnold Thackray (Philadelphia: University of Pennsylvania Press, 1998): 39–62. Outside of biology, see David Noble, *America By Design: Science, Technology, and the Rise of Corporate Capitalism* (London: Oxford University Press, 1977).

5. Kohler, "The Management of Science," p.281. Kohler is quoting the following document from the Rockefeller Foundation Archives: AF.900.22.168. Agenda for Meeting, 11 April, 1933, 61–5. Kohler's extremely informative primary research on the managerial approach of the Foundation necessarily forms the basis for any discussion of pre-war biological research.

6. Kohler, "The Management of Science," p.288.

7. Kohler, "The Management of Science," p.298.

8. Creager, "Biotechnology and Blood," p.46.

9. Martin Kenney, *Biotechnology: The University-Industrial Complex* (New Haven: Yale University Press, 1986), 13.

10. Yoxen, "Life as a Productive Force," p.94.

11. Kenny, *Biotechnology,* pp.16–9; Yoxen, "Life as a Productive Force," p.95.

12. Yoxen, "Life as a Productive Force," p.95.

13. Kay, "Problematizing Basic Research," p.34.

14. Yoxen, "Life as a Productive Force," pp.105–6.

15. Sheldon Krimsky, *Genetic Alchemy: The Social History of the Recombinant DNA Controversy* (Cambridge, MA: MIT University Press, 1982), 85–7. Krimsky's authority on this debate derives largely from his in-depth research and elucidation of the material in MIT's archival collection on the rDNA debate. As his rendition of events is both thorough and compelling, I rely heavily on his depiction of this period.

16. Krimsky, *Genetic Alchemy,* p.151.

17. Krimsky, *Genetic Alchemy,* p.110.

18. An expression of the general principles, presented by Maxine Singer of the RAC, quoted by Krimsky, *Genetic Alchemy,* p.182.

19. Krimsky, *Genetic Alchemy,* p.198.

20. Krimsky, *Genetic Alchemy,* p.330.

21. Philip Handler, then President of the National Academy of Sciences, quoted in Susan Wright, "Molecular Politics in a Global Economy," ed. Arnold Thackray, *Private Science: Biotechnology and the Rise of the Molecular Sciences* (Philadelphia: University of Pennsylvania Press, 1998), 91.

22. Sherwood Gorbach, quoted in Krimsky, *Genetic Alchemy*, p.216, emphasis added.

23. Indeed, according to Wright, "the meeting reached consensus on the need for further experimental work to address these questions. Nevertheless, what reached the wider scientific community and the public through the circulation of the summary report written by the conference chair was an essentially soothing view that *E coli* K12 was incapable of pathogenic transformation. As a *New York Times* headline put it: 'No Sci-Fi Nightmare After All.'" See Wright, "Molecular Politics," p.88.

24. Wright, "Molecular Politics," p.90

25. Protocol for risk-experiments, quoted in Krimsky, *Genetic Alchemy*, pp.255–6, emphasis added.

26. Krimsky, *Genetic Alchemy*, p.258.

27. Krimsky makes the claim that *Science* tends to remain in accord with the interests of the NIH, because its editorial review board has a great deal of overlap and relation with the NIH. The paper was later published in the journal *Nature*. See Krimsky, *Genetic Alchemy*, p.259.

28. Sinsheimer, quoted in Krimsky, *Genetic Alchemy*, p.265.

29. Erwin Chargaff, quoted in Krimsky, *Genetic Alchemy*, p.267.

30. Krimsky, *Genetic Alchemy*, p.272.

31. Kenney, *Biotechnology*, p.25.

32. Sheldon Krimsky, "Regulating Recombinant DNA Research," *Controversy: Politics of Technical Decisions*, ed. D. Nelkin (London: Sage, 1979), 237.

33. Some reject even the suggestion that industrial pressures had any significance before the 1990s. Dr. Charles Cantor, famous for his development of DNA sequencing techniques, recently stated that there is nothing to the argument that commercial motives play any serious role in the development of genome sciences. His rather anecdotal evidence consists of an inability, along with Walter Gilbert, to find a commercial outlet for their research in the 1980s. Charles Cantor, "Introductory Remarks," (paper presented at Human Genome Project: Commercial Implications, San Francisco, May, 1999).

34. Susan Wright, "The Social Warp of Science: Writing the History of Genetic Engineering Policy," *Science, Technology and Human Values* 18, no.1 (1993): 79–101.

35. Wright, "The Social Warp of Science," p.96.

36. Wright, "Molecular Politics in a Global Economy," p.92.

37. Martin Kenney, "Biotechnology and a New Economic Space," *Private Science: Biotechnology and the Rise of the Molecular Sciences*, ed. Arnold Thackray (Philadelphia: University of Pennsylvania Press, 1998), 137; Kenney, *Biotechnology*, p.140.

38. Daniel J. Fairbanks and W. Ralph Anderson, *Genetics: The Continuity of Life* (Toronto: Brooks/Cole Publishing, 1999), 95.

39. The story of the manner in which David Botstein and Ronald Davis seem to have literally stumbled on this method, by way of a graduate student workshop, is outlined in Jerry E. Bishop and Michael Waldholz, *Genome: The Story of the Most Astonishing Scientific Adventure of Our Time—The Attempt to Map All the Genes in the Human Body* (New York: Simon and Schuster, 1990), 49–68. Legend has it that, when a graduate student expressed dissatisfaction with the lack of markers available on the human genome, Botstein and Davis looked at each other with the simultaneous recognition that RFLPs could be used to do precisely this and that its wider ramifications were immense.

40. Robert Cook-Deegan, *The Gene Wars: Science, Politics, and the Human Genome* (New York: W.W. Norton & Company, 1995), 37.

41. For an interesting discussion of such cloning mechanisms, as well as problems with recent constructions, see Christopher Anderson, "Genome shortcut leads to problems," *Science* 259, no. 5102 (1993): 1684–8.

42. PCR, or polymerase chain reaction, credited to Kerry Mullis, was developed in the Cetus Corporation during the mid–1980s. The process uses different temperature cycles to induce DNA polymerases to replicate DNA. By repeating these cycles, it is possible to obtain exponential reproduction of exact segments of DNA. See Fairbanks and Anderson, *Genetics: The Continuity of Life,* pp.277–8. For the story of PCR's development, see Paul Rabinow, *Making PCR: A Story of Biotechnology* (Chicago: University of Chicago Press, 1996).

43. "Briefing on DNA Sequencing: Methods and Applications," *Futuretech,* May 21, 2001, 3.

44. R. Waterston, J.E. Sulston, "Human Genome Project: reaching the finish line," *Science* 282, no.5386 (1998): 53–4.

45. J. Craig Venter, Mark D. Adams, "Shotgun sequencing of the human genome," *Science* 280, no.5369 (1998): 1540–3.

46. On the Drosophila project, see Leslie Roberts, "The lords of the flies," *U.S. News & World Report* 127, no.11 (1999): 52.

47. Waterston and Sulston, "Human Genome Project," p.54.

48. See, for instance, Dorothy Nelkin, "The Social Power of Genetic Information," and Evelyn Fox-Keller, "Nature, Nurture, and the Human Genome Project," in *The Code of Codes: Scientific and Social Issues in the Human Genome Project,* eds. Daniel J. Kevles and Leroy Hood (Cambridge, MA: Harvard University Press, 1992), 177–90, 281–99; Ruth Hubbard, "Genomania and health: arguments against genetic prediction," *American Scientist* 83, no.1 (1995): 8–11.

49. Amy Harman, "In New Tests for Fetal Defects, Agonizing Choices," *New York Times,* June 20, 2004, Health Section.

50. This has been explored, for instance, in Barbara Katz Rothman, *Genetic Maps and Human Imaginations: The Limits of Science in Understanding Who We Are* (New York: W.W. Norton, 1998).

51. Deborah Stone has made a very compelling argument concerning the futility of public regulation access to personal genomic information. She points out, quite rightly, that there can be no question of restraining insurance

companies and employers concerning their disposition towards this knowl-edge, given the present structure and practices related to medical insurance in the United States. See: Deborah Stone, "The Implications of the Human Genome Project for Access to Health Insurance," *The Human Genome Project and the Future of Health Care*, eds. Thomas H. Murray, Mark A. Rothstein, and Robert F. Murray, Jr. (Indianapolis, Indiana University Press, 1996), 133–57.

52. Miller Freeman, "Biopharmaceuticals increase their share of the market," *Manufacturing Chemist* 68, no.2 (1997): 28–9.

53. While Congress passed legislation in 1990 prohibiting the use of hGH on those without a 'recognized disease,' the interpretation of medical deficien-cies is a very fluid one. Eli Lilly has proposed the use of hGH being applied to the 3 percent of children with the lowest height in the US population. Of course, this is a self-perpetuating category and represents a guaranteed mar-ket for the company. For the other questions concerning hGH, including its dubious 'deficiency' in small children and the potential hazards of its long-term use, see Andrew Kimbrell, *The Human Body Shop: The Engineering and Marketing of Life* (San Francisco: Harper Collins), 142–57.

54. The ongoing public debate concerning stem-cell research is, of course, re-lated to the prospects for germ-line therapy. While embryonic stem cells are being explored for a variety of medical applications, the knowledge derived will be of considerable interest to those interested in delivering germ-line therapies.

55. The story of this process can be read in Jeff Lyon and Peter Gorner, *Altered Fates: Gene Therapy and the Retooling of Human Life* (New York: W.W. Norton, 1996).

56. See, for instance, Eric Grace, "Better health through gene therapy," *The Futurist* 32, no.1 (1998): 39–43; C. Thomas Caskey, "DNA-Based Medicine: Prevention and Therapy," *The Code of Codes: Scientific and Social Issues in the Human Genome Project*, eds. Daniel J. Kevles and Leroy Hood (Cambridge, MA: Harvard University Press, 1992), 112–35.

57. "Overview: Prospects for Germline Gene Therapy," UCLA Center for the Study of Evolution and the Origin of Life, 1998, www.ess.ucla/huge/frames19.html. The results of gene therapy trials have been 'disappoint-ing' over the course of the 1990s, but recent cases of success are emerg-ing, causing a considerable degree of excitement in the scientific community. An informative source on this topic is *BBC Online* (www.bbc.co.uk). For a small sample, see: "Scientists quarrel over gene therapy," *BBC Online*, November 10, 1999; "Hundreds of gene therapy experiments failed," *BBC News Online*, February 1, 2000; "Surprise gene therapy a success," *BBC Online*, March 2, 2000; "Gene therapy frees 'bubble babies,'" *BBC Online*, April 27, 2000; "Gene therapy cancer treatment success," *BBC Online*, August 1, 2000; "Diabetes gene therapy draws closer," *BBC Online*, December 7, 2000; "Gene therapy restores dogs' sight," *BBC Online*, April 27, 2001; "Gene trickery cons cancer," *BBC Online*, November 22, 2001; "Gene therapy hope for sickle cell dis-ease," *BBC Online*, December 14, 2001.

58. Of course, a major part of this velocity must be squarely attributed to the emergence of Celera as a corporate competitor to the HGP. See "Genomic Pronouncements," *Economist*, December 2, 1999, 77; Nicholas Wade, "Company Nears Last Leg of Genome Project," *New York Times*, January 11, 2000, D3.

NOTES TO CHAPTER THREE

1. Some examples include: Christopher T. Hill, " Technology and International Competitiveness: Metaphor for Progress," and Carl Mitcham, "Science, Technology, and the Theory of Progress," in *Science, Technology, and Social Progress: Research in Technology Studies Volume 2*, ed. Stephen Goldman (Toronto: Associated University Presses, 1989), 33–47, 241–52; Chris Freeman, "Technical Change and Future Trends in the World Economy," *Futures* 25, no.6 (1993): 621–35.
2. R.K. Merton, *The Sociology of Science: theoretical and empirical investigations* (Chicago: University of Chicago Press, 1973).
3. See, for instance, Marc Berg, "The Politics of Technology: On Bringing Social Theory into Technological Design," *Science, Technology and Human* Values 23, no.4 (1998): 456–90; and Michael Mulkay, "The Mediating Role of the Scientific Elite," *Social Studies of Science* 6 (1976): 445–70.
4. Langdon Winner, "Upon Opening the Black Box and Finding It Empty: Social Constructivism and the Philosophy of Technology," *Science, Technology & Human Values* 18, no.3 (1993): 364–5. Importantly, Winner is a critic of this social constructivism. From various perspectives, advocates include: Steven Woolgar, "The Turn to Technology in Social Studies of Science," *Science, Technology & Human Values* 16, no.1 (1991): 20–50; Trevor Pinch and Wiebe Bijker, "Science, Relativism and the New Sociology of Technology: Reply to Russell," *Social Studies of Science* 16 (1986): 347–60; Bruno Latour, "Technology is society made durable," in *A Sociology of Monsters: Essays on Power, Technology and Domination*, ed. John Law (London: Routledge, 1991), 103–31; see also *Science in Action* (Cambridge, MA: Harvard University Press, 1987).
5. Winner, "Upon Opening the Black Box," p.369. By this, Winner is noting the failure in social constructivism to delineate how and why groups are systematically excluded from power, and the social structures that maintain this exclusion. As Winner states it, social constructivism seems, "not to have noticed the problem of elitism, the ways in which even a broad, multicentered spectrum of technical possibilities is skewed in ways that favor some social interests while excluding others." (p.370)
6. While these may, at first glance, appear to be similar undertakings, they are not. Of the former, Bruno Latour offers a telling example. Latour's conception of the progress of scientific research revolves around individual experiences through exposure to various networks. While this tells us something about social inputs during critical junctures of scientific practice, it overemphasizes individual agency in the development of this practice. Most

importantly, it fails to account, or even mention, large social processes, which may have a resoundingly more powerful effect on the direction of scientific research. See: Latour, "Technology is society made durable"; *Science in Action* (Cambridge, MA: Harvard University Press, 1987).

7. Sheila Jasanoff, "Beyond Epistemology: Relativism and Engagement in the Politics of Science," *Social Studies of Science* 26 (1996): 393–418.

8. Hans K. Klein and Daniel Lee Kleinman, "The Social Construction of Technology: Structural Considerations," *Science, Technology & Human Values* 27, no.1 (2002): 40.

9. Stanley Aronowitz, *Science as Power: Discourse and Ideology in Modern Society* (Minneapolis: University of Minnesota Press, 1988), 29.

10. On the latter, see Chris Freeman, "Economics of Research and Development," in *Science, Technology and Society: A Cross-Disciplinary Perspective*, eds. Ina Spiegel-Rösing and Derek de Solla Price (London: Sage, 1977), 223–75; "Technical Change and Future Trends in the World Economy," *Futures* 25, no.6 (1993): 621–35. On the former, see Ernest Mandel, *Late Capitalism* (London: Verso, 1978); *Long Waves of Capitalist Development: A Marxist Interpretation* (New York: Verso, 1995). See also: Carlota Peretz, "Structural Change and Assimilation of New Technologies in the Economic and Social Systems," *Futures* (October, 1983): 357–75.

11. Joseph Schumpeter, *Business Cycles: A Theoretical, Historical and Statistical Analysis of the Capitalist Process* (New York: McGraw Hill, 1939), 72–109.

12. Schumpeter, *Business Cycles*, p.104.

13. Manuel Castells, *The Rise of the Network Society* (Cambridge, M.A.: Blackwell, 1996), 51.

14. Castells, *The Rise of the Network Society*, p.51.

15. Ellen Wood, *Democracy Against Capitalism: Renewing Historical Materialism* (New York: Cambridge University Press, 1995), 111. Wood is quoting John Roemer, *Free to Lose* (Cambridge, MA: Cambridge University Press, 1988), 126.

16. Wood, *Democracy Against Capitalism*, p.132.

17. Wood, *Democracy Against Capitalism*, p.138.

18. Karl Marx, *Capital: A Critique of Political Economy, Volume I*, trans. Samuel Moor and Edward Aveling (New York: Modern Library, 1936), 397.

19. Marx, *Capital, Vol.I*, p.504.

20. Marx, *Capital, Vol.I*, p.42.

21. Paul Sweezy, *The Theory of Capitalist Development: Principles of Marxian Political Economy* (New York: Monthly Review Press, 1942), 26.

22. Marx, *Capital, Vol.I*, p.45.

23. Marx, *Capital, Vol.I*, pp.188–9. Of course, here, much of the literature concerning the transition to capitalism is instructive. See Rodney Hilton, et al., *The Transition from Feudalism to Capitalism* (New York: Verso, 1976); T.H Aston and C.H.E. Philpin, *The Brenner Debate: Agrarian Class Structure and Economic Development in Pre-Industrial Europe* (New York: Cambridge University Press, 1985); see also Ellen Wood, "From

Opportunity to Imperative: the History of the Market," *Monthly Review* 46, no.3 (1994): 14–40.

24. Marx, *Capital, Vol.I*, p.189. Pursuant to this, Marx states in a footnote on the same page that "The capitalist epoch is thus characterised by this, that labour-power takes in the eyes of the labourer himself the form of a commodity which is his property; his labour consequently becomes wage labour. On the other hand, it is only from this moment that the produce of labour universally becomes a commodity."

25. On this point, see Marx, *Capital, Vol.I*, pp.173–85. As is well known, this stage of Marx's theorization intentionally holds value equivalent to price, although Marx freely admits that, in reality, they regularly deviate from one another. In *Vol.III*, he reintroduces the problem of price, opening the door to the so-called transformation problem.

26. For an interesting review of this part of Marx's arguments, see George Caffentzis, "Why Machines Cannot Create Value: or, Marx's Theory of Machines," in *Cutting Edge: Technology, Information, Capitalism and Social Revolution*, eds. Jim Davis, Thomas Hirschl and Michael Stack (London: Verso, 1997), 29–56.

27. Marx, *Capital, Vol.I*, pp.185–96.

28. Marx delays until a later point in *Capital* any explanation as to why and how the laborer accepts this unprecedented situation. In his discussion of value theory, he states merely that "The question why this free labourer confronts him [the capitalist] in the market, has no interest for the owner of money, who regards the labour market as a branch of the general market for commodities. And for the present it interests us just as little. We cling to the fact theoretically, as he does practically. One thing, however, is clear—nature does not produce on the one side owners of money or commodities, and on the other men possessing nothing but their own labour-power. This relation has no natural basis, neither is its social basis one that is common to all historical periods." See Marx, *Capital, Vol.I*, p.188. On the historical development of labor power as a commodity, see pp.784–837.

29. Marx, *Capital, Vol.I*, p.190.

30. Marx deals with both absolute and relative surplus value in Marx, *Capital, Vol.I*, and pp.342–53.

31. See, for instance, Hilary Rose and Steven Rose, eds., *The Political Economy of Science: Ideology of/in the Natural Sciences* (London: MacMillan, 1976).

32. Hans Ehrbar and Mark Glick, "The Labour Theory of Value and its Critics," *Science & Society* 50, no.4 (1986): 473–4; See also: Paul Mattick Jr., "Some aspects of the value-price problem," *Économies et Sociétés* 15, nos.6–7 (1981): 725–81.

33. Karl Marx, *Capital: A Critique of Political Economy, Vol.III* (New York: International Publishers, 1967), 173.

34. Marx, *Capital, Vol.III*, p.177.

35. Guglielmo Carchedi, *Frontiers in Political Economy* (London: Verso, 1991), 71. Here, I am referring to the sense of supply and demand intended by Marx, whereby " . . . the ratio of supply to demand does not explain the

market value, but conversely, the latter rather explains the fluctuations of supply and demand." See Marx, *Capital, Vol.III*, p.192.

36. Marx, *Capital, Vol.III*, p.198.
37. This is, simultaneously, precisely the manner in which the tendency towards equalization is enforced, although never wholly realized. See Marx, *Capital, Vol.III*, pp.195–6.
38. Chidem Kurdas, "Accumulation and Technical Change: Marx Revisited," *Science and Society* 59, no.1 (1995): 52–68.
39. Kurdas, "Accumulation and Technical Change," p.64.
40. Kurdas, "Accumulation and Technical Change," p.65. Importantly, it is Kurdas' view that, here, there is a necessity to account for Schumpeter and 'entrepreneurialism.' In particular, Marx's picture of capitalist innovation needs to be augmented by one which understands those special individuals who do more than just 'follow the script' concerning accumulation and investment. Radical change is better explained by pointing to those investors who, "are behaving not as lemmings but as Schumpeterian entrepreneurs who 'reform or revolutionize the pattern of production.'" See Kurdas, pp.62–4.
41. Marx, *Capital, Vol.III*, pp.211–31.
42. Joachim Hirsch, "The State Apparatus and Social Reproduction: Elements of a Bourgeois State," in *State and Capital: A Marxist Debate*, eds. John Holloway and Sol Picciotto (London: Edward Arnold, 1978), 76.
43. Chris Harman, "Footnotes and Fallacies: A Comment on Robert Brenner's 'The Economics of Global Turbulence,'" *Historical Materialism* 4 (1999): 98–100.
44. Hirsch, "The State Apparatus and Social Reproduction," p.76.
45. Hirsch, "The State Apparatus and Social Reproduction," p.77.
46. Marx, *Grundrisse: Foundations of the Critique of Political Economy* (London: Penguin, 1973), 408–9.
47. Hirsch, "The State Apparatus and Social Reproduction," p.79.
48. Sweezy, *The Theory of Capitalist Development*, p.219.
49. Hirsch, "The State Apparatus and Social Reproduction," p.81
50. Richard Florida and Martin Kenney, "The New Age of Capitalism: Innovation-mediated production," *Futures* 25, no.6 (1993): 637–51.
51. Florida and Kenney, "The New Age of Capitalism," p.640.
52. To be clear (and fair), it should be noted that Florida and Kenney are opposed to any 'post-capitalist' explanation of information-based production. "While we would agree . . . that knowledge is increasingly important as a source of value, we do not believe that the increasing role played by knowledge, intelligence and innovation in the economy represents a shift to a new, post-capitalist form of economic and social organization. In our view, capitalism has evolved in a dynamic way to harness and integrate knowledge and intellectual labour as sources of value within the boundaries of capitalist progress." See Florida and Kenney, "The New Age of Capitalism," p.639. That said, the authors also do not go out of their way to point to the ways in which technology serves the vertical relations of capitalist

production. On this issue, see Peter Meiksins, "Work, New Technology, and Capitalism," *Monthly Review* 48, no.3 (1996), 99–114; Christopher May, "Information society, task mobility and the end of work," *Futures* 32 (2000), 399–416.

53. Ellen Wood, "A Reply to Sivanandan," *Monthly Review* 48, no.9 (1997): 22.

54. Florida and Kenney, "The New Age of Capitalism," p.640. In another work, Martin Kenney has taken a stand that is far more consistent with the position of the present work. See Kenney, "Value Creation in the Late Twentieth Century: The Rise of the Knowledge Worker," in *Cutting Edge: Technology, Information, Capitalism and Social Revolution*, eds. Jim Davis, Thomas Hirschl and Michael Stack (London: Verso, 1997), 87–102.

55. Guglielmo Carchedi, "Between Class Analysis and Organization Theory: Mental Labour," in *Organization Theory and Class Analysis: New Approaches and New Issue*, ed. Stewart Clegg (New York: Walter de Gruyter, 1990), 434. My understanding of knowledge and its internal interaction with the production process relies heavily on Carchedi's work.

56. Carchedi, "Between Class Analysis and Organization Theory," p.434.

57. Carchedi, "Between Class Analysis and Organization Theory," pp.435–6. It should be noted here that Carchedi is referring to two different senses of 'new.' On the one hand, knowledge is new if it leads to a different relation to the material world. But it is also 'new' if it reproduces the validity of an already existing knowledge, thus furthering the latter's longevity.

58. Carchedi, *Frontiers of Political Economy*, p.23.

59. Hirsch, "The State Apparatus and Social Reproduction," p.80.

60. Kenney, "Value Creation in the Late Twentieth Century," p.89.

61. Marx, *Capital, Volume I*, pp.443–4, emphasis added. Of course, this passage remains entirely consistent with Marx's insistence on the relationship between labor and surplus value.

62. For reviews of this debate, see Bob Jessop, *The Capitalist State: Marxist Theories and Methods* (New York: New York University Press, 1982); Clyde W. Barrow, "The Marx Problem in Marxian State Theory," *Science and Society* 64, no.1 (2000): 87–118; Raju Das, "State Theories: A Critical Analysis," *Science and Society* 60, no.1 (1996): 27–57; Haldun Gulalp, "Capital Accumulation, Classes and the Relative Autonomy of the State," *Science and Society* 51, no.3 (1987): 287–313; John Bellamy Foster, "Marxian Economics and the State," *Science and Society* 46, no.3 (1982): 257–83. On the initial debates concerning the degree to which the state could be understood as autonomous within capitalist social relations, see Nicos Poulantzas, "The Problem of the Capitalist State," *New Left Review* 58 (1969): 67–78; "The Capitalist State: A Reply to Miliband and Laclau," *New Left Review* 95 (1976): 63–83; Ralph Miliband, "The Capitalist State: Reply to Nicos Poulantzas," *New Left Review* 59 (1970): 53–60; "Poulantzas and the Capitalist State," *New Left Review* 82 (1973): 83–92.

63. Ellen Wood, *Democracy Against Capitalism*, p.47.

64. Heide Gerstenberger, "Class Conflict, Competition and State Functions," in *State and Capital: A Marxist Debate*, eds. John Holloway and Sol Picciotto (London: Edward Arnold, 1978), 154.

65. Regarding this point and the development of capitalism in Europe, see Ellen Wood, *The Pristine Culture of Capitalism: A Historical Essay on Old Regimes and Modern States* (London: Verso, 1991); Colin Mooers, *The Making of Bourgeois Europe*, (New York: Verso, 1991). On the manner in which biotechnology and genome science are affected by this reality, see Rodney, "History, Technology and the Capitalist State: The Comparative Political Economy of Biotechnology and Genomics," *Review of International Political Economy* 12, no. 2 (2005, forthcoming).

66. Hirsch, "The State Apparatus and Social Reproduction," p.76.

67. Gerstenberger, "Class conflict, Competition and State Functions," p.159.

68. Hirsch, "The State Apparatus and Social Reproduction," p.61.

69. This is not to say that the political-legal terrain of the capitalist state form has not been subject to unintended historical consequences. It is precisely the point that, as a field of struggle, countless victories can be enumerated that were not the immediate preference of either the ruling class or those in charge of the state apparatus.

70. Hirsch, "The State Apparatus and Social Reproduction," p.83.

71. Hirsch, "The State Apparatus and Social Reproduction," p.83.

72. Hirsch, "The State Apparatus and Social Reproduction," p.88. Robert Brenner has also makes this historical point as a corrective to the 'wage-squeeze' theory of capitalist crisis. See Robert Brenner, "Uneven Development and the Long Downturn," *New Left Review* 229 (1998): 95–9.

73. It is for this reason that although the effects of the unproductive state sphere is recognized, as well as the state's introduction of essentially demand-driven policies, the argument presented here should not be equated with either the underconsumption or disproportionality theses. Both describe processes that are functional to crises, but neither is their explanation. To assume that they are, in my opinion, is to imply that it is only 'regulation,' either of 'demand' or the balance between industrial 'departments,' that is necessary to avert crises. In contrast, the view taken here is that there are inherently contradictory tendencies within capitalist development that bring about both consumption and proportion problems. For a perspective on underconsumption, see: Paul Sweezy, *A Theory of Capitalist Development*. On disproportionality, see Simon Clarke, "The Marxist Theory of Overaccumulation and Crisis," *Science and Society* 54, no.4 (1990–91), 442–67.

74. Hirsch, "The State Apparatus and Social Reproduction," p.92.

75. Hirsch, "The State Apparatus and Social Reproduction," p.94.

76. Guglielmo Carchedi, "A Missed Opportunity: Orthodox vs. Marxist Crises Theories," *Historical Materialism* 4 (1999): 48.

77. Hirsch, "The State Apparatus and Social Reproduction," p.96.

78. Gerstenberger, "Class conflict, Competition and State Functions," p.158.

79. For some of the early recognition of this process, see Robin Murray, "The Internationalization of Capital and the Nation State," *New Left Review* 67 (1971): 84–109; Bill Warren, "Imperialism and Capitalist Industrialization," *New Left Review* 81 (1973): 1–44.

80. Leo Panitch, "Globalisation and the State," in *Socialist Register 1994*, eds. Leo Panitch and R. Miliband (London: Merlin Press, 1994), 64.

81. Panitch, "Globalisation and the State," p.82.
82. Here, a cautionary note is warranted. That this author recognizes the increasing prevalence of international political structures, which extend the reach of capital and the market, should not be equated with a wholesale acceptance of the 'globalization' thesis. It is one thing to account for the manner in which a capitalist 'logic of motion' plays itself out at the international level, but entirely another to adopt uncritically a discourse which virtually naturalizes this process and drains it of its social and political content. While there is, to put it mildly, an overabundance of literature on this topic, some samples include: Peter Evans, "The Eclipse of the State? Reflections on Stateness in an era of Globalization," *World Politics* 50 (1997): 62–87; Paul Hirst and Grahame Thompson, *Globalization in Question: The International Economy and the Possibilities of Governance* (Cambridge: Polity Press, 1996); Harry Magdoff, "A Letter to a Contributor: The Same Old State," *Monthly Review* 49, no.8 (1998): 1–10; Philip McMichael, "Globalization: Myths and Realities." *Rural Sociology* 61, no.1 (1996): 25–55; Hugo Radice, "Taking Globalization Seriously," in *Socialist Register 1999*, eds. Leo Panitch and Colin Leys (New York: Merlin Press, 1999); Ellen Wood, "A Reply to Sivanandan," *Monthly Review* 48, no.9 (1997): 21–32; "Class Compacts, the Welfare State, and Epochal Shifts," *Monthly Review* 49/8 (1998): 25–43; Rodney Loeppky, "Problematising Technology and 'Globalisation,'" in *Globalization 2000: Convergence or Divergence?* ed. Axel Hueselmeyer (Basingstoke: Palgrave, 2003), 33–48.

NOTES TO CHAPTER FOUR

1. "Genetic warfare," *Economist*, May 16, 1998, 87–8; Elizabeth Pennisi, "Funders reassure genome sequencers," *Science* 280, no.5367 (1998): 1185; Eliot Marshall, "NIH to produce a 'working draft' of the genome by 2001," *Science* 281, no.5384 (1998): 1774–5.
2. US Congress, Office of Technology Assessment, *Biotechnology in a Global Economy* (Washington, DC: US Government Printing Office, 1991), 45.
3. Luigi Orsenigo, *The Emergence of Biotechnology: Institutions and Markets in Industrial Innovation* (London: Pinter, 1989), 109.
4. Ann-Marie McIntyre, *Key Issues in the Pharmaceutical Industry* (New York: John Wiley & Sons, 1999), 14.
5. McIntyre, *Key Issues in the Pharmaceutical Industry*, p.15.
6. Heinz Redwood, *The Pharmaceutical Industry: Trends, Problems and Achievements* (Suffolk: Oldwicks Press, 1987), 217.
7. Redwood, *The Pharmaceutical Industry*, p.217.
8. Redwood, *The Pharmaceutical Industry*, p.219.
9. Robert Brenner, "Uneven Development and the Long Downturn," *New Left Review* 229 (1998): 1–265.
10. Brenner, "Uneven Development and the Long Downturn," p.137.
11. Brenner, "Uneven Development and the Long Downturn," pp.147–52. Particularly on its theoretical terms, Brenner's analysis of the post-war

situation has stirred up considerable controversy in Marxist circles. There is no space here for an account of squabbles over anybody's Marxist credentials (some have, very unfairly, labelled Brenner a neo-Smithian). Indeed, while Brenner's analytical explanation may not be complete, his overall historical explanation remains largely consistent with the theoretical position presented here. For an array of discussions concerning Brenner's work, see "Symposium: Robert Brenner and the World Crisis (Part 1)," *Historical Materialism* 4 (1999). For a flavor of the falling rate of profit debate, see David S. Yaffe, "The Marxian Theory of Crisis, Capital and the State," *Economy and Society* 2, no.2 (1973): 186–232; John E. Roemer, "Technological Change on the Real Wage and Marx's Falling Rate of Profit," *Australian Economic Papers* 17, no.30 (1978): 152–66; John Weeks, "Equilibrium, Uneven Development and the Tendency of the Rate of Profit to Fall," *Capital and Class* 16 (1982): 62–77; Mario Cogoy, "The Falling Rate of Profit and the Theory of Accumulation," *International Journal of Political Economy* 17, no.2 (1987): 55–74.

12. Fred Mosely, *The Falling Rate of Profit in the Postwar United States Economy* (New York: St.Martin's Press, 1991), 48–100; see also: "The United States Economy at the Turn of the Century: Entering a New Era of Prosperity?" *Capital and Class* 67 (1999): 28–45; "The Decline in the Rate of Profit in the Post-War US Economy: Regulation and Marxian Explanations," *International Journal of Political Economy* 19, no.1 (1989): 48–66; and "The Rate of Surplus Value, the Organic Composition, and the General Rate of Profit in the U.S. Economy, 1947–1967: A Critique and Update of Wolff's Estimates," *The American Economic Review* 78, no.1 (1988): 298–303. For an alternative analysis, see Anwar M. Shaikh and E. Ahmet Tonak, *Measuring the wealth of nations: The political economy of national accounts* (New York: Cambridge University Press, 1994); Murray Smith, measuring for Canada, finds a drop in the rate of profit from 14 percent in 1947 to 9 percent in 1991. At the same time, the rate of surplus value went from 0.4764 to 0.7366 and organic composition rose from 2.362 to 4.801. Murray Smith, "The Necessity of Value Theory: Brenner's Analysis of the 'Long Downturn' and Marx's Theory of Crisis," *Historical Materialism* 4 (Summer, 1999): 165.

13. McIntyre, *Key Issues in the Pharmaceutical Industry*, p.17.

14. Redwood, *The Pharmaceutical Industry*, p.49; McIntyre, *Key Issues in the Pharmaceutical Industry*, p.22; Madhu Agrawal, *Global Competitiveness in the Pharmaceutical Industry: The Effect of Regulatory, Economic and Market Factors* (New York: Haworth Press, 1999), 6.

15. Stuart O. Schweizer, *Pharmaceutical Economics and Policy* (New York: Oxford University Press, 1997), 106.

16. Schweitzer, *Pharmaceutical Economics and Policy*, p.58.

17. This perception has continued to hold sway throughout the 1980s and 1990s. See, for instance, Brian O'Reilly, "Drugmakers Under Attack," *Fortune*, July 29, 1991, 48–83; Leonard Zehr, "Drug firms facing short-term financial pressures, study says," *Globe and Mail*, January 21, 1999, B5; McIntyre, *Key Issues in the Pharmaceutical Industry*, pp.89–90.

18. U.S. Congress, Office of Technology Assessment, *Pharmaceutical R&D: Costs, Risks and Rewards,* (Washington, DC: U.S Government Printing Office, 1993), 21.

19. The precursor to this act, the 1906 Pure Food and Drug Act, was put in place after the widespread use of soothing syrup concocted out of ethylene glycol, otherwise known as radiator fluid.

20. In 1958, a German company, *Chemie-Grunenthal,* gained approval for thalidomide as an antidote to 'morning sickness' during pregnancy. Having gained approval in many countries (although not in the United States), the drug was administered widely. By the end of one year, reports emerged that "over 50% of children born to mothers who had taken thalidomide early during their pregnancies were born with phocolemia, a strange deformity marked by seal-like flippers in place of arms and legs. At the end, it was estimated that the thalidomide tragedy afflicted some 10,000 babies in at least 20 countries. See: Schweitzer, *Pharmaceutical Economics and Policy,* pp.173–4.

21. That is to say that since the state itself was not the primary provider for healthcare payment, it was less inclined to impose cost controls on the powerful U.S. pharmaceutical industry. Indeed, even in the current context, the pharmaceutical lobby has moved to hinder cost control on those drugs for U.S. senior citizens that are now to be supplied by medicare. See Jacob Hacker, Jacob Hacker, *The Divided Welfare State: The Battle Over Public and Private Social Benefits in the United States* (Cambridge: Cambridge University Press, 2002); Gardiner Harris, "Drugmakers Move Closer to Big Victory," *New York Times,* November 25, 2002, A20.

22. O'Reilly, "Drugmakers Under Attack," p.60.

23. Schweitzer, *Pharmaceutical Economics and Policy,* p.171.

24. This situation did not prove permanent, as pharmaceutical and health maintenance corporations strategically bargained with employers (who provide the majority of healthcare coverage in the U.S.) to give the latter the impression that they could control costs *via* the market. This completely undermined any possibility for reform at the political level—a fact made clear by the death of the Clinton Administration's healthcare proposals. See: Peter Swenson and Scott Greer, "Foul Weather Friends: Big Business and Health Care Reform in the 1990s in Historical Perspective," *Journal of health Politics, Policy and Law* 27, no.4 (2002): 605–38.

25. Bruce Agnew, "When Pharma Merges, R&D is the Dowry," *Science* 287, no. 5460 (2000): 1952; see also: Geoffrey Carr, "Beyond the behemoths," *Economist,* February 19, 1998, 16–8; Peter Mash, "Mergers in the drug industry," *British Medical Journal* 299, no. 6703 (1989): 813–4.

26. Shawn Tully, "Pill pushers get merger fever," *Fortune,* May 30, 1994, 14; Schweitzer, *Pharmaceutical Economics and Policy,* p.119.

27. Quoted in Alan Hall, "The Race for Miracle Drugs," *Business Week,* July 22, 1985, 96.

28. Redwood, *The Pharmaceutical Industry,* p.228.

29. Orsenigo, *The Emergence of Biotechnology,* pp.73–7.

30. Sheldon Krimsky, *Biotechnics and Society: The Rise of Industrial Genetics* (New York: Praeger, 1991), 23.
31. One could argue that such a strategy was also under way in the United Kingdom, although on a lesser scale.
32. Margaret Young, "The legacy of Cohen-Boyer," *Signals Magazine Online*, June 12, 1998, www.signalsmag.com.
33. Koyin Chang, "The Organization of the R&D Intensive Firm: An Application to the Biotechnology Industry," (Ph.D. diss., University of Kentucky, 1998), 17.
34. Orsenigo, *The Emergence of Biotechnology*, p.147; Cynthia Robbins-Roth, *From Alchemy to IPO: the Business of Biotechnology* (Cambridge, MA: Perseus, 2000), 135.
35. Chang, "The Organization of the R&D Intensive Firm," p.17.
36. Robbins-Roth, *From Alchemy to IPO*, p.140.
37. Alice Sapienza, "Collaboration as a global competitive tactic—biotechnology and the ethical pharmaceutical industry," *R&D Management* 19, no.4 (1989): 286.
38. Orsenigo, pp.111–2.
39. J. Rogers Hollingsworth, "The Institutional Embeddedness of American Capitalism," in *Political Economy of Modern Capitalism: Mapping Convergence & Diversity*, eds. Colin Crouch and Wolfgang Streeck (London: Sage Publications, 1997), 133–47.
40. Alfonso Gambardella, *Science and Innovation: the US Pharmaceutical Industry During the 1980s* (New York: Cambridge University Press, 1995), 23.
41. Gambardella, *Science and Innovation*, p.26.
42. Redwood, *The Pharmaceutical Industry*, pp.173–5.
43. Gambardella, *Science and Innovation*, pp.23–6.
44. Gambardella, *Science and Innovation*, p.25.
45. Stuart Gannes, "Merck Has Made Biotech Work," *Fortune*, January 19, 1987, 59. As an important note, the reader should not develop the impression that these competitive, horizontal relations among capitals in the pharmaceutical industry were the only important social relation. Simultaneously, Gannes (in an almost celebratory manner) makes clear that Merck also "got tough on labor relations and sweated out a four-month strike by the Oil, Chemical and Atomic workers union in 1984 to push through a two-tier wage structure similar to those in the airline industry." As was made clear in the previous chapter, periods of devalorization and restructuring, in order to optimize value appropriation on behalf of individual capitals, always rests on a variety of tactics aimed both vertically at capital-labor relations and horizontally at competitive relations between capitals in the marketplace.
46. George Post, "Untitled," (paper presented at Foresight Seminar on Biotechnology and the Regulation of Pharmaceuticals, Alexandria, VA, March 18, 1987) 5.
47. Gambardella, *Science and Innovations*, p.27.
48. Gambardella, *Science and Innovations*, p.40.

49. Included in this group are McIntyre, Arawal and Schweitzer.
50. US Congress, OTA, *Pharmaceutical R&D*, p.24.
51. Marx would find this attempted quantification, based on the unique characteristics of the sector, difficult to swallow. His own sense of the cost of capital is related (albeit flexibly) to the general rate of profit, and not that of particular sectors. "In so far as the rate of interest is determined by the rate of profit, this is always the general rate of profit and not any specific rate of profit prevailing in some particular branch of industry, and still less any extra profit which an individual capitalist may make in a particular sphere of business." See: Karl Marx, *Capital: A Critique of Political Economy, Vol.III* (New York: International Publishers, 1967), 365. And, indeed, the next paragraph of the report seems to admit so much: "the cost of capital can vary widely over time with underlying interest rates and expected inflation, so precise measurement of each group's cost of capital over the study period is impossible." It is notable that there is no meaningful connection between 'risk' and capital costs. Rather, it is the generalized conditions of capital acquisition that matter far more in capital costs.
52. This may also explain the fact that, despite the much-touted 'technological revolution' within the industry, approval numbers of new drugs have not grown back to their 'golden era' levels. For statistics, see: Marshal, "Autonomy and Sovereignty," p.120.
53. Gambardella, *Science and Innovation*, p.44.
54. Mark Crawford, "Patent claim buildup haunts biotechnology," *Science* 239, no.4841 (1988): 723.
55. Daniel J. Kevles, "Ananda Chakrabarty wins a patent: Biotechnology, law, and society, 1972–1980," *HSPS: Historical Studies in the Physical and Biological Sciences* 25, no.1 (1994): 111–36.
56. Kevles, "Ananda Chakrabarty wins a patent," p.125.
57. Kevles, "Ananda Chakrabarty wins a patent," p.131.
58. Christopher May, "Fishing with Dynamite: Knowledge commons in the global political economy," Annual Meeting of the International Studies Association, Chicago, 2001.
59. Orsenigo, *The Emergence of Biotechnology*, p.140.
60. Wallace Walrod, "Knowledge, Trust and Cooperative Relationships in the U.S. Biotechnology Industry," (Ph.D. diss., University of California, Irvine, 1999), 5.
61. US Congress, OTA, *Biotechnology in a Global Economy*, p.88, note 16.
62. Martin Kenney, *The University-Industrial Complex* (New Haven: Yale University Press, 1986), 200.
63. Kenney, *The University-Industrial Complex*, p.240.
64. Kenney, *The University-Industrial Complex*, p.240.
65. Stuart Gannes, "The Big Boys Are Joining the Biotech Party," *Fortune*, July 6, 1987, 61.
66. Linda Marsa, *Prescription for Profits: How the Pharmaceutical Industry Bankrolled the Unholy Marriage Between Science and Business* (New York: Scribner, 1997), 170.
67. Gambardella, *Science and Innovation*, pp.42–3, emphasis added.

68. Marsa, *Prescription for Profit*, p.264.
69. U.S. Congress, Office of Technology Assessment, *Mapping Our Genes— Genome Projects: How Big? How Fast?* (Washington: U.S. Government Publishing Office, 1988), 108–9.
70. U.S. Congress, Hearing on OTA Report on the Human Genome Project, Subcommittee on Oversight and Investigations, House Committee on Energy and Commerce (Washington: U.S. Government Publishing Office), statement of Richard Godown, 134.
71. U.S. Congress, Hearing on OTA Report, p.134.
72. U.S. Congress, OTA, *Mapping Our Genes*, p.109.
73. James Watson, "The Human Genome Project: Past, Present and Future," *Science* 248, no.4951 (1990): 44–50.
74. U.S. Congress, Hearing on OTA Report, p.76.
75. The more prominent role of the DOE during the initial formulation of the HGP will be discussed in the next chapter. Here, it is important to state only that it was the DOE, and not the NIH, which was the first government body to encourage the formation of a mapping project, then titled the Human Genome Initiative.
76. Beverly Merz, "Senate committee sees NIH-DOE partnership in genome project," *Journal of the American Medical Association* 259, no.1 (1988): 16.
77. Quoted in Michael Fortun, "Mapping and making genes and histories: The genomics project in the United States, 1980–1990," (Ph.D. diss., Harvard University, 1993), 266.
78. U.S. Congress, OTA, *Mapping Our Genes*, p.165.
79. U.S. Congress, Hearing on OTA Report, p.44.
80. U.S. Congress, Hearing on OTA Report, p.45.
81. U.S. Congress, Hearing on The Human Genome Project, Subcommittee on Energy research and Development, Senate Committee on Energy and Natural Resources (Washington: U.S. Government Printing Office, 1990), 101–2.
82. Post, "Untitled," p.9
83. John Carey, "This Genetic Map Will Lead to a Pot of Gold," *Business Week*, March 2, 1992, 74.
84. U.S. Congress, Hearing on OTA Report, pp.71–5.
85. Quoted in Robert Cook-Deegan, *The Gene Wars: Science, Politics, and the Human Genome* (New York: W.W. Norton & Company, 1995), 110. See also Robert Cook-Deegan, "Origins of the Human Genome Project," *Risk: Health, Safety and Environment* 5 (1994), 97–111.
86. Quoted in Robert Cook-Deegan, *The Gene Wars*, p.111.
87. Quoted in Robert Cook-Deegan, *The Gene Wars*, p.114.
88. Leslie Roberts, "Genome backlash going full force," *Science* 248, no.4957 (1990): 804.
89. This is not to suggest that such controversies were meaningless. They were the subject matter of crucial political processes, as will be pointed out in a later chapter. It is only to point out that the perspective of dominant scientific players seemed often to converge with those of investing capitals.

90. Roger Lewin, "Shifting sentiments over sequencing the human genome," *Science* 233, no. 4764 (1986): 620.
91. Cook-Deegan, "Origins of the Human Genome Project," p.97.
92. Charles Cantor, "Introductory Remarks," (paper presented at Human Genome Project: Commercial Implications, San Francisco, May 1999).
93. Susan Wright, "Varieties of Secrets and Secret Varieties: The Case of Biotechnology," *Politics and the Life Sciences* 19/1 (2000): 47; this view is also expressed in Richard Lewontin, "The Dream of the Human Genome," in *Politics and the Human Body: Assault on Dignity,* eds. Jean Bethke Elshtain and J. Timothy Cloyd (Nashville: Vanderbilt University Press, 1995), 41–6.
94. In fact, as an interesting contrast to Botstein's early reservations, international meetings in Valencia over how to share the HGP's information were steered away from any prohibitive actions. When Jean Dausset of the Centre d'Etude Polymorphism Humain in Paris suggested, primarily on moral grounds, that there should be an agreement to ban genetic manipulation in germline cells, the possibility was averted by Norman Zinder of Rockefeller University, soon to be Chair of the NIH Human Genome Advisory Committee. Zinder reminded the meeting "that, no matter what they thought, Valencia was no Asilomar—the groundbreaking 1975 meeting where molecular biologists drafted guidelines to govern recombinant DNA research." Although the Asilomar meetings should not be romanticized, one cannot help but notice the striking alterations with respect to the scientific community's disposition toward self-regulation. See: Leslie Roberts, "Carving up the genome," *Science* 242, no.4883 (1988): 1246.
95. U.S. Congress, Hearing on The Human Genome Project, pp.23–4.
96. U.S. Congress, Hearing on The Human Genome Project, p.8
97. U.S. Congress, Hearing on The Human Genome Project, pp.91–2.
98. John Savill, "Prospecting for gold in the human genome," *British Medical Journal* 314, no.7073 (1997): 44.
99. Ernst & Young, "The Economic Contributions of the Biotechnology Industry to the U.S. Economy," (report prepared for the Biotechnology Industry Organization, May, 2000).
100. Carey, "This Genetic Map Will Lead to a Pot of Gold," p.74.
101. This HGP-related increase in industrial biotechnology and pharmaceutical production was the subject of considerable media attention. See, for example, Joan O'C. Hamilton, et al., "Biotech: America's Dream Machine," *Business Week,* March 2, 1992, 66–74; David Stipp, "Hatching a DNA Giant," *Fortune,* May 24, 1999, 179–86; John Carey, "The Genome Gold Rush: Who will be the first to hit pay dirt?" *Business Week,* June 12, 2000, 147–58; "Genomics Advances Expected to Aid Growth of Biotechnology Industry," Biotechnology Industry Organization, Press Release, June 27, 2000; Michael D. Lemonick, "The Genome Is Mapped: Now What?" *Time,* July 3, 2000, 24.
102. Ralph Christoffersen, "Untitled," (paper presented at Foresight Seminar on Biotechnology and Pharmaceutical Regulation, Alexandria, VA, March 18, 1987).

103. Jennifer Van Brunt, "Grand Ambitions," *Signals Online Magazine*, February 24, 2001, www.signalsmag.com.

104. Biotechnology Industry Organization (BIO), *Editors' and Reporters' Guide* (Washington: Biotechnology Industry Organization, 2004), 3.

105. Wade Roush, "Biotech Finds a Growth Industry," *Science* 273, no.5273 (1996): 300.

106. Jennifer Van Brunt, "Antisense: Poised to Strike," *Signals Online Magazine*, January 5, 2001, www.signalsmag.com.

107. Boston Consulting Group, "A Revolution in R&D: Part II The Impact of Genetics," Consulting Report, July 2001.

108. Jennifer Van Brunt, "Biotech's Tsunami," *Signals Online Magazine*, August 18, 2000; "Borderless Biotech," *Signals Online Magazine*, December 13, 2000, www.signalsmag.com.

109. "Drugs ex machina," *Economist* (Technology Quarterly), September 22, 2001, 30. This, of course, accepts *uncritically* the circulating figure of $800 million in development costs for each successful drug.

110. Craig Venter and Mark Adams, "Shotgun sequencing of the human genome," *Science* 280, no.5369 (1998), 1540–2.

111. See, for instance, "Genetic Warfare," *Economist*, May 16, 1998, 88–9; "Private venture to sequence human genome launched," *Issues in Science and Technology* 15, no.1 (1998): 28–9; James Shreeve, "The code breaker," *Discover* 19, no.5 (1998): 44–52; Michael D. Lemonick and Dick Thompson, "Racing to Map Our DNA: Completion from private labs has forced the Human Genome Project into a frantic rush to finish first," *Time*, January 11, 1999, 44.

112. Kevin Davies, *Cracking the Genome: Inside the Race to Unlock Human DNA* (New York: The Free Press, 2001), 165. Of course, Lander himself was no stranger to commercial enterprises in molecular biology, as co-founder of Millennium Pharmaceuticals, one of the most successful biotechnology corporations in the industry.

113. Stipp, "Hatching a DNA Giant," p.179–80.

114. Nor is this to claim in any way that Venter's deal with *Perkin-Elmer* was without important economic consequences. Certainly Celera's program was scoffed at by other biotechnology leaders, including Incyte, HGS and Millennium. Millennium's Steven Holtzman stated that "the race at this point is not for the DNA," and Bill Haseltine of HGS claimed that Celera's program was like racing NASA to the moon and asked "where is the business plan?" For his own part, Incyte's Roy Whitfield asserted that from "a commercial point of view, sequencing the genome is just a complete waste of time." These perspectives, however, were just as naïve as those exaggerating the Celera/HGP competition. Besides the major pharmaceutical firms that Celera had signed up for license-based access to its data base (licenses which are reputed to cost as much as $ 50 million), it is critical not to forget the role of Celera's close relatives, PE and Applied Biosystems. The latter capital, not by coincidence, was the leading producer of automated sequencers in the U.S. market. Celera's obvious choice to utilize Applied Biosystems' PRISM 3700 meant that the public project,

if it were to keep up, would need to follow suit. By March, 1999 over 500 orders had been received, and by the end of 1999, there were over 1000 orders—at $300,000 per unit. What business plan, indeed. See "Washington Diary," *New Scientist* 167, no.2249 (2000): 61; Carey, "The Genome Gold Rush," pp.153–4; Davies, *Cracking the Genome*, pp.145, 167, 242.

115. Jennifer Van Brunt, "A Matter of Expression," *Signals Online Magazine*, July 3, 2001, www.signalsmag.com.

116. Jenniver Van Brunt, "Pharmacogenomics Gets Clinical," *Signals Online Magazine*, April 25, 2003, www.signalsmag.com.

117. See Unmesh Kher, "The Next Frontier: Proteomics," *Time*, July 3, 2000, 29; Jennifer Van Brunt, "Proteomics Gears Up," *Signals Online Magazine*, May 9, 2001, www.signalsmag.com.

118. "Drugs ex machina," *Economist*, p.30.

119. BIO, *Editors' and Reporters' Guide*, p.4.

120. Siddhartha Mukherjee, "Wrong Map—Why public science can't really be public," *New Republic*, May 8, 2000, 14.

NOTES TO CHAPTER FIVE

1. Nathan Rosenberg, *Exploring the Black Box: Technology, economics and history* (Cambridge: Cambridge University Press, 1994), 109.

2. According to Charles Post, "[by] the 1840s and 1850s, at the latest, agrarian self-organized commodity production in the Northeast and West was governed by the law of value. Merchant capital, through the mechanisms of land law, land speculation and the *promotion of internal improvements*, was responsible for the enforced dependence of free farmers on commodity production for the economic reproduction. . . . The portions of the public domain reserved for free settlement tended to be of the worst soil quality and distant from the railroads. The railroads, on the other hand, were given, under the provisions of the Homestead corollary land-grant acts, large alternating blocks of the public domain along their routes, while the Federal government reserved the other blocks of land for sale at public auction. This plundering of the public domain through huge land grants to railroads and mining companies, and the sale government land at public auction, provided a tremendous lever for the commodification of the land and created a permanent obstacle to 'natural economy.'" See Charles Post, "The American Road to Capitalism," *New Left Review* 133 (1982), 43–51, emphasis added.

3. Charles Post, "The American Road to Capitalism," p.48.

4. Bruce L.R. Smith, *American Science Policy Since World War II* (Washington: Brookings Institution, 1990), 22.

5. Of course, land grant colleges, such as MIT or Cornell, played an important role in this process.

6. David Mowery and Nathan Rosenberg, *Paths of Innovation: Technological Change in 20th Century America* (Cambridge: Cambridge University Press, 1998), 16. Moreover, while the Sherman Act of 1890 and Clayton Act of

1914 were, respectively, aimed at reining in 'trusts' and 'mergers,' each approached these problems solely in terms of anti–competitive behavior. In other words, the logic of capitalist accumulation, which tends toward centralization and concentration, was not in question—rather it was a question of only specific acts endangering market logic. And while Standard Oil bore the brunt of this suspicion in 1911, its breakup was based on its 're-straint of trade,' not its size—six of the other major trusts formed in the 1880s survived. As the state was attempting to outlaw 'trusts,' it was simultaneously legalizing (in 1889) the acquisition of 'holding companies,' creating the legal framework for firm integration, and setting the groundwork for the extraordinary merger wave at the turn of the century. 'Antitrust' has never been equated with anti-bigness in the US, and the government has (and could have) never opposed the ongoing 'rationalization' of capitalist social relations through mergers, acquisition, and decentralized financial structures. See Thomas McGraw, *Creating Modern Capitalism: How Entrepreneurs, Companies, and Countries Triumphed in Three Industrial Revolutions* (Cambridge, MA: Harvard University Press, 1997), 330; Richard DuBoff, *Accumulation and Power: An Economic History of the United States* (New York: ME Sharpe, 1989), 43–9.

7. Mowery and Rosenberg, *Paths of Innovation*, pp.17–8.
8. Mowery and Rosenberg, *Paths of Innovation*, pp.27–8.
9. Smith, *American Science Policy Since World War II*, p.81.
10. Smith, *American Science Policy Since World War II*, pp.73–7.
11. David Hart, "Managing Technology at the White House," in *Investing in Innovation: Creating a Research and Innovation Policy That Works*, eds. Lewis M. Branscomb and James H. Keller (Cambridge, MA: MIT Press, 1998), 438–61.
12. J. Rogers Hollingsworth, "The Institutional Embeddedness of American Capitalism," in Colin Crouch and Wolfgang Streeck (eds.) *Political Economy of Modern Capitalism: Mapping Convergence & Diversity* (London: Sage Publications, 1997), 133–47.
13. U.S. Congress, Hearing on Commercialization of Academic Biomedical Research, Subcommittee on Investigations and Oversight and the Subcommittee on Science, Research and Technology, House Committee on Science and Technology (Washington, DC: US Government Printing Office, 1981), 1.
14. U.S. Congress, Office of Technology Assessment (OTA), *Federal Technology Transfer and the Human Genome Project* (Washington, DC: US Government Printing Office, 1995), 46.
15. OTA, *Federal Technology Transfer*, p.50.
16. U.S. Congress, OTA, *Pharmaceutical R&D: Costs, Risks and Rewards* (Washington, DC: US Government Printing Press, 1993), 16.
17. Stuart Schweizer, *Pharmaceutical Economics and Policy* (Oxford: Oxford University Press, 1997), 124.
18. OTA, *Federal Technology Transfer*, p.47.
19. U.S. Congress, Hearing on Commercialization of Academic Biomedical Research, p.65.

20. U.S. Congress, Hearing on Commercialization of Academic Biomedical Research, p.78.
21. Marjorie Sun, "White House enters fray on DNA regulation," *Science* 224, no.4651 (1984): 855.
22. Barbara J. Culliton, "NIH role in biotechnology debated," *Science* 229, no.4709 (1985): 147–9.
23. U.S. Congress, Office of Technology Assessment, *Mapping Our Genes— Genome Projects: How Big? How Fast?* (Washington: U.S. Government Publishing Office, 1988), 167.
24. Smith, *American Science Policy Since WWII*, p.136.
25. OTA, *Federal Technology Transfer*, pp.12–8.
26. Martin Kenney, *Biotechnology: The University-Industrial Complex* (London: Yale University press, 1986), 62–72.
27. U.S. Congress, Hearing on Commercialization of Academic Biomedical Research, pp.90–2.
28. U.S. Congress, Hearing on The Human Genome Project, Subcommittee on Energy Research and Development, Senate Committee on Energy and Natural Resources (Washington DC: US Government Printing Office, 1990), 121.
29. Robert Cook-Deegan, *The Gene Wars: Science, Politics, and the Human Genome* (New York: W.W. Norton & Company, 1995), 81. Although in Cook-Deegan's own account, it is the actions of DOE that really gave rise to sustainable efforts at genome mapping, he also suggests, in a not-very-convincing manner, that it is Sinsheimer who 'passes the torch' to actors within that government department.
30. There is some controversy over which of these meetings constitutes the exact 'origin' of the HGP, but the 'correct' answer is of little import to this study. Michael Fortun makes a considerable issue out of this, claiming that events are characterized and then re-characterized in order to fit a neat and tidy sequence of historical events. See Michael Fortun, "Mapping and making genes and histories: The genomics project in the United States, 1980–1990," (Ph.D. diss., Harvard University, 1993), chapter 2.
31. Cook-Deegan, *The Gene Wars*, p.104. This argument is also accepted in Daniel Kevles, "Big Science and Big Politics in the United States: Reflections on the Death of the SSC and the Life of the Human Genome Project," *HSPS: Historical Studies in the Physical and Biological Sciences* 27, no.2 (1997): 269–98.
32. Fortun, "Mapping and making genes and histories," pp.241–3
33. U.S. Congress, Workshop on Human Genome Mapping, Senate Committee on Energy and Natural Resources (Washington DC: US Government Printing Office, 1987), 1.
34. Kevles, "Big Science and big politics in the United States," p.275.
35. Even if one does not accept Cook-Deegan's 'weapons and defense' arguments, there is an argument to be made that Domenici, as Senator for New Mexico, had an obvious and somewhat pork barrel-oriented interest in this project. It is certainly true that his spirited enthusiasm seems somewhat overplayed. But it would be a mistake to dismiss the Senator's capacity to

differentiate what he judges to be the 'value' of a scientific project from the political capital it brings due to its location. In the above cited workshop, Domenici was perfectly frank about what he thought of the Superconducting Super Collider, another project sacred to the National Labs: "You know, if anything—I hate to say it—but with reference to super conducting materials, regrettably, I believe the White House was given some great ideas, spent a hell of a lot of time with very bright people and called a great big, marvelous national conference, and I'm not at all convinced that they gave birth to much." See OTA, Workshop on Human Genome Mapping, p.21.

36. "Bush boosts big programmes," *Chemistry & Industry* 5 (1990): 120.
37. Pat Janowski and Peter G. Brown, "Science, technology and the U.S. economy," *The Sciences* 33, no.4 (1993): 7–9.
38. Kevles, "Big Science and big politics in the United States," p.292.
39. Kevles, "Big Science and big politics in the United States," pp.290–1.
40. Cook-Deegan, *The Gene Wars*, p.172.
41. Kevles, "Big Science and big politics in the United States," p.295. Of course, this was part of the debate over mapping *versus* sequencing, and the argument to undertake mapping immediately while developing cheaper and faster technology for sequencing was an *economic* argument as much as it was a *scientific* one. See: Roger Lewin, "Politics of the genome," *Science* 235 (1987): 1453.
42. Quoted in Fortun, "Mapping and making genes and histories," p.254. Domenici goes on in this hearing to extol the virtues of the free market and entrepreneurial spirit in U.S. society, warning detractors that passing up on this endeavor would be a failure to provide the country with the technological base necessary for a vibrant economy. In an ensuing footnote, Fortun highlights the 'irony' of extolling the marketplace while trying to arrange massive government financial support. While for Fortun this may constitute irony, it is precisely in keeping with the expected behavior of the strategic capitalist state, *intervening* in order to ensure the reproducibility of the marketplace.
43. Kirschstein was head of the National Institute of General Medical Sciences, the NIH body which had been responsible for the vast majority of funding related to genetic research.
44. OTA, Workshop on Human Gene Mapping, p.11.
45. OTA, Workshop on Human Gene Mapping, pp.20–1. DeLisi also makes the point that "the country, the nation has to pay the bill for these [technological advancements]."
46. OTA, Workshop on Human Gene Mapping, p.39.
47. U.S. Congress, Hearing on OTA Report on the Human Genome Project, Subcommittee on Oversight and Investigations, House Committee On Energy and Commerce (Washington, DC: US Government Printing Office, 1988), 2.
48. U.S. Congress, Hearing on The Human Genome Initiative and the Future of Biotechnology, Subcommittee on Science, Technology, and Space, Senate Committee on Commerce, Science, and Transportation (Washington, DC: US Government Printing Office, 1989), 9.

49. U.S. Congress, Hearing on The Human Genome Initiative, p.9.
50. Fortun, "Mapping and making genes and histories," p.251.
51. The NIH reacted with mixed signals toward the initial genome initiative as conceptualized by the DOE. Clearly the NIH should play a central role, but there existed a prevailing mindset that this would draw the NIH into 'big science' in a manner inconsistent with the philosophy of its normal operations. See Leslie Roberts, "Agencies vie over human genome project," *Science* 237, no.4814 (1987): 487.
52. Quoted in Fortun, "Mapping and making genes and histories," p.252 and Cook-Deegan, *The Gene Wars*, p.153.
53. Testimony of James Wyngaarden, quoted in Fortun, "Mapping and making genes and histories," p.260.
54. U.S. Congress, OTA, Workshop on Mapping the Human Genome, p.32.
55. U.S. Congress, Hearing on the Human Genome Project, Statement of Richard D. Godown, pp.135–6.
56. U.S. Congress, OTA, *Mapping Our Genes*, pp.13–4.
57. Cook-Deegan, *The Gene Wars*, p.152; Fortun, "Mapping and making genes and histories," p.272.
58. Kevles, "Big Politics and big science in the United States," p.277.
59. U.S. Congress, Report to House of Representatives, *The Biotechnology Science Coordination and Competitiveness Act*, September 28, 1988, 8.
60. The panel was to be composed of the following: Secretary of Energy, Director of NIH, Director of the NSF, Director of the National Library of Medicine, four individuals from industry, four individuals from university community, two individuals from DOE National libraries, one expert in biomedical ethics, one individual representing the national foundations, medical institutions and philanthropic organizations. Except for the first three positions, all other positions would be appointed by the President.
61. James D. Watson, "The Human Genome Project: Past, Present and Future," *Science* 248, no.4951 (1990): 47.
62. Fortun quite rightly points out that the NIH, at this point, utilized completely the opposite logic as in its struggle against the DOE. While its earlier claims were related to the need to utilize the NIH's capacity for decentered, investigator-led research structure, suddenly it was advocating the need for a centralized coordinating structure, to ensure that there would be 'central planning, coordination and direction.' See Fortun, "Mapping and making genes and histories," p.330.
63. The Centre's first Director, James Watson, states that Wyngaarden informed him of his intentions as Watson came to work for him at OHGR. See Watson, "The Human Genome Project," p.47. The NCHGR would eventually be renamed the National Human Genome Research Institute (NHGRI).
64. Watson, "The Human Genome Project," p.47.
65. Christopher J. Harnett, "The Human Genome Project and the Downside of Federal Technology Transfer," *Risk: Health, Safety & Environment* 5 (1995): 151–62.
66. Anna Maria Gillis, "The patent question of the year," *BioScience* 42, no.5 (1992): 337. In its 1992 extension of the application, the NIH dropped the requests concerning proteins.

67. This widely cited statement is found in Keith Davies, *Cracking the Genome: Inside the Race to Unlock Human DNA* (New York: The Free Press, 2001): 62.
68. Davies, *Cracking the Genome*, p.63.
69. Leslie Roberts, "Genome patent fight erupts," *Science* 254, no.5029 (1991): 184.
70. Davies, *Cracking the Genome*, p.58.
71. Thomas D. Kiley, "Patents on random complementary DNA fragments?" *Science* 257, no.5072 (1992): 916.
72. Rebecca Eisenberg, "Genes, patents, and product development," *Science* 257, no.5072 (1992): 904.
73. Reid Adler, "Genome research: fulfilling the public's expectations for knowledge and commercialization," *Science* 257, no.5072 (1992): 908.
74. Quoted in Davies, *Cracking the Genome*, p. 63.
75. Roberts, "Patent fight erupts," *Science* 254, no.5029 (1991): 1.
76. Eisenberg, "Genes, patents, and product development," p. 907.
77. Kiley, "Patents on random complementary DNA fragments?" p. 915. Kiley, who at one time was Vice President and general counsel at Genentech, expressed his frustration within corporate law: "patents are avidly pursued all along the lengthy road from the most basic science through to the market place for pharmaceuticals. Because every step along the way draws another patent application, the path toward public possession of real benefit is increasingly obscured by dense thickets of intersecting, overlapping, and cross-blocking patents. . . . The system is abused if those who benefit in this way from the later labors of others can posit patents on the most strained utilities imaginable."(p.918) However, a little earlier on, Kiley also reveals that his interests are not abstractly concerned with 'fair' market practice: "because NIH seeks patents on encoding sequencing but not encoded proteins, the very manufacturers whose cause NIH purports to promote would be competitively disadvantaged by either grant. Such patents would be enforceable here against expression of encoded sequences but not against overseas manufacturers who export the unpatented protein to American shores. . . . If these patents are issued to NIH, companies will face the usual choices—pay up (assuming licenses are available at any price), fight, or switch." (p.917)
78. According to the PTO, 'blocking' patents are those which, "have claims that overlap each other in a manner that the invention claimed in one patent cannot be practiced without infringing the claims of the other patent and vice versa," while 'stacking' licenses "give the owner of a patented invention used in upstream research rights in subsequent downstream inventions." See Jeanne Clark, Joe Piccolo, Brian Stanton and Karin Tyson, "Patent Pools: A Solution to the Problem of Access in Biotechnology Patents?" Policy Paper, United States Patent and Trademark Office, Washington, DC, December 5, 2000, 8.
79. Eisenberg, "Genes, patents, and product development," p. 902. Interestingly, in a footnote Eisenberg explains the ABC's support *versus* IBA's opposition: "ABC is a larger organization than IBA whose roster of voting members includes not only companies that develop products but also

numerous law firms and other entities that speculate in biotechnology. One might speculate that these other entities, particularly law firms, have more to gain from a proliferation of patent rights in the human genome than do the companies that need to decide about whether to commit capital to the development of biotechnology products. IBA's voting membership is comprised solely of such companies." (note 30)

80. Dr. Charles Sanders, CEO of then Glaxo Inc. and advocate of the genome project, went so far in 1991 to state in government testimony that if "intellectual property protection were not available in the whole [sic], we could not exist as an industry. It is just that simple." See U.S. Congress, Hearing on Biotechnology and Technology Transfer, Subcommittee on Technology and Competitiveness, House Committee on Science, Space and Technology (Washington, DC: US Government Printing Office, 1991), 24.

81. Mark Crawford, "Patent claim buildup haunts," *Science* 239, no.4841 (1988): 723.

82. Eliot Marshall and David P. Hamilton, "The patent game: raising the ante," *Science* 253, no.5015 (1991): 21.

83. U.S. Congress, Hearing on the Human Genome Initiative, pp.58–9.

84. The NIH, under the direction of Healy, largely refused to give way on the issue of EST patents. It was not until 1994 that Harold Varmus, Healy's successor, announced that the NIH would not pursue its application any further. See Davies, *Cracking the Genome*, pp.61–2.

85. Roberts, "Gene patent fight erupts," p.185.

86. Eisenberg, "Genes, patents, and product development," p. 903.

87. Adler, "Genome Research," p. 909.

88. Eliot Marshall, "Biotech leaders give patent office a litany of complaints," *Science* 266, no.5185 (1994): 537.

89. "BIO files Comments on Proposed Guidelines From PTO For Patenting Gene-Based Inventions," Biotechnology Industry Organization, Press Release, March 22, 2000; "BIO Issues Statement On PTO's Final Gene-Based Patent Guidelines," Biotechnology Industry Organization, Press Release, January 5, 2001; Dennis J. Henner, Genentech Senior Vice President of Research, statement before United States House of Representatives Judiciary Subcommittee On Courts and Intellectual Property, July 13, 2000, URL: www.bio.org. For a perspective imploring more leeway from the PTO, see Randal Scott, President and Chief Scientific Officer of Incyte Genomics Inc., testimony before U.S. House of Representatives Judiciary Subcommittee on Courts and Intellectual Property, July 13, 2000, URL: www.bio.org. This is not to suggest that the intergovernmental and industrial concerns over the patent office have disappeared. For example, there is a continuing question as to whether the PTO should be granted some responsibility to enforce how patents are utilized once they are awarded. This would be especially pertinent to the 1000 genes already patented and the scores of ESTs patented prior the PTO's recent rule changes. See Nicholas Thompson, "Gene Blues: United States Patent and Trademark Office Overloaded," *Washington Monthly* 33, no.4 (2001): 9.

90. Thompson, "Gene Blues," p.9.

91. That Venter would continuously be held up as the solid public scientist 'gone morally wrong' remains deeply problematic. It is certainly true that Venter's interaction with the corporate world, as well as NIH's legal counsel, may have led him to avoid immediate release. But on several occasions he continued to demonstrate that the results of his scientific productivity were to be released into the public domain. Even if this had not been the case, Venter pales in comparison to the many biotech and pharmaceutical firms who have sought patent protection and maintained large degrees of trade secrecy.

92. Nicholas Wade, "Scientist's Plan: Map All DNA Within 3 Years," *New York Times*, May 10, 1998, A1, A10; "Genetic Warfare," *Economist*, May 16, 1998, 87–8.

93. By 1999, Venter approached Gerald Rubin, who had been working on a project to sequence the genome of *Drosophila Melongaster* (the fruit fly), with a proposal to test his methods on this most beloved of model organisms. The effects were astonishingly effective, as the full sequence was reassembled within months, and publicly released. See: Leslie Roberts, "The lords of the flies," *U.S. News & World Report* 127, no.11 (1999): 52.

94. Elizabeth Pennisi, "Funders reassure genome sequencers," *Science* 280, no.5367 (1998): 1185.

95. Davies, *Cracking the Genome*, pp.162–3.

96. U.S. Congress, Hearing on the Human Genome Project: How Private Sector Developments Affect the Government Program, Subcommittee on Energy and Environment, House Committee on Science (Washington, DC: US Government Printing Office, 1998), 55–7.

97. Sulston derided *Celera*'s proposed version of the sequence as 'intermediate' and 'transitory' while Waterston equated it to "an encyclopedia ripped to shreds and scattered on the floor." See Davies, *Cracking the Genome*, p.151.

98. Venter publicly called the collective directors of the genome centers 'the liars club' and claimed that the NIH's decision had 'nothing to do with reality.' Francis Collins retorted that Venter's plan was the equivalent of the 'Cliff Notes version of the genome.' See: Davies, *Cracking the Genome*, p.163.

99. U.S. Congress, Hearing on the Human Genome Project: How Private Sector Developments, p.78.

100. Davies, *Cracking the Genome*, p.198.

101. U.S. Congress, Hearing on the Human Genome Project: How Private Sector Developments, p.2.

102. U.S. Congress, Hearing on the Human Genome Project: How Private Sector Developments, p.16.

103. U.S. Congress, Hearing on the Human Genome Project: How Private Sector Developments, p.6.

104. U.S. Congress, Hearing on the Human Genome Project: How Private Sector Developments, p.80.

105. U.S. Congress, Hearing on the Human Genome Project: How Private Sector Developments, p.72.

106. It is precisely in this context that one needs to view reactions to the now infamous Clinton-Blair speech of March 14, 2000. Although these state officials expressed their preference for the important role of intellectual

property protection, a subsequent reference to the need to put raw DNA sequence information in the public domain sent markets crumbling and
elicited an intense reaction from industry. The statement, obviously aimed
at Celera after reports of that company's expanded patent application effort,
drew a visceral reaction, because it infringed on the general conditions
which the pharmaceutical and biotechnology industries view as critical to
their development. See: Davies, *Cracking the Genome*, pp.205–7; "BIO Responds to Clinton, Blair Statement on Gene-Based Health-Care Research,"
Biotechnology Industry Organization, Press Release, March 14, 2000; "BIO
Praises Clinton Reassurances Regarding Gene Patents and PTO Leadership," Biotechnology Industry Organization, Press Release, April 5, 2000.

107. John Braithwaite and Peter Drahos, *Global Business Regulation*
(Cambridge: Cambridge University Press, 2000) 59–60.

108. This is not to assert that the United States had no access to, or did not enjoy
the protection of, the Berne Convention. Dealing largely with published materials, the Convention extended copyright protection to material published
in any member state, regardless of the nationality of the publisher. With
Canada's ascension to the Berne Convention in 1928, United States authors
were afforded protection through simultaneous publication in the United
States and Canada. See: Mark L. Damschroder, "Intellectual Property
Rights and the GATT: United States Goals in the Uruguay Round,"
Vanderbilt Journal of Transnational Law 21, no. 2 (1988): 381.

109. The thirteen corporations included Bristol-Myers Co., EI du Pont de
Nemours & Co, Johnson & Johnson, Merck & Co., Monsanto, Pfizer Inc.,
Rockwell International Corp., Warner Communications, FMC Corpora-
tion, General Electric, General Motors, Hewlett-Packard and International
Business Machines. See Braithwaite and Drahos, Global Business Regula-
tion, p.165, note 122.

110. Jacque J. Gorlin, "The Business Community and the Uruguay Round," in
Intellectual Property Rights and Capital Formation in the Next Decade, eds.
Charles E. Walker and Mark A. Bloomfield (New York: University Press of
America, 1988), 172.

111. Gail E. Evans, "Intellectual Property as a Trade Issue: The Making of the
Agreement on Trade-Related Aspects of Intellectual Property Rights,"
World Competition: Law and Economics Review 18, no.2 (1994): 165.

112. David Dickson, "OECD to set rules for international science," *Science*
238/4828 (1987) p.743.

113. Peter Drahos and John Braithwaite, *Information Feudalism: Who Owns the
Knowledge Economy?* (New York, New Press, 2003), 19–38.

114. Evans, "Intellectual Property as a Trade Issue," p.161.

115. Evans, "Intellectual Property as a Trade Issue," p.144.

116. Evans, "Intellectual Property as a Trade Issue," p.144.

117. Bernard M. Hoekman, "New Issues in the Uruguay Round and Beyond,"
The Economic Journal 103 (1993): 1531–2.

118. Philippe Cullet, "Patents and medicines: the relationship between TRIPS
and the human right to health," *International* Affairs 79, no.1 (2003):
139–60; Meri Koivusalo, "World Trade Organisation and Trade-Creep in

Health and Social Policies," Occasional Paper, Globalism and Social Policy Programme, Helsinki, 1999. On the openings in the TRIPs agreement for public health exemptions, as well as a conservative view of them as regrettable, see Peggy E. Chaudhry and Michael G. Walsh, "Intellectual Property Rights: Changing Levels of Protection Under GATT, NAFTA and the EU," *Columbia Journal of Business* 30, no.2 (1995): 81–92.

119. Susan K. Sell, "Intellectual property protection and antitrust in the developing world: crisis, coercion, and choice," *International Organization* 49, no.2 (1995): 322.

120. Evans, "Intellectual Property as a Trade Issue," p.152.

121. Susan Sell, "Intellectual Property Rights After TRIPS," (paper presented at the Annual Meeting of the International Studies Association, Chicago, IL, February 2001).

122. Sell, "Intellectual property protection and antitrust in the developing world," p.349.

NOTES TO CHAPTER SIX

1. Consider the comments in 1982 by A. Bartlett Giamatti, then President of Yale University. On the subject of university-industry linkages, Giamatti speaks of the need to " . . . sustain the university's commitment to free inquiry by fostering a spirit of collegiality, a shared sense of respect for and trusteeship of shared values of openness and intellectual freedom that the university exists to embody in the larger society. . . . And . . . members of the faculty, collectively and individually, are at the core of the university; and that, on behalf of members of the faculty, it is essential to protect academic freedom as well as to foster traditions of faculty self-regulation and self-government." See A. Bartlett Giamatti, "The University, Industry, and Cooperative Research," *Science* 218, no.4579 (1982): 1278.

2. Jon Cohen, "The Culture of Credit," *Science* 268, no.5218 (1995): 1706.

3. This should in no way romanticize the post-war competitive environment of American science. To be sure, not only were their problematic incidents within scientific fields, but the entire network of scientific 'credibility' and patron-client structure could easily be subject to its own critique. That said, it is not the place of this work to do so. The claim here is that there were, especially prior to the 1980s, a set of practices in molecular biology that had a strong normative grounding considered integral to the academic process, ensuring autonomy, creativity and protection from political and economic influence.

4. U.S. Congress, Hearing on Commercialization of Academic Biomedical Research, Subcommittee on Investigations and Oversight and the Subcommittee on Science, Research and Technology, House Committee on Science and Technology (Washington, DC: US Government Printing Office, 1981): 63.

5. This is not to suggest that Bayh-Dole or the FTTA *caused* an increase in patenting. Rather, in keeping with the analysis presented in the previous three chapters, both would be seen as manifestations of capitalist social

relations as they increasingly relate to scientific labor, knowledge production and value accumulation. The important, but not causative, role of the Bayh-Dole Act is discussed in David C. Mowery, Richard R. Nelson, Bhaven N. Sampat, and Arvids A. Ziedonis, "The Effects of the Bayh-Dole Act on U.S. Research and Technology Transfer," in *Industrializing Knowledge: University-Industry Linkages in Japan and the United States,* eds. Lewis M. Branscomb, Fumio Kodama, and Richard Florida (Cambridge, MA: MIT Press, 1999), 269–306.

6. The point is made in Walter W. Powell and Jason Owen-Smith, "Universities and the Market for Intellectual Property in the Life Sciences," *Journal of Policy Analysis and Management* 17, no.2 (1998): 259–60. Powell and Smith draw on Rebecca Henderson, Adam B. Jaffe and Manuel Trajtenberg, "Universities as a Source of Commercial Technology: A Detailed Analysis of University Patenting 1965–1988," National Bureau of Economic Research, Working Paper No.5068 (March, 1995). I have extended the data for leading university patents classes by consulting the National Science Board, *Science & Engineering Indicators-2000* (Washington, DC: US Government Printing Office, 2000).

7. Powell and Smith, p.260; See National Science Board, *Science & Engineering Indicators-2000,* Appendix A-476.

8. Kathryn Packer and Andrew Webster, "Patenting Culture in Science: Reinventing the Scientific Wheel of Credibility," *Science, Technology, and Human Values* 21, no.4 (1996): 427–53.

9. Packer and Webster, "Patenting Culture in Science," p.435.

10. Packer and Webster, "Patenting Culture in Science," p.439.

11. Packer and Webster, "Patenting Culture in Science," p.442. The authors highlight the resistance to using patents in teaching because of their tendency to make overly casual claims and deliberately obscure important detail. Especially interesting is their reference to a professor who does use patents in teaching, but only to contrast with academic papers. Students had to "examine a patent in their area of study to see what information it disclosed and, more important, what further information one would require if one wanted actually to reduce the patent to practice."

12. Michael Mackenzie, Peter Keating and Alberto Cambrosio, "Patents and Free Scientific Information in Biotechnology: Making Monoclonal Antibodies Proprietary," *Science, Technology and Human Values* 15, no.1 (1990): 77.

13. This is certainly corroborated in a much-cited story on so-called 'knock-out' model organisms. See: Jon Cohen, "Research Materials: Share and Share Alike Isn't Always the Rule in Science," *Science* 268, no.5218 (1995): 1715–8.

14. Quoted in Cohen, "The Culture of Credit," p.1706.

15. Rebecca Eisenberg, "Proprietary Rights and the Norms of Science in Biotechnology Research," *The Yale Law Journal* 97, no.2 (1987): 199–205. In a footnote, Eisenberg refers to a facetious form letter circulating in the scientific community, given to her in an interview by a practicing molecular biologist:

> I regret to inform you that we are unable to send the strains you wish because* we have a graduate student who is studying this particular strain and it would be unfair to distribute it at this time/ the problem you outline does not seem very significant/we have just concluded your particular study/we suspect you are lying about the purpose for which you want the strain/we suspect you are the referee with whom we had considerable trouble recently.
>
> I might add that I, personally, am not in favour of withholding mutant strains.
>
> *Delete as appropriate.

16. Packer and Webster, "Patenting Culture in Science," p.444.

17. David Blumenthal et al., "University-Industry Research Relationships in Biotechnology: Implications for the University," *Science* 232, no.4756 (1986): 1361–6.

18. For these figures see: Blumenthal et al., "University-Industry Research Relationships," pp.1362–4.

19. David Blumenthal et al., "Industrial Support of University Research in Biotechnology," *Science* 231, no.4735 (1986): 242–6; see also Mary Murray, "Professors minding their own business: survey of university biotechnology researchers with industry ties," *Science News* 129 (1986): 374.

20. Blumenthal et al., "Industrial Support of University Research," p.242.

21. Blumenthal et al., "Industrial Support of University Research," p.245.

22. Sheldon Krimsky, James G. Ennis, and Robert Weissman, "Academic-Corporate Ties in Biotechnology: A Quantitative Study," *Science, Technology, and Human Values* 16, no.3 (1991): 275–87.

23. Krimsky, Ennis and Weissman, "Academic-Corporate Ties in Biotechnology," pp.283–4. The top ten institutions were as follows: MIT, Stanford, Harvard, University of California-Davis, University of California-San Francisco, University of California-Berkeley, University of Washington, University of California-Los Angeles, University of California-San Diego, and Yale.

24. Horace Freeland Judson, "Structural Transformation of the sciences and the end of peer review," *Journal of the American Medical Association* 272, no.2 (1994): 92.

25. This is Freeland Judson's point in "Structural Transformation of the sciences and the end of peer review," p.93.

26. Krimsky, Ennis and Weissman, "Academic-Corporate Ties in Biotechnology," p.286.

27. David Blumenthal et al., "Relationships Between Academic Institutions and Industry in the Life Sciences—An Industry Survey," *New England Journal of Medicine* 334, no.6 (1996): 368–73.

28. Blumenthal et al., "Relationships Between Academic Institutions and Industry," p.369.

29. Blumenthal et al., "Relationships Between Academic Institutions and Industry," p.371.

30. David Blumenthal et al., "Participation of Life-Science Faculty in Research Relationships with Industry," *New England Journal of Medicine* 335, no.23 (1996): 1734–9.
31. This statistic held on average, until a researcher had more than two-thirds of his/her research underwritten by industry, at which point their productivity fell below that of researchers without industrial support.
32. Blumenthal et al. note the fact that the ratios between industrially-affiliated and non-affiliated scientists remain largely similar over time. That is certainly true, but they also conclude their discussion with concern over the degree of trade secrecy, withholding of data and commercial influence—a fact probably attributable to *absolute* numerical increases on such issues. While commercial influence on the research agenda of those with and without linkages in 1986 was reported as 30 percent and 7 percent, respectively, the numbers in 1996 were 35 percent and 14 percent. That now twice as many scientists without industrial funding have explicit commercial considerations shaping their work is, in the opinion of this author, indicative of considerable change. See: Blumenthal et al., "Participation of Life-Science Faculty in Research Relationships with Industry," pp.1737–8.
33. David Blumenthal et al., "Withholding Research Results in Academic Life Science: Evidence From a National Survey of Faculty," *Journal of the American Medical Association* 277, no.15 (1997) pp.1224–8.
34. Blumenthal et al., "Withholding Research Results in Academic Life Science," p.1226.
35. Eric G. Campbell, Karen Seashore Louis and David Blumenthal, "Looking a Gift Horse in the Mouth: Corporate Gifts Supporting Life Sciences Research," *Journal of the American Medical Association* 279, no.13 (1998): 995–9.
36. The authors included under gifts discretionary funds for research, biomaterials, student support, research equipment and trips to professional meetings.
37. Campbell, Seashore Louis and Blumenthal, "Looking a Gift Horse in the Mouth," p.998.
38. A recent study, reviewing all studies to date dealing with industrial influence on biomedical research, concluded that "the financial ties that intertwine industry, investigators and academic institutions can influence the research process. Strong and consistent evidence shows that industry-sponsored research tends to draw pro-industry conclusions. By combining data from articles examining 1140 studies, we found that industry-sponsored studies were significantly more likely to reach conclusions that were favorable to the sponsor than were non-industry studies." See: Justin E. Bekelman, Yan Li and Cary P. Gross, "Scope and Impact of Financial Conflicts of Interest in Biomedical Research: A Systematic Review," *Journal of the American Medical Association* 289, no.4 (2003): 463.
39. Quoted in Tim Beardsley, "Big-Time Biology," *Scientific American*, November 1994, 77.
40. Stanley G. Korenman et al., "Evaluation of the Research Norms of Scientists and Administrators Responsible for Academic Research Integrity," *Journal of the American Medical Association* 279, no.1 (1998): 41–7.

41. Eisenberg, "Proprietary Rights and the Norms of Science in Biotechnology Research," p.205.
42. Frank W. Fitch, quoted in Beardsley, "Big Time Biology," p.77.
43. Henry Etzkowitz, Andrew Webster and Peter Healey, eds., *Capitalizing Knowledge: New Intersections of Industry and Academia* (Albany, NY: State University of New York Press, 1998), 4; Henry Etzkowitz, "Knowledge as Property: The Massachusetts Institute of Technology and the Debate Over Academic Patent Policy," *Minerva: A Review of Science Learning and Policy* 32, no.4 (1994): 383–421.
44. Blumenthal, et al., "Relationship Between Academic Institutions and Industry," p.372.
45. Sheryl Gay Stolberg, "Financial ties in Biomedicine Get Closer Look," *New York Times,* February 20, 2000, A1.
46. Henry Etzkowitz, "Bridging the Gap: The Evolution of Industry-University Links in the United States," in *Industrializing Knowledge: University-Industry Linkages in Japan and the United States,* eds. Lewis M. Branscomb, Fumio Kodama, and Richard Florida (Cambridge, MA: MIT Press, 1999), 206.
47. Etzkowitz, Webster and Healey, *Capitalizing Knowledge,* p.15.
48. Roli Varma and Richard Worthington, "Immiseration of Industrial Scientists in Corporate Laboratories in the United States," *Minerva: A Review of Science Policy and Learning* 33 (1995): 325–38.
49. Tom Abate, "Scientists' 'publish or perish' credo now 'patent and profit': 'Recombinant U.' phenomenon alters academic culture," *San Francisco Chronicle,* August 13, 2001, Section 6.
50. Abate, "Scientists' 'publish or perish' credo now 'patent and profit,'" Section 6.
51. Etzkowitz, "Bridging the Gap," p.207.
52. Karl Marx, *Capital: A Critique of Political Economy, Volume I,* trans. Samuel Moor and Edward Aveling (New York: Modern Library, 1936), 809.
53. For this, we would require 'lab-less' biologists roaming the campus, forced back as part-time technicians to private 'research parks' (located adjunct to campus) under threat of arrest by campus security. Humor aside, there are certain elements of truth in this scenario.
54. Marx, *Capital, Vol.I,* p.188. A similar problem is posed much earlier by Marx in the *Philosophical and Economic Manuscripts,* where he states at the end of the first manuscript that the 'non-worker does everything against the worker which the worker does to himself." See Karl Marx, *Economic and Philosophical Manuscripts of 1844,* trans. Martin Milligan (New York: International Publishers, 1964).
55. Marx, *Capital, Vol.I,* p.809.
56. Michel Foucault, "Truth and Power," in *The Foucault Reader,* ed. Paul Rabinow (New York: Pantheon, 1984), 61.
57. Here, the regular dismissals of Marxism as 'totalitarian meta-narrative' by those invoking Foucault is equaled by caustic Marxist analyses of 'postmodernism' and 'poststructuralism,' under which Foucault generally gets

positioned. See: Ellen Wood, "Modernity, Postmodernity or Capitalism?" *Review of International Political Economy* 4, no.3 (1997): 539–60; Alex Callinicos, *Against Postmodernism: A Marxist Critique* (New York: St.Martin's Press, 1990); Peter Dews, *Logics of Disintegration: post-structuralist thought and the claims of critical theory* (London: Verso, 1987).

58. Foucault's presentation of 'history' is, of course, at once suspect. He does not present the rigorously detailed work of, say, an E.P. Thompson but, instead, tends to draw general historical conclusions from a series of anecdotes. However, the general assertions that he does put forward are suggestive, and they can be subjected to historical periods other than those contained in his own work.

59. Michel Foucault, *Discipline and Punish: The Birth of the Prison*, trans. Alan Sheridan (New York: Vintage, 1995), 138.

60. Foucault, *Discipline and Punish*, p.218. In referring to the 'surveillance' necessary for discipline to operate effectively, Foucault defers directly to Marx himself: "Surveillance thus becomes a decisive economic operator both as an internal part of the production machinery and as a specific mechanism in disciplinary power. 'The work of directing, superintending and adjusting becomes one of the functions of capital, from the moment that the labour under the control of capital, becomes cooperative. Once a function of capital, it requires special characteristics.'" See Foucault, *Discipline and Punish*, p.175.

61. Michel Foucault, *The History of Sexuality, Volume I*, trans. Robert Hurley (New York: Vintage, 1990), 99–100.

62. Foucault, *Discipline and Punish*, p.221, emphasis added.

63. Foucault, *The History of Sexuality, Volume I*, p.141.

64. Castells has been the most prominent advocate of this mode of thought. See Manuel Castells, *The Rise of the Network Society* (Cambridge, M.A.: Blackwell, 1996).

65. Powell and Owen-Smith, "Universities and the Market for Intellectual Property," p.266.

66. John Portz and Peter Eisinger, "Biotechnology and Economic Development: the Role of the States," *Politics and the Life Sciences* 9, no.2 (1991), 226.

67. William P. Browne, "Biotechnology, State Economic Development, and Interest Politics: A Troublesome Trinity," *Politics and the Life Sciences* 9, no.2 (1991), 245–50.

68. Powell and Owen-Smith are insistent that the perceived drop in federal support, while discursively alive, in no way constitutes an adequate explanation for university behavior in the life sciences. The authors state that, "[in] contrast to many other areas of academic research, the life sciences do not suffer from declining resources. The life sciences presently receive more than 55 percent of all federal research support. The NIH is now by far the largest supporter of academic research, and between 1981 and 1990, its budget increased by 50 percent (in constant dollars), a figure two thirds greater than the increase in total federal outlays. At the end of the 1980s, the government began to fund the Human Genome Project at the rate of 3 billion dollars over 15 years. In fiscal year 1996, while most branches of government

limped along on partial and continuing funding extensions, the NIH received a firm commitment from the Congress and the president, with a 5.6 percent increase, the largest in the federal budget. And, more recently, the 1997 appropriations bill gives the NIH an increase of 6.9 percent to a budget of $12.7 billion." See Powell and Owen-Smith, "Universities and the Market for Intellectual Property," pp.264–5.

69. Henry Etzkowitz and Andrew Webster, "Entrepreneurial Science: the Second Academic Revolution," in *Capitalizing Knowledge: New Intersections of Industry and Academia*, eds. Henry Etzkowitz, Andrew Webster and Peter Healey (Albany, NY: State University of New York Press, 1998), 21–46.

70. Etzkowitz and Webster, "Entrepreneurial Science," p.22.

71. Powell and Owen-Smith, "Universities and the Market for Intellectual Property," p.269

72. Irwin Feller, "Universities as engines of R&D-based economic growth: They think they can," *Research Policy* 19 (1990): 341.

73. Etzkowitz and Webster, "Entrepreneurial Science," pp.37–8.

74. Marx himself asserted that "the process of production, separated from capital, is simply a labour-process. Therefore, the industrial capitalist, as distinct from the owner of capital, does not appear as operating capital, but rather as a functionary irrespective of capital, or, as a simple agent of the labour-process in general, as a labourer, and indeed as a wage labourer." See Karl Marx, *Capital: A Critique of Political Economy, Vol. III* (New York: International Publishers, 1967), 382.

75. Irwin Feller, "The American University System as a Performer of Basic and Applied Research," in *Industrializing Knowledge: University-Industry Linkages in Japan and the United States*, eds. Lewis M. Branscomb, Fumio Kodama, and Richard Florida (Cambridge, MA: MIT Press, 1999), 65–101.

76. Etzkowitz and Webster, "Entrepreneurial Science," p.36. The uniqueness of the U.S. system is particularly evident when compared with the national state-led systems prevalent on the European continent. As Etzkowitz and Webster point out, " . . . the experience of those countries with a more interventionist industrial policy, such as France, Germany, Japan, and more recently Australia and Brazil . . . need to be properly explored and evaluated." There is, unfortunately, no space to pursue such questions here. However, in a separate work, I take up a comparative analysis of the rise of biotechnology genome sciences in the United States and Germany. Germany offers a striking contrast to the United States, as an advanced industrial country highly reliant on technology development, active in molecular biology, but over 15 years 'late' in entering the rush to develop this kind of industrial potential. See; Rodney Loeppky, "History, Technology, and the Capitalist State: The Comparative Political Economy Biotechnology and Genomics," *Review of International Political Economy* (2005, forthcoming).

77. Note that this statement should be strenuously contrasted from the following: the 'new' was always contained in the 'old.' This more deterministic logic is heavily utilized in reference to market-oriented change. In relation to this study, it would imply that it has always just been a question of removing

'barriers,' such that the 'natural' inclination of scientific practice (of course, along market lines) could realize itself. In this work, this method of historical thinking is explicitly rejected. For a very useful discussion of this topic, see Ellen Wood, "From Opportunity to Imperative: the History of the Market," *Monthly Review* 46, no.3 (1994): 14–40.

78. Foucault, "Truth and Power," p.54.
79. Foucault, "Truth and Power," p.61.
80. Feller, "Universities as engines of R&D-based economic growth," p.344.
81. Jonathan R. Cole, "Balancing Acts: Dilemmas of Choice Facing Research Universities," *Dædalus: Journal of the American Academy of Arts and Sciences* 122, no.4 (1993): 12.
82. Quoted in Feller, "Universities as engines of R&D-based economic growth," p.336.
83. Tellingly, by the late 1980s, Harvard University had entirely reversed its position.
84. U.S. Congress, Hearing on Commercialization of Academic Biomedical Research, p.58.
85. Karen Seashore Louis and Melissa Anderson, "The Changing Context of Science and University-Industry Relations," in *Capitalizing Knowledge: New Intersections of Industry and Academia*, eds. Henry Etzkowitz, Andrew Webster and Peter Healey (Albany, NY: State University of New York Press, 1998), 79.
86. See, for instance, Simon Moffat, "Pharmaceuticals: good opportunities in small packages," *Science* 261, no.5129 (1993): 788–9; Nicole Ruediger, "Out of college and into a rewarding biotech career," *Science* 278, no.5344 (1997): 1823.
87. Marcia Barinaga, "The attractions of biotech careers over academia," *Science* 257, no.5077 (1992): 1718.
88. Powell and Owen-Smith, "Universities and the Market for Intellectual Property in the Life Sciences," p.7.
89. Quoted in Tim Beardsley, "Big Time Biology," p.79.
90. Etzkowitz, "Bridging the Gap," p.223.
91. Martin Kenney, *Biotechnology: The University-Industrial Complex* (London: Yale UP, 1986), 113.
92. Etzkowitz, Webster and Healey, eds., *Capitalizing Knowledge*, p.14.
93. Christopher Anderson, "Genome project goes commercial," *Science* 259, no.5093 (1993), 300–2; Bruce Goldman, "Patient, Diagnose Thyself," *Signals Online Magazine*, February 1, 2001, www.signalsmag.com; Jennifer Van Brunt, "30,000 Genes? No Way, Claims Haseltine," *Signals Online Magazine*, March 18, 2001, www.signalsmag.com.
94. Blumenthal et al., "Withholding Research Results in Academic Life Science," p.1228.
95. Robert Weinberg and David Botstein, quoted in, Robert Cook-Deegan, *The Gene Wars: Science, Politics, and the Human Genome* (New York: W.W. Norton & Company, 1995), 111, 114.
96. Roger Lewin, "Shifting sentiments over sequencing the human genome," *Science* 233, no.4764 (1986): 621.

97. Leslie Roberts, "Tough times ahead for the genome project," *Science* 248, no.4963 (1990): 1601.
98. Quoted in Michael Fortun, "Mapping and making genes and histories: The genomics project in the United States, 1980–1990" (Ph.D. diss., Harvard University, 1993), 368–9.
99. Fortun, "Mapping and making genes and histories," p.374.
100. U.S. Congress, Hearing on The Human Genome Project, Subcommittee on Energy Research and Development, Senate Committee on Energy and Natural Resources (Washington DC: US Government Printing Office, 1990), 89.
101. U.S. Congress, Hearing on The Human Genome Project, p.119.
102. U.S. Congress, Hearing on The Human Genome Project, pp.130–1.
103. U.S. Congress, Hearing on The Human Genome Project, p.131; for the referred to *Science* article, see Bernard Davis, "The human genome and other initiatives," *Science* 249, no.4967 (1990): 342–3.
104. U.S. Congress, Hearing on The Human Genome Project, p.132.
105. U.S. Congress, Hearing on The Human Genome Project, p.182.
106. The point concerning 'opposition' and the quotation are attributable to Fortun, "Mapping and making genes and histories," p.397, note 22.
107. U.S. Congress, Hearing on The Human Genome Project, p.133.
108. National Science Board, Science and Engineering Indicators—1993, *www.nsf.gov/sbe/srs/seind93/chap5/doc/5s293.htm*.
109. Powell and Owen-Smith, "Universities and the Market for Intellectual Property in the Life Science," pp.16–7.
110. In a 1987 workshop on genome mapping, Domenici outlined this suspicion of peer-review to the Director of the National Institute of General Medical Sciences: "There are plenty of people in the Congress who want to do away with it right now. . . . As a matter of fact, as one of those, Ruth, who leads peer review, I will give you my stock lecture. I really believe that it is most important that you stimulate the peer reviewers to a high level of consideration of what they're doing, because they are quite properly accused of becoming very sedentary, very rote." See U.S. Congress, Workshop on Human Genome Mapping, Senate Committee on Energy and Natural Resources (Washington DC: US Government Printing Office, 1987), 38.
111. Cook-Deegan, *The Gene Wars*, pp.157–8.
112. Leon Jaroff, "The Gene Hunt: scientists launch a $3 billion project to map the chromosomes and decipher the complete instructions for making a human being," *Time*, March 20, 1989, 66.
113. Quoted in Fortun, "Mapping and making genes and histories," pp.399–400; see also Leslie Roberts, "A Meeting of the Minds on the Genome Project?" *Science* 250, no.4982 (1990): 756–7.
114. U.S. Congress, Workshop on Human Genome Mapping, p.27.
115. U.S. Congress, Workshop on Human Genome Mapping, p.28, emphasis added.
116. Keith Davies, *Cracking the Genome: Inside the Race to Unlock Human DNA* (New York: The Free Press, 2001), 165.
117. Etzkowitz, Webster, and Healy, eds., *Capitalizing Knowledge*, p.16.

NOTES TO CHAPTER SEVEN

1. Quoted in Michael Fortun, "Mapping and making genes and histories: The genomics project in the United States, 1980–1990," (Ph.D. diss., Harvard University, 1993), 424.
2. In 1996, Jeremy Rifkin unsuccessfully attempted to block patents on breast cancer genes BRCA 1 and BRCA 2 by *Myriad Genetics Inc.* One of his claims was that such patents make diagnostics products much more expensive. Telling is Myriad's subsequent drive to enforce its patent exclusivity and administer all diagnostics in its own lab at a cost $3,850 per test (against a non-Myriad performed test cost of approximately $800). It has pressed, and continues to press, its monopoly rights against public institutions not adhering to its patent coverage. See: Eliot Marshall, "Rifkin's latest target: genetic testing," *Science* 272, no.5265 (1996): 1094; Nicholas Thompson, "Gene Blues: United States Patent and Trademark Office Overloaded," *Washington Monthly* 33, no.4 (2001): 9; Caroline Mallan, "Gene tests for cancer won't stop," *Toronto Star,* September 20, 2001, A3.
3. Arnold S. Relman and Marcia Angell, "America's other drug problem: how the drug industry distorts medicine and politics," *The New Republic,* December 16, 2002, 30.
4. Relman and Angell, "America's other drug problem," pp.28–30; James Love, "How much does it cost to develop a new drug?" paper presented at MSF Working Group, Geneva, 2 April (2000), www.cptech.org/ip/health/econ/howmuch.html; Merrill Goozner, "The Price Isn't Right," *The American Prospect* 11, no.20 (2000): 25–8. On the Orphan Drug Act, see Janice Marchiafava Hogan, "Revamping the Orphan Drug Act: potential impact on the world pharmaceutical market," *Law and Policy in International Business* 26, no.2 (1995): 523–61.
5. Linda Marsa, *Prescription for Profit: How the Pharmaceutical Industry Bankrolled the Unholy Marriage Between Science and Business* (New York: Scribner, 1997), 264. Marsa goes on to state that in " . . . 1991 alone, the NIH, or researchers supported through extramural grants, had 121 drugs under development—more than any single drug company. In that same year, the FDA approved 327 new drugs and products, yet only 5 of them were considered a significant advance, 9 were targeted to 'severely debilitating or life-threatening illness,' and 2 were for the treatment of AIDS. *All 5* of the therapies deemed an important therapeutic gain, 6 of the 9 drugs for treatment of serious ills, and both of the AIDS drugs were devised with federal funds."
6. Relman and Angell, "America's other drug problem," p.32.
7. Peter Conrad, "Medicalization and Social Control," *Annual Review of Sociology* 18 (1992): 209–32; Ray Moynihan, Iona Heath and David Henry, "Selling sickness: the pharmaceutical industry and disease mongering," *British Medical Journal* 324 (2002): 886–91; J. Bancroft, "The medicalization of female sexual dysfunction: the need for caution," *Archives of Sexual Behaviour* 31, no.3 (2002): 451–5; Ray Moynihan, "The making of a disease: female sexual dysfunction," *British Medical Journal* 326 (2003):

45–7; Leonore Tiefer, "Sexology and the pharmaceutical industry: the threat of co-optation," *Journal of Sex Research* 37, no.3 (2000): 273–83; Regina H. Kenan, "The At-Risk Health Status and Technology: A Diagnostic Invitation and the Gift of Knowing," *Social Science and Medicine* 42 (1996): 1545–53; Simon J. Williams and Michael Calnan, "The Limits of Medicalization?: Modern Medicine and the Lay Populace In 'Late Modernity,'" *Social Science and Medicine* 42 (1996): 1609–20.

8. Jordan Mejias, "Research Always Runs the Risk of Getting Out of Control (Interview with Erwin Chargaff)," *Frankfurter Allgemeine Zeitung* (English ed.), June 4, 2001, www.faz.com.

9. Consider, in relation to the HGP, the extraordinary vilification of Craig Venter, both over the issue of NIH patenting and Celera's corporate production of a genome map. Corporate scientists are not the only target of questioning here, evident in a critical issue of *Science* that highlights individual researchers that have 'gone too far' from norms of practice, as well as the special responsibility carried by scientists. See "Conduct in Science," *Science* 268, no.5218 (1995): 1706–18.

10. UNESCO, "Introductory Note" in *Science Agenda—Framework for Action*," General Conference, 30th Session, Paris, 1999, 4.

11. Darryl Macer, "Whose Genome Project?" *Bioethics* 5 (1991): 202; Robert Bohrer, "Future Fall-Out From The Genetic Revolution," *Futures* 24 (1992): 681–8.

12. See, for instance, Barbara Katz Rothman, *Genetic Maps and Human Imaginations: The Limits of Science in Understanding Who We Are* (New York: W.W. Norton, 1998); "Not All That Glitters Is Gold," *Hastings Center Report* 22, no.4 (1992); Robert Weir, Susan Lawrence, and Evan Fales, eds. *Genes and Human Self-knowledge: Historical and Philosophical Reflections on Modern Genetics* (Iowa City: Iowa University Press, 1994); Thomas H. Murray, Mark A. Rothstein, and Robert F. Murray, Jr., eds., *The Human Genome Project and the Future of Health Care* (Indianapolis, Indiana University Press, 1996).

13. Patricia Kaufert, "Health Policy and the New Genetics," *Social Science and Medicine* 51 (2000): 823.

14. Chantelle M. Wolpert, "Human Genomics in Clinical Practice," *Clinician Review* 10, no.7 (2000): 67.

15. Chargaff, quoted in Mejias, "Research Always Runs the Risk," www.faz.com.

16. Sheryl Gay Stolberg, "Bioethicists Find Themselves the Ones Being Scrutinized," *New York Times*, August 2, 2001, A1. Bioethicists have been in high demand from many companies and institutions participating in genome research. It is now being reported that ethical review committees that pay bioethicists a consulting fee are becoming increasingly problematic. Daniel Callahan, a prominent bioethicist in the United States: "This is a semi-scandalous situation for my field . . . These companies are smart enough to know that there are a variety of views on these subjects, and with a little bit of asking and shopping around you can find a group that will be congenial to what you are doing."

17. For instance, Congress has only begun to grapple seriously with these questions, particularly concerning the future trajectory of healthcare in relation to its undying support for an innovative health industry. In the wake of the HGP's completion, one Congressional member hit on several pertinent questions: "[W]hile this Human Genome Project is a key to unlocking many of life's mysteries, it also opens up a whole host of questions, many of which will be up to Congress to answer. . . . [H]ow do we protect against genetic discrimination? How do we ensure that everyone, across all social and economic divides, have access to the miracles that genomics bring? How does our healthcare system bear the costs associated with knowing about disease years in advance? How will Medicare handle the costs of a potentially elongated life span?" See: U.S. Congress, Hearing on The National Institutes of Health: Decoding Our Federal Investment in Genome Research, Subcommittee on Health, House Committee on Energy and Commerce (Washington DC: US Government Printing Office, 2003), 6.

Bibliography

Abate, Tom. "Scientists' 'publish or perish' credo now 'patent and profit': 'Recombinant U.' phenomenon alters academic culture." *San Francisco Chronicle*, August 13, 2001, Section 6.

Adler, Reid. "Genome research: fulfilling the public's expectations for knowledge and commercialization." *Science* 257, no.5072 (1992): 908–17.

Agnew, Bruce. "When Pharma Merges, R&D is the Dowry." *Science* 287, no.5460 (2000): 1952.

Agrawal, Madhu. *Global Competitiveness in the Pharmaceutical Industry: The Effect of Regulatory, Economic and Market Factors.* New York: Haworth Press, 1999.

Anderson, Christopher. "Genome shortcut leads to problems." *Science* 259, no.5102 (1993): 1684–8.

——. "Genome project goes commercial." *Science* 259, no.5093 (1993): 300–2.

Aronowitz, Stanley. *Science as Power: Discourse and Ideology in Modern Society.* Minneapolis: University of Minnesota Press, 1988.

Bancroft, J. "The medicalization of female sexual dysfunction: the need for caution." *Archives of Sexual Behaviour* 31, no.3 (2002): 451–5.

Barinaga, Marcia. "The attractions of biotech careers over academia." *Science* 257, no.5077 (1992): 1718–22.

Barrow, Clyde W. "The Marx Problem in Marxian State Theory." *Science and Society* 64, no.1 (2000): 87–118.

Beardsley, Tim. "Big-Time Biology." *Scientific American*, November 1994, 72–9.

Bekelman, Justin E., Yan Li, and Cary P. Gross. "Scope and Impact of Financial Conflicts of Interest in Biomedical Research: A Systematic Review." *Journal of the American Medical Association* 289, no.4 (2003): 454–65.

Bellamy Foster, John. "Marxian Economics and the State." *Science and Society* 46, no.3 (1982): 257–83.

Berg, Marc. "The Politics of Technology: On Bringing Social Theory into Technological Design." *Science, Technology and Human Values* 23, no.4 (1998): 456–90.

"BIO Responds to Clinton, Blair Statement on Gene-Based Health-Care Research." Biotechnology Industry Organization. Press Release, March 14, 2000.

"BIO files Comments on Proposed Guidelines From PTO For Patenting Gene-Based Inventions." Biotechnology Industry Organization. Press Release, March 22, 2000.

"BIO Praises Clinton Reassurances Regarding Gene Patents and PTO Leadership."
    Biotechnology Industry Organization. Press Release, April 5, 2000.
"BIO Issues Statement On PTO's Final Gene-Based Patent Guidelines." Biotech-
    nology Industry Organization. Press Release, January 5, 2001.
"Biotech Drug Approvals Top 90 With Hundreds More In Late-Stage Clinical
    Trials." Biotechnology Industry Organization. Press Release, January 18,
    2000.
Biotechnology Industry Organization. Editors' and Reporters' Guide. Washington:
    Biotechnology Industry Organization, 2004.
Bishop, Jerry, and Michael Waldholz. Genome: The Story of the Most Astonishing
    Scientific Adventure of Our Time—The Attempt to Map All the Genes in the
    Human Body. New York: Simon and Schuster, 1990.
Blumenthal, David, Michael Gluck, Karen Seashore Louis, Michael A. Stoto, and
    David Wise. "University-Industry Research Relationships in Biotechnology:
    Implications for the University." Science 232, no.4756 (1986): 1361–6.
Blumenthal, David, Michael Gluck, Karen Seashore Louis, and David Wise.
    "Industrial Support of University Research in Biotechnology." Science 231,
    no.4735 (1986): 242–6.
Blumenthal, David, Nancyanne Causino, Eric Campbell, and Karen Seashore
    Louis." Relationships Between Academic Institutions and Industry in the Life
    Sciences—An Industry Survey." New England Journal of Medicine 334, no.6
    (1996): 368–73
Blumenthal, David, Eric G. Campbell, Nancyanne Causino, and Karen Seashore
    Louis. "Participation of Life-Science Faculty in Research Relationships with
    Industry." New England Journal of Medicine 335, no.23 (1996) 1734–9.
Blumenthal, David, Eric G. Campbell, Melissa Anderson, Nancyanne Causino, and
    Karen Seashore Louis. "Withholding Research Results in Academic Life
    Science: Evidence From a National Survey of Faculty." Journal of the
    American Medical Association 277, no.15 (1997): 1224–8.
Bohrer, Robert. "Future Fall-Out From The Genetic Revolution." Futures 24
    (1992): 681–8.
Boston Consulting Group. "A Revolution in R&D: Part II The Impact of Genetics."
    Consulting Report, July 2001.
Braithwaite, John, and Peter Drahos. Global Business Regulation. Cambridge:
    Cambridge University Press, 2000.
——. Information Feudalism: Who Owns the Knowledge Economy? New York,
    New Press, 2003.
Brenner, Robert. "Uneven Development and the Long Downturn: The Advanced
    Capitalist Economies from Boom to Stagnation, 1950–1998." New Left
    Review 229 (1998): 1–265.
"Briefing on DNA Sequencing: Methods and Applications." Futuretech, May 21,
    2001, 1–23.
Broad, William J. "Who Built the H-Bomb? Debate Revives." New York Times,
    April 24, 2001, F1.
Browne, William P. "Biotechnology, State Economic Development, and Interest
    Politics: A Troublesome Trinity." Politics and the Life Sciences 9, no.2
    (1991): 245–50.

"Bush boosts big programmes." *Chemistry & Industry* 5 (1990): 120.

Buttel, Frederick. "Biotechnology: An Epoch-Making Technology." In *The Biotechnology Revolution?* Edited by Martin Fransman, Gerd Junne and Annemieke Roobeek. Oxford: Blackwell, 1995.

Caffentzis, George. "Why Machines Cannot Create Value: or, Marx's Theory of Machines." In *Cutting Edge: Technology, Information, Capitalism and Social Revolution.* Edited by Jim Davis, Thomas Hirschl and Michael Stack. London: Verso, 1997.

Callinicos, Alex. *Against Postmodernism: A Marxist Critique.* New York: St. Martin's Press, 1990.

Campbell, Eric G., Karen Seashore Louis, David Blumenthal. "Looking a Gift Horse in the Mouth: Corporate Gifts Supporting Life Sciences Research." *The Journal of the American Medical Association* 279, no.13 (1998): 995–9.

Cantor, Charles. "Introductory Remarks." Paper presented at Human Genome Project: Commercial Implications, San Francisco, May 1999.

Carchedi, Guglielmo. "Between Class Analysis and Organization Theory: Mental Labour." In *Organization Theory and Class Analysis: New Approaches and New Issues.* Edited by Stewart Clegg. New York: Walter de Gruyter, 1990.

———. *Frontiers in Political Economy.* London: Verso, 1991.

———. "A Missed Opportunity: Orthodox vs. Marxist Crises Theories." *Historical Materialism* 4 (1999): 33–55.

Carey, John. "This Genetic Map Will Lead to a Pot of Gold." *Business Week,* March 2, 1992, 74.

———. "The Genome Gold Rush: Who will be the first to hit pay dirt?" *Business Week,* June 12, 2000, 147–58.

Carr, Geoffrey. "Beyond the behemoths." *Economist,* February 19, 1998, survey 16–8.

Caskey, C. Thomas. "DNA-Based Medicine: Prevention and Therapy." In *The Code of Codes: Scientific and Social Issues in the Human Genome Project.* Edited by Daniel J. Kevles and Leroy Hood. Cambridge, MA: Harvard University Press, 1992.

Castells, Manuel. *The Rise of the Network Society.* Cambridge, M.A.: Blackwell, 1996.

Chang, Koyin. "The Organization of the R&D Intensive Firm: An Application to the Biotechnology Industry." Ph.D. diss., University of Kentucky, 1998.

Chaudhry, Peggy E., and Michael G. Walsh. "Intellectual Property Rights: Changing Levels of Protection Under GATT, NAFTA and the EU." *Columbia Journal of Business* 30, no.2 (1995): 81–92.

Christoffersen, Ralph. "Untitled." Paper presented at Foresight Seminar on Biotechnology and Pharmaceutical Regulation, Alexandria, VA, March 18, 1987.

Clark, Jeanne, Joe Piccolo, Brian Stanton and Karin Tyson. "Patent Pools: A Solution to the Problem of Access in Biotechnology Patents?" Policy Paper, United States Patent and Trademark Office, Washington, DC, December 5, 2000.

Clarke, Simon. "The Marxist Theory of Overaccumulation and Crisis." *Science and Society* 54, no.4 (1990–1): 442–67.

Coghlan, Andy. "Land of Opportunity." *New Scientists* 168, no.2263 (2000): 30.

Cogoy, Mario. "The Falling Rate of Profit and the Theory of Accumulation." *International Journal of Political Economy* 17, no.2 (1987): 55–74.

Cohen, Jon. "The Culture of Credit." *Science* 268, no.5218 (1995): 1706–11.

———. "Research Materials: Share and Share Alike Isn't Always the Rule in Science." *Science* 268, no.5218 (1995): 1715–8.

Cole, Jonathan R. "Balancing Acts: Dilemmas of Choice Facing Research Universities." *Dædalus: Journal of the American Academy of Arts and Sciences* 122, no.4 (1993): 1–36.

"Conduct in Science." *Science* 268, no.5218 (1995): 1706–18.

Conrad, Peter. "Medicalization and Social Control." *Annual Review of Sociology* 18 (1992): 209–32.

Cook-Deegan, Robert. *The Gene Wars: Science, Politics, and the Human Genome*. New York: W.W. Norton & Company, 1995.

———. "Origins of the Human Genome Project." *Risk: Health, Safety and Environment* 5 (1994): 97–111.

Crawford, Mark. "Patent claim buildup haunts biotechnology." *Science* 239, no.4841 (1988): 723.

Creager, Angela. "Biotechnology and Blood: Edwin Cohn's Plasma Fractionation Project, 1940–1953." In *Private Science: Biotechnology and the Rise of the Molecular Sciences*. Edited by Arnold Thackray. Philadelphia: University of Pennsylvania Press, 1998.

Cullet, Philippe. "Patents and medicines: the relationship between TRIPS and the human right to health." *International* Affairs 79, no.1 (2003): 139–60.

Culliton, Barbara J. "NIH role in biotechnology debated." *Science* 229, no.4709 (1985): 147–9.

Damschroder, Mark L. "Intellectual Property Rights and the GATT: United States Goals in the Uruguay Round." *Vanderbilt Journal of Transnational Law* 21, no.2 (1988): 367–400.

Das, Raju. "State Theories: A Critical Analysis." *Science and Society* 60, no.1 (1996): 27–57.

Davies, Kevin. *Cracking the Genome: Inside the Race to Unlock Human DNA*. New York: The Free Press, 2001.

Davis, Bernard. "The human genome and other initiatives." *Science* 249, no.4967 (1990): 342–3.

Department of Energy. Human Genome Project Information Website, www.ornl.gov/hgmis/project/budget.html.

Dews, Peter. *Logics of Disintegration: post-structuralist thought and the claims of critical theory*. London: Verso, 1987.

"Diabetes gene therapy draws closer." *BBC Online*, December 7, 2000, www.bbc.co.uk.

Dickson, David. "OECD to set rules for international science." *Science* 238, no.4828 (1987): 743.

"Drugs ex machina." *Economist*, September 22, 2001, 30.

DuBoff, Richard. *Accumulation and Power: An Economic History of the United States*. New York: ME Sharpe, 1989.

Ehrbar Hans and Mark Glick. "The Labour Theory of Value and its Critics." *Science & Society* 50, no.4 (1986): 464–78.

Ernst & Young. "The Economic Contributions of the Biotechnology Industry to the U.S. Economy." Report prepared for the Biotechnology Industry Organization, May 2000.

Eisenberg, Rebecca. "Genes, patents, and product development." *Science* 257, no.5072 (1992): 904–9.

——. "Proprietary Rights and the Norms of Science in Biotechnology Research." *The Yale Law Journal* 97, no.2 (1987): 177–231.

Etzkowitz, Henry. "Knowledge as Property: The Massachusetts Institute of Technology and the Debate Over Academic Patent Policy." *Minerva: A Review of Science Learning and Policy* 32, no.4 (1994): 383–421.

——. "Bridging the Gap: The Evolution of Industry-University Links in the United States." In *Industrializing Knowledge: University-Industry Linkages in Japan and the United States*. Edited by Lewis M. Branscomb, Fumio Kodama, and Richard Florida. Cambridge, MA: MIT Press, 1999.

Etzkowitz, Henry, and Andrew Webster. "Entrepreneurial Science: the Second Academic Revolution." In *Capitalizing Knowledge: New Intersections of Industry and Academia*. Edited by Henry Etzkowitz, Andrew Webster and Peter Healey. Albany, NY: State University of New York Press, 1998.

Etzkowitz, Henry, Andrew Webster and Peter Healey, eds., *Capitalizing Knowledge: New Intersections of Industry and Academia*. Albany, NY: State University of New York Press, 1998.

Evans, Gail E. "Intellectual Property as a Trade Issue: The Making of the Agreement on Trade-Related Aspects of Intellectual Property Rights." *World Competition: Law and Economics Review* 18, no.2 (1994): 137–80.

Evans, Peter. "The Eclipse of the State? Reflections on Stateness in an era of Globalization." *World Politics* 50 (1997): 62–87.

Fairbanks, Daniel J., and W. Ralph Anderson. *Genetics: The Continuity of Life*. Toronto: Brooks/Cole Publishing, 1999.

Feller, Irwin. "Universities as engines of R&D-based economic growth: They think they can." *Research Policy* 19 (1990): 335–48.

——. "The American University System as a Performer of Basic and Applied Research." In *Industrializing Knowledge: University-Industry Linkages in Japan and the United States*. Edited by Lewis M. Branscomb, Fumio Kodama, and Richard Florida. Cambridge, MA: MIT Press, 1999.

Florida, Richard and Martin Kenney. "The New Age of Capitalism: Innovation-mediated production." *Futures* 25, no.6 (1993):637–51.

Fortun, Michael. "Mapping and making genes and histories: The genomics project in the United States, 1980–1990." Ph.D. diss., Harvard University, 1993.

——. "The Human Genome Project and the Acceleration of Biotechnology." In *Private Science: Biotechnology and the Rise of the Molecular Sciences*. Edited by Arnold Thackray. Philadelphia: University of Pennsylvania Press, 1998.

Foucault, Michel. "Truth and Power." In *The Foucault Reader*. Edited by Paul Rabinow. New York: Pantheon, 1984.

——. *Discipline and Punish: The Birth of the Prison*. Translated by Alan Sheridan. New York: Vintage, 1995.

——. *The History of Sexuality, Volume I*. Translated by Robert Hurley. New York: Vintage, 1990.

Fox-Keller, Evelyn. "Nature, Nurture, and the Human Genome Project." In *The Code of Codes: Scientific and Social Issues in the Human Genome Project*. Edited by Daniel J. Kevles and Leroy Hood. Cambridge, MA: Harvard University Press, 1992.

——. *Refiguring Life: Metaphors of Twentieth-Century Biology*. New York: Columbia University Press, 1995.

Freeland Judson, Horace. "Structural Transformation of the sciences and the end of peer review." *Journal of the American Medical Association* 272, no.2 (1994): 92–4.

Freeman, Chris. "Technical Change and Future Trends in the World Economy." *Futures* 25, no.6 (1993): 621–35.

Freeman, Miller. "Biopharmaceuticals increase their share of the market." *Manufacturing Chemist* 68, no.2 (1997): 28–30.

Gambardella, Alfonso. *Science and Innovation: the US Pharmaceutical Industry During the 1980s*. New York: Cambridge University Press, 1995.

Gannes, Stuart. "Merck Has Made Biotech Work." *Fortune*, January 19, 1987, 58–64.

——. "The Big Boys Are Joining the Biotech Party." *Fortune*, July 6, 1987, 58–64.

Gearan, Anne. "Clinton finds inspiration in Human Genome Project." *Globe and Mail*, December 25, 1999, A1.

"Gene therapy cancer treatment success." *BBC Online*, August 1, 2000, www.bbc.co.uk.

"Gene therapy frees 'bubble babies.'" *BBC Online*, April 27, 2000, www.bbc.co.uk.

"Gene therapy hope for sickle cell disease." *BBC Online*, December 14, 2001, www.bbc.co.uk.

"Gene therapy restores dogs' sight." *BBC Online*, April 27, 2001, www.bbc.co.uk.

"Gene trickery cons cancer." *BBC Online*, November 22, 2001, www.bbc.co.uk.

"Genetic warfare." *Economist*, May 16, 1998, 87–8.

"Genomic Pronouncements." *Economist*, December 2, 1999, 77.

"Genomics Advances Expected to Aid Growth of Biotechnology Industry." Biotechnology Industry Organization. Press Release. June 27, 2000.

Gerstenberger, Heide. "Class Conflict, Competition and State Functions." In *State and Capital: A Marxist Debate*. Edited by John Holloway and Sol Picciotto. London: Edward Arnold, 1978.

Giamatti, A. Bartlett. "The University, Industry, and Cooperative Research." *Science* 218, no.4579 (1982): 1278–9.

Gillis, Anna Maria. "The patent question of the year." *BioScience* 42, no.5 (1992): 336–9.

Goldman, Bruce. "Patient, Diagnose Thyself." *Signals Online Magazine*, February 1, 2001, www.signalsmag.com.

Goozner, Merrill. "The Price Isn't Right." *The American Prospect* 11, no.20 (2000): 25–8.

Gorlin, Jacque J. "The Business Community and the Uruguay Round." In *Intellectual Property Rights and Capital Formation in the Next Decade*. Edited by Charles E. Walker and Mark A. Bloomfield. New York: University Press of America, 1988.

Grace, Eric. "Better health through gene therapy." *The Futurist* 32, no.1 (1998): 39–43.

Gulalp, Haldun. "Capital Accumulation, Classes and the Relative Autonomy of the State." *Science and Society* 51, no.3 (1987): 287–313

Hacker, Jacob. *The Divided Welfare State: The Battle Over Public and Private Social Benefits in the United States*. Cambridge: Cambridge University Press, 2002.

Hall, Alan. "The Race for Miracle Drugs." *Business Week,* July 22, 1985, 92–6.

Harman, Chris. "Footnotes and Fallacies: A Comment on Robert Brenner's 'The Economics of Global Turbulence.'" *Historical Materialism* 4 (1999): 95–103.

Harman, Amy. "In New Tests for Fetal Defects, Agonizing Choices." *New York Times,* June 20, 2004, Health Section.

Harnett, Christopher J. "The Human Genome Project and the Downside of Federal Technology Transfer." *Risk: Health, Safety & Environment* 5 (1995): 151–62.

Harris, Gardiner. "Drugmakers Move Closer to Big Victory." *New York Times,* November 25, 2003, A20.

Hart, David. "Managing Technology at the White House." In *Investing in Innovation: Creating a Research and Innovation Policy That Works*. Edited by Lewis M. Branscomb and James H. Keller. Cambridge, MA: MIT Press, 1998.

Henderson, Rebecca, Adam B. Jaffe and Manuel Trajtenberg. "Universities as a Source of Commercial Technology: A Detailed Analysis of University Patenting 1965–1988." National Bureau of Economic Research. Working Paper No.5068, March 1995.

Henner, Dennis J., Statement before the United States House of Representatives Judiciary Subcommittee on Courts and Intellectual Property, July 13, 2000, www.bio.org.

Hill, Christopher T. "Technology and International Competitiveness: Metaphor for Progress." In *Science, Technology, and Social Progress: Research in Technology Studies Volume 2*. Edited by Stephen Goldman. Toronto: Associated University Presses, 1989.

Hirsch, Joachim. "The State Apparatus and Social Reproduction: Elements of a Bourgeois State." In *State and Capital: A Marxist Debate*. Edited by John Holloway and Sol Picciotto. London: Edward Arnold, 1978.

Hirst, Paul, and Grahame Thompson. *Globalization in Question: The International Economy and the Possibilities of Governance*. Cambridge: Polity Press, 1996.

Hoekman, Bernard M. "New Issues in the Uruguay Round and Beyond." *The Economic Journal* 103 (1993): 1531–2.

Hollingsworth, J. Rogers. "The Institutional Embeddedness of American Capitalism." In *Political Economy of Modern Capitalism: Mapping Convergence & Diversity*. Edited by Colin Crouch and Wolfgang Streeck. London: Sage Publications, 1997.

Hubbard, Ruth. "Genomania and health: arguments against genetic prediction." *American Scientist* 83, no.1 (1995): 8–11.

"Hundreds of gene therapy experiments failed." *BBC News Online*, February 1, 2000, www.bbc.co.uk.

Jaroff, Leon. "The Gene Hunt: scientists launch a $3billion project to map the chromosomes and decipher the complete instructions for making a human being." *Time*, March 20, 1989, 62–7.

Jasanoff, Sheila. "Beyond Epistemology: Relativism and Engagement in the Politics of Science." *Social Studies of Science* 26 (1996): 393–418.

Janowski, Pat, and Peter G. Brown. "Science, technology and the U.S. economy." *The Sciences* 33, no.4 (1993): 7–9.

Jessop, Bob. *The Capitalist State: Marxist Theories and Methods.* New York: New York University Press, 1982.

Katz Rothman, Barbara. "Not All That Glitters Is Gold." *Hastings Center Report* 22, no.4 (1992).

——. *Genetic Maps and Human Imaginations: The Limits of Science in Understanding Who We Are.* New York: W.W. Norton, 1998.

Kaufert, Patricia. "Health Policy and the New Genetics." *Social Science and Medicine* 51 (2000): 821–9.

Kay, Lily. "Problematizing Basic Research in Molecular Biology." In *Private Science: Biotechnology and the Rise of the Molecular Sciences,* Edited by Arnold Thackray. Philadelphia: University of Pennsylvania Press, 1998, 20–38.

Kher, Unmesh. "The Next Frontier: Proteomics." *Time*, July 3, 2000, 29.

Kenan, Regina H. "The At-Risk Health Status and Technology: A Diagnostic Invitation and the Gift of Knowing." *Social Science and Medicine* 42 (1996): 1545–53.

Kenney, Martin. *Biotechnology: The University-Industrial Complex.* New Haven: Yale University Press, 1986.

——. "Value Creation in the Late Twentieth Century: the Rise of the Knowledge Worker." In *Cutting Edge: Technology, Information, Capitalism and Social Revolution.* Edited by Jim Davis, Thomas Hirschl and Michael Stack. London: Verso, 1997.

——. "Biotechnology and a New Economic Space." In *Private Science: Biotechnology and the Rise of the Molecular Sciences.* Edited by Arnold Thackray. Philadelphia: University of Pennsylvania Press, 1998.

Kevles, Daniel J. "Ananda Chakrabarty wins a patent: Biotechnology, law, and society, 1972–1980." *HSPS: Historical Studies in the Physical and Biological Sciences* 25, no.1 (1994): 111–36.

——. "Big Science and Big Politics in the United States: Reflections on the Death of the SSC and the Life of the Human Genome Project." *HSPS: Historical Studies in the Physical and Biological Sciences* 27, no.2 (1997): 269–98.

Kiley, Thomas D. "Patents on random complementary DNA fragments?" *Science* 257, no.5072 (1992): 915–9.

Kimbrell, Andrew. *The Human Body Shop: The Engineering and Marketing of Life.* San Francisco: Harper Collins, 1993.

King, Jonathan. "The Biotechnology Revolution: Self-Replicating Factories and the Ownership of Life Forms." In *Cutting Edge: Technology, Information, Capitalism and Social Revolution*. Edited by Jim Davis, Thomas Hirschl and Michael Stack. London: Verso, 1997.

Klein, Hans K., and Daniel Lee Kleinman. "The Social Construction of Technology: Structural Considerations." *Science, Technology & Human Values* 27, no.1 (2002): 28–52.

Kohler, Robert E. "The Management of Science: The Experience of Warren Weaver and the Rockefeller Foundation Programme in Molecular Biology." *Minerva* 14 (1976): 279–306.

Koivusalo, Meri. "World Trade Organisation and Trade-Creep in Health and Social Policies." Occasional Paper, Globalism and Social Policy Programme, Helsinki, 1999.

Korenman, Stanley G., Richard Berk, Neil Wenger, and Vivian Lew. "Evaluation of the Research Norms of Scientists and Administrators Responsible for Academic Research Integrity." *Journal of the American Medical Association* 279, no.1 (1998): 41–7.

Koshland, Daniel E. "Sequences and consequences of the human genome." *Science* 246, no.4927 (1989): 189.

Krimsky, Sheldon. *Biotechnics and Society: The Rise of Industrial Genetics*. New York: Praeger, 1991.

———. *Genetic Alchemy: The Social History of the Recombinant DNA Controversy*. Cambridge, MA: MIT University Press, 1982.

———. "Regulating Recombinant DNA Research." In *Controversy Politics of Technical Decisions*. Edited by Dorothy Nelkin. London: Sage, 1979.

Krimsky, Sheldon, James G. Ennis, and Robert Weissman. "Academic-Corporate Ties in Biotechnology: A Quantitative Study." *Science, Technology, and Human Values* 16, no.3 (1991): 275–87.

Kurdas, Chidem. "Accumulation and Technical Change: Marx Revisited." *Science and Society* 59, no.1 (1995): 52–68.

Latour, Bruno. "Technology is society made durable." In *A Sociology of Monsters: Essays on Power, Technology and Domination*. Edited by John Law. London: Routledge, 1991.

———. *Science in Action*. Cambridge, MA: Harvard University Press, 1987.

Lee, Thomas. *Gene Future: The Promise and Peril of the New Biology*. New York: Plenum, 1993.

Lemonick, Michael D. "The Genome Is Mapped: Now What?" *Time*, July 3, 2000, 24.

Lemonick, Michael D., and Dick Thompson. "Racing to Map Our DNA: Completion from private labs has forced the Human Genome Project into a frantic rush to finish first." *Time*, January 11, 1999, 44.

Lewin, Roger. "Shifting sentiments over sequencing the human genome." *Science* 233, no.4764 (1986): 620–2.

Lewin, Roger. "Politics of the genome." *Science* 235, no.4795 (1987): 1453.

Lewontin, Richard. "The Dream of the Human Genome." In *Politics and the Human Body: Assault on Dignity*. Edited by Jean Bethke Elshtain and J. Timothy Cloyd. Nashville: Vanderbilt University Press, 1995.

Loeppky, Rodney. "Problematising Technology and 'Globalisation.'" In *Globalization 2000: Convergence or Divergence?* Edited by Axel Hueselmeyer. Basingstoke: Palgrave Press, 2003.

———. "History, Technology, and the Capitalist State: The Comparative Political Economy of Genome Science." *Review of International Political Economy* (2005, forthcoming).

Love, James. "How much does it cost to develop a new drug?" Paper presented at MSF Working Group, Geneva, April 2, 2000, www.cptech.org/ip/health/econ/howmuch.html.

Lyon, Jeff, and Peter Gorner. *Altered Fates: Gene Therapy and the Retooling of Human Life.* New York: W.W. Norton, 1996.

Macer, Darryl. "Whose Genome Project?" *Bioethics* 5 (1991): 183–211.

Mackenzie, Michael, Peter Keating and Alberto Cambrosio. "Patents and Free Scientific Information in Biotechnology: Making Monoclonal Antibodies Proprietary." *Science, Technology and Human Values* 15, no.1 (1990): 65–83.

Magdoff, Harry. "A Letter to a Contributor: The Same Old State." *Monthly Review* 49, no.8 (1998): 1–10.

Mallan, Caroline. "Gene tests for cancer won't stop." *Toronto Star,* September 20, 2001, A3.

Mandel, Ernest. *Late Capitalism.* London: Verso, 1978.

———. *Long Waves of Capitalist Development: A Marxist Interpretation.* New York: Verso, 1995.

Marchiafava Hogan, Janice. "Revamping the Orphan Drug Act: potential impact on the world pharmaceutical market." *Law and Policy in International Business* 26, no.2 (1995): 523–61.

Marsa, Linda. *Prescription for Profits: How the Pharmaceutical Industry Bankrolled the Unholy Marriage Between Science and Business.* New York: Scribner, 1997.

Marshall, Eliot. "Biotech leaders give patent office a litany of complaints." *Science* 266, no.5185 (1994): 537

———. "Rifkin's latest target: genetic testing." *Science* 272, no.5265 (1996): 1094.

———. "NIH to produce a 'working draft' of the genome by 2001." *Science* 281, no.5384 (1998): 1774–5.

Marshall, Eliot, and David P. Hamilton. "The patent game: raising the ante." *Science* 253, no.5015 (1991): 20–4.

Marshall, Robert. "Autonomy and Sovereignty in the Era of Global Restructuring." *Studies in Political Economy* 59 (1999): 115–47.

Marx, Karl. *Capital: A Critique of Political Economy, Volume I.* Translated by Samuel Moor and Edward Aveling. New York: Modern Library, 1936.

———. *Capital: A Critique of Political Economy, Volume III.* New York: International Publishers, 1967.

———. *Economic and Philosophical Manuscripts of 1844.* Translated by Martin Milligan. New York: International Publishers, 1964.

Mash, Peter. "Mergers in the drug industry." *British Medical Journal* 299, no.6703 (1989): 813–4.

Mattick, Paul Jr. "Some aspects of the value-price problem." *Économies et Sociétés* 15, nos.6–7 (1981): 725–81.

May, Christopher. "Information society, task mobility and the end of work." *Futures* 32 (2000): 399–416.

——. "Fishing with Dynamite: Knowledge commons in the global political economy." Paper presented at Annual Meeting of the International Studies Association, Chicago, IL, February 2001.

McGraw, Thomas. *Creating Modern Capitalism: How Entrepreneurs, Companies, and Countries Triumphed in Three Industrial Revolutions.* Cambridge, MA: Harvard University Press, 1997.

McIntyre, Ann-Marie. *Key Issues in the Pharmaceutical Industry.* New York: John Wiley & Sons, 1999.

McMichael, Philip. "Globalization: Myths and Realities." *Rural Sociology* 61, no.1 (1996): 25–55.

Mejias, Jordan. "Research Always Runs the Risk of Getting Out of Control (Interview with Erwin Chargaff)." *Frankfurter Allgemeine Zeitung* (English ed.), June 4, 2001.

Meiksins, Peter. "Work, New Technology, and Capitalism." *Monthly Review* 48, no.3 (1996): 99–114.

Merton, R.K. *The Sociology of Science: theoretical and empirical investigations.* Chicago: University of Chicago Press, 1973.

Merz, Beverly. "Senate committee sees NIH-DOE partnership in genome project." *Journal of the American Medical Association* 259, no.1 (1988): 15–8.

Miliband, Ralph. "The Capitalist State: Reply to Nicos Poulantzas." *New Left Review* 59 (1970): 53–60;

——. "Poulantzas and the Capitalist State." *New Left Review* 82 (1973): 83–92.

Mitcham, Carl. "Science, Technology, the Theory of Progress." In *Science, Technology, and Social Progress: Research in Technology Studies, Volume 2.* Edited by Stephen Goldman. Toronto: Associated University Presses, 1989.

Moffat, Simon. "Pharmaceuticals: good opportunities in small packages." *Science* 261, no.5129 (1993): 788–9.

Mooers, Colin. *The Making of Bourgeois Europe.* New York: Verso, 1991.

Mosely, Fred. "The United States Economy at the Turn of the Century: Entering a New Era of Prosperity?" *Capital and Class* 67 (1999): 25–45.

——. *The Falling Rate of Profit in the Postwar United States Economy.* New York: St.Martin's Press, 1991.

——. "The Decline in the Rate of Profit in the Post-War US Economy: Regulation and Marxian Explanations." *International Journal of Political Economy* 19, no.1 (1989): 48–66.

——. "The Rate of Surplus Value, the Organic Composition, and the General Rate of Profit in the U.S. Economy, 1947–1967: A Critique and Update of Wolff's Estimates." *The American Economic Review* 78, no.1 (1988): 298–303.

Mowery, David and Nathan Rosenberg. *Paths of Innovation: Technological Change in 20th Century America.* Cambridge: Cambridge University Press, 1998.

Mowery, David C., Richard R. Nelson, Bhaven N. Sampat, and Arvids A. Ziedonis. "The Effects of the Bayh-Dole Act on U.S. Research and Technology Transfer." In *Industrializing Knowledge: University-Industry Linkages in Japan and the United States.* Edited by Lewis M. Branscomb, Fumio Kodama, and Richard Florida. Cambridge, MA: MIT Press, 1999.

Moynihan, Ray, Iona Heath, and David Henry. "Selling sickness: the pharmaceutical industry and disease mongering." *British Medical Journal* 324 (2002): 886–91.

Moynihan, Ray. "The making of a disease: female sexual dysfunction." *British Medical Journal* 326 (2003): 45–7.

Mukherjee, Siddhartha. "Wrong Map—Why public science can't really be public." *The New Republic*, May 8, 2000, 14.

Mulkay, Michael. "The Mediating Role of the Scientific Elite." *Social Studies of Science* 6 (1976): 445–70.

Munro, Margaret. "The moon walk of medicine." *National Post*, March 13, 2000, www.nationalpost.com/content/features/genome/0313001.html.

Murray, Mary. "Professors minding their own business: survey of university biotechnology researchers with industry ties." *Science News* 129 (1986): 374.

Murray, Robin. "The Internationalization of Capital and the Nation State." *New Left Review* 67 (1971): 84–109.

Nelkin, Dorothy. "The Social Power of Genetic Information." In *The Code of Codes: Scientific and Social Issues in the Human Genome Project*. Edited by Daniel J. Kevles and Leroy Hood. Cambridge, MA: Harvard University Press, 1992.

National Science Board. *Science and Engineering Indicators—1993*, www.nsf.gov/sbe/srs/seind93/chap5/doc/5s293.htm.

———. *Science & Engineering Indicators—2000*. Washington, DC: U.S Government Printing Office, 2000.

Noble, David. *America By Design: Science, Technology, and the Rise of Corporate Capitalism*. London: Oxford University Press, 1977.

O'C Hamilton, Joan. "Biotech: America's Dream Machine." *Business Week*, March 2, 1992, 66–74.

O'Reilly, Brian. "Drugmakers Under Attack." *Fortune*, July 29, 1991, 48–83.

Orsenigo, Luigi. *The Emergence of Biotechnology: Institutions and Markets in Industrial Innovation*. London: Pinter, 1989.

"Overview: Prospects for Germline Gene Therapy." UCLA Centre for the Study of Evolution and the Origin of Life, 1998, www.ess.ucla/huge/frames19.html.

Packard, Kathryn, and Andrew Webster. "Patenting Culture in Science: Reinventing the Scientific Wheel of Credibility." *Science, Technology, and Human Values* 21, no.4 (1996): 427–53.

Panitch, Leo. "Globalisation and the State." In *Socialist Register 1994*. Edited by Leo Panitch and R. Miliband. London: Merlin Press, 1994.

Pennisi, Elizabeth. "Funders reassure genome sequencers." *Science* 280, no.5367 (1998): 1185.

Peretz, Carlota. "Structural Change and Assimilation of New Technologies in the Economic and Social Systems." *Futures* 15, no.10 (1983): 357–75.

Pharmaceutical Research and Manufacturers of America (PhRMA). *Pharmaceutical Industry Profile 2000*. Washington DC: PhRMA, 2000.

———. *Pharmaceutical Industry Profile 2004*. Washington DC: PhRMA, 2004.

Pinch, Trevor, and Wiebe Bijker. "Science, Relativism and the New Sociology of Technology: Reply to Russell." *Social Studies of Science* 16 (1986): 347–60.

Portz, John, and Peter Eisinger. "Biotechnology and Economic Development: the Role of the States." *Politics and the Life Sciences* 9, no.2 (1991): 225–39.

Post, Charles. "The American Road to Capitalism." *New Left Review* 133 (1982): 30–51.

Post, George. "Untitled." Paper presented at Foresight Seminar on Biotechnology and the Regulation of Pharmaceuticals, Alexandria, VA, March 18, 1987.

Poulantzas, Nicos. "The Problem of the Capitalist State." *New Left Review* 58 (1969): 67–78.

———. "The Capitalist State: A Reply to Miliband and Laclau." *New Left Review* 95 (1976): 63–83

Powell, Walter W., and Jason Owen-Smith. "Universities and the Market for Intellectual Property in the Life Sciences." *Journal of Policy Analysis and Management* 17, no.2 (1998): 253–77.

"Private venture to sequence human genome launched." *Issues in Science and Technology* 15, no.1 (1998): 28–9.

Radice, Hugo. "Taking Globalization Seriously." In *Socialist Register 1999*. Edited by Leo Panitch and Colin Leys. New York: Merlin Press, 1999.

Redwood, Heinz. *The Pharmaceutical Industry: Trends, Problems and Achievements*. Suffolk: Oldwicks Press, 1987.

Relman, Arnold S., and Marcia Angell. "America's other drug problem: how the drug industry distorts medicine and politics." *The New Republic,* December 16, 2002, 27–41.

Rifkin, Jeremy. *The Biotech Century: Harnessing the Gene and Remaking the World* (New York: Putnam, 1998).

Roberts, Leslie. "Agencies vie over human genome project." *Science* 237, no.4814 (1987): 486–7.

———. "Carving up the genome." *Science* 242, no.4883 (1988): 1244–6.

———. "Report card on the genome project." *Science* 253, no.5018 (1991): 376.

———. "Genome backlash going full force." *Science* 248, no.4957 (1990): 804.

———. "A Meeting of the Minds on the Genome Project?" *Science* 250, no.4982 (1990): 756–7.

———. "Genome patent fight erupts." *Science* 254, no.5029 (1991): 184–6.

———. "The lords of the flies." *U.S. News & World Report* 127, no.11 (1999): 52.

Robbins-Roth, Cynthia. *From Alchemy to IPO: the Business of Biotechnology.* Cambridge, MA: Perseus, 2000.

Roemer, John E. "Technological Change on the Real Wage and Marx's Falling Rate of Profit." *Australian Economic Papers* 17, no.30 (1978): 152–66.

Rose, Hilary, and Steven Rose (eds.) *The Political Economy of Science: Ideology of/in the Natural Sciences.* London: MacMillan, 1976.

Rosenberg, Nathan. *Exploring the Black Box: Technology, economics and history.* Cambridge: Cambridge University Press, 1994.

Roush, Wade. "Biotech Finds a Growth Industry." Science. 273, no.5273 (1996): 300.

Ruediger, Nicole. "Out of college and into a rewarding biotech career." *Science* 278, no.5344 (1997): 1823.

Sapienza, Alice. "Collaboration as a global competitive tactic—Biotechnology and the ethical pharmaceutical industry." *R&D Management* 19, no.4 (1989): 285–95.

Savill, John. "Prospecting for gold in the human genome." *British Medical Journal* 314, no.7073 (1997): 43–6.

Schumpeter, Joseph. *Business Cycles: A Theoretical, Historical and Statistical Analysis of the Capitalist Process.* New York: McGraw Hill, 1939.

Schweitzer, Stuart O. *Pharmaceutical Economics and Policy.* New York: Oxford University Press, 1997.

"Scientists quarrel over gene therapy." *BBC Online,* November 10, 1999, www. bbc.co.uk.

Scott, Randal. Testimony before the United States House of Representatives Judiciary Subcommittee on Courts and Intellectual Property, July 13, 2000, www.bio.org.

Seashore Louis, Karen, and Melissa Anderson. "The Changing Context of Science and University-Industry Relations." In *Capitalizing Knowledge: New Intersections of Industry and Academia.* Edited by Henry Etzkowitz, Andrew Webster and Peter Healey. Albany, NY: State University of New York Press, 1998.

Sell, Susan K. "Intellectual property protection and antitrust in the developing world: crisis, coercion, and choice." *International Organization* 49, no.2 (1995): 315–49.

——. "Intellectual Property Rights After TRIPS." Paper presented at Annual Meeting of the International Studies Association, Chicago, IL, February 2001.

Shaikh, Anwar M., and E. Ahmet Tonak. *Measuring the wealth of nations: The political economy of national accounts.* New York: Cambridge University Press, 1994.

Shreeve, James. "The code breaker." *Discover* 19, no.5 (1998): 44–52.

Smith, Bruce L.R. *American Science Policy Since World War II.* Washington: Brookings Institution, 1990.

Smith, Murray. "The Necessity of Value Theory: Brenner's Analysis of the 'Long Downturn' and Marx's Theory of Crisis." *Historical Materialism* 4 (Summer, 1999): 149–69.

Stipp, David. "Hatching a DNA Giant." *Fortune,* May 24, 1999, 179–86.

Stolberg, Sheryl Gay. "Financial ties in Biomedicine Get Closer Look." *New York Times,* February 20, 2000, A1.

——. "Bioethicists Find Themselves the Ones Being Scrutinized." *New York Times,* August 2, 2001, A1.

Stone, Deborah. "The Implications of the Human Genome Project for Access to Health Insurance." In *The Human Genome Project and the Future of Health Care.* Edited by Thomas H. Murray, Mark A. Rothstein, and Robert F. Murray, Jr. Indianapolis, Indiana University Press, 1996. 133–57.

Sun, Marjorie. "White House enters fray on DNA regulation." *Science* 224, no.4651 (1984): 855.

Sweezy, Paul. *The Theory of Capitalist Development: Principles of Marxian Political Economy.* New York: Monthly Review Press, 1942.

Swenson, Peter and Scott Greer. "Foul Weather Friends: Big Business and Health Care Reform in the 1990s in Historical Perspective." *Journal of health Politics, Policy and Law* 27, no.4 (2002): 605–38.

"The proper study of mankind." *Economist,* September 14, 1996, 19–21.

Thompson, Nicholas. "Gene Blues: United States Patent and Trademark Office Overloaded." *Washington Monthly* 33, no.4 (2001): 9.

Tiefer, Leonore. "Sexology and the pharmaceutical industry: the threat of co-optation." *Journal of Sex Research* 37, no.3 (2000): 273–83.

Tully, Shawn. "Pill pushers get merger fever." *Fortune*, May 30, 1994, 14.

United Nations Education, Science and Cultural Organization (UNESCO). *Science Agenda—A Framework for Action*, General Conference, 30th Session, Paris, 1999.

U.S. Congress. Hearing on Commercialization of Academic Biomedical Research. Subcommittee on Investigations and Oversight and the Subcommittee on Science, Research and Technology. House Committee on Science and Technology. Washington, DC: U.S. Government Printing Office, 1981.

———. Workshop on Human Genome Mapping. Senate Committee on Energy and Natural Resources. Washington DC: U.S. Government Printing Office, 1987.

———. Office of Technology Assessment. *New Developments in Biotechnology: U.S Investments in Biotechnology—Special Report*. Washington, DC: U.S. Government Printing Office, 1988.

———. Office of Technology Assessment, *Mapping Our Genes—Genome Projects: How Big, How Fast?* Washington, DC: U.S. Government Printing Office, 1988.

———. Hearing on OTA Report on the Human Genome Project. Subcommittee on Oversight and Investigation. House Committee on Energy and Commerce. Washington, DC: U.S. Government Printing Office, 1988.

———. Hearing on The Human Genome Initiative and the Future of Biotechnology. Subcommittee on Science, Technology, and Space. Senate Committee on commerce, Science, and Transportation. Washington, DC: U.S. Government Printing Office, 1989.

———. Hearing on The Human Genome Project. Subcommittee on Energy Research and Development. Senate Committee on Energy and Natural Resources. Washington DC: U.S. Government Printing Office, 1990.

———. Hearing on Biotechnology and Technology Transfer. Subcommittee on Technology and Competitiveness. House Committee on Science, Space and Technology. Washington, DC: U.S. Government Printing Office, 1991.

———. Office of Technology Assessment. *Biotechnology in a Global Economy*. Washington, DC: U.S. Government Printing Office, 1991.

———. Office of Technology Assessment. *Pharmaceutical R&D: Costs, Risks and Rewards*. Washington, DC: U.S. Government Printing Office, 1993.

———. Office of Technology Assessment. *Federal Technology Transfer and the Human Genome Project*. Washington, DC: U.S. Government Printing Office, 1995.

———. Hearing on the Human Genome Project: How Private Sector Developments Affect the Government Program. Subcommittee on Energy and Environment. House Committee on Science. Washington, DC: U.S. Government Printing Office, 1998.

———. Hearing on The National Institutes of Health: Decoding Our Federal Investment in Genome Research. Subcommittee on Health. House Committee on Energy and Commerce. Washington DC: U.S. Government Printing Office, 2003.

Van Brunt, Jennifer. "Biotech's Tsunami." *Signals Online Magazine,* August 18, 2000, www.signalsmag.com.

——. "Borderless Biotech." *Signals Online Magazine,* December 13, 2000, www.signalsmag.com.

——. "Antisense: Poised to Strike." *Signals Online Magazine,* January 5, 2001, www.signalsmag.com.

——. "Biotechs Weigh In." *Signals Online Magazine,* February 2, 2001, www.signalsmag.com.

——. "Grand Ambitions." *Signals Online Magazine,* February 24, 2001, www.signalsmag.com.

——. "30,000 Genes? No Way, Claims Haseltine." *Signals Online Magazine,* March 18, 2001, www.signalsmag.com.

——. "Proteomics Gears Up." *Signals Online Magazine,* May 9, 2001, www.signalsmag.com.

——. "A Matter of Expression." *Signals Online Magazine,* July 3, 2001, www.signalsmag.com.

——. "Pharmacogenomics Gets Clinical." *Signals Online Magazine,* April 25, 2003, www.signalsmag.com.

Varma, Roli and Richard Worthington. "Immiseration of Industrial Scientists in Corporate Laboratories in the United States." *Minerva: A Review of Science Policy and Learning* 33 (1995): 325–38.

Venter, J. Craig and Mark D. Adams. "Shotgun sequencing of the human genome." *Science* 280, no.5369 (1998): 1540–3.

Wade, Nicholas. "Scientist's Plan: Map All DNA Within 3 Years." *New York Times,* May 10, 1998, A1.

——. "Company Nears Last Leg of Genome Project." *New York Times,* January 11, 2000, D3.

Walrod, Wallace. "Knowledge, Trust and Cooperative Relationships in the U.S. Biotechnology Industry." Ph.D. diss., University of California, Irvine, 1999.

Warren, Bill. "Imperialism and Capitalist Industrialization." *New Left Review* 81 (1973): 1–44.

"Washington Diary." *New Scientist* 167, no.2249 (2000): 61.

Waterston, R and J.E. Sulston. "Human Genome Project: reaching the finish line." *Science* 282, no.5386 (1998): 53–4.

Watson, James. "The Human Genome Project: Past, Present and Future." *Science* 248, no.4951 (1990): 44–50.

Weeks, John. "Equilibrium, Uneven Development and the Tendency of the Rate of Profit to Fall." *Capital and Class* 16 (1982): 62–77.

Williams, Simon J., and Michael Calnan. "The Limits of Medicalization?: Modern Medicine and the Lay Populace In 'Late Modernity.'" *Social Science and Medicine* 42, (1996): 1609–20.

Winner, Langdon. "Upon Opening the Black Box and Finding It Empty: Social Constructivism and the Philosophy of Technology." *Science, Technology & Human Values* 18, no.3 (1993): 362–78.

Wolpert, Chantelle M. "Human Genomics in Clinical Practice." *Clinician Review* 10, no.7 (2000): 67.

Wood, Ellen. *The Pristine Culture of Capitalism: A Historical Essay on Old Regimes and Modern States.* London: Verso, 1991.

———. "From Opportunity to Imperative: the History of the Market." *Monthly Review* 46:3 (1994): 14–40.

———. *Democracy Against Capitalism: Renewing Historical Materialism.* New York: Cambridge University Press, 1995.

———. "Modernity, Postmodernity or Capitalism?" *Review of International Political Economy* 4, no.3 (1997): 539–60.

———. "A Reply to Sivanandan." *Monthly Review* 48, no.9 (1997): 21–32.

———. "Class Compacts, the Welfare State, and Epochal Shifts." Monthly Review 49, no.8 (1998): 25–43.

Woolgar, Steven. "The Turn to Technology in Social Studies of Science." *Science, Technology & Human Values* 16, no.1 (1991): 20–50

Wright, Susan. "The Social Warp of Science: Writing the History of Genetic Engineering Policy." *Science, Technology and Human Values* 18, no.1 (1993): 79–101.

———. "Molecular Politics in a Global Economy." In *Private Science: Biotechnology and the Rise of the Molecular Sciences.* Edited by Arnold Thackray. Philadelphia: University of Pennsylvania Press, 1998.

———. "Varieties of Secrets and Secret Varieties: The Case of Biotechnology." *Politics and the Life Sciences* 19, no.1 (2000) 45–57.

Yaffe, David S. "The Marxian Theory of Crisis, Capital and the State." *Economy and Society* 2, no.2 (1973) 186–232.

Yanchinski, Stephanie. *Setting Genes to Work: The Industrial Era of Biotechnology* (New York: Viking Penguin, 1985).

Young, Margaret. "The legacy of Cohen-Boyer." *Signals Online Magazine,* June 12, 1998, www.signalsmag.com.

Yoxen, Edward. "Life as a Productive Force: Capitalising the Science and Technology of Molecular Biology." In *Science, Technology and the Labour Process.* Edited by Les Levidow and Bob Young. London: CSE Books, 1981.

Zehr, Leonard. "Drug firms facing short-term financial pressures, study says." *Globe and Mail,* January 21, 1999, B5.

Index

For Product Safety Concerns and Information please contact our EU
representative GPSR@taylorandfrancis.com Taylor & Francis Verlag GmbH,
Kaufingerstraße 24, 80331 München, Germany

Printed and bound by CPI Group (UK) Ltd, Croydon, CR0 4YY
08/05/2025
01864532-0002